LIVING MESSAGES
OF THE
BOOKS OF THE BIBLE

Living Messages
of the
Books of The Bible

BY THE REV.
G. CAMPBELL MORGAN, D.D.

MATTHEW TO REVELATION

WIPF & STOCK · Eugene, Oregon

Wipf and Stock Publishers
199 W 8th Ave, Suite 3
Eugene, OR 97401

Living Messages of The Books of The Bible
Matthew to Revelation
By Morgan, G. Campbell and Morgan, Richard L.
Copyright©1912 by Morgan, G. Campbell
ISBN 13: 978-1-60899-293-5
Publication date 5/28/2010
Previously published by Fleming H. Revell Co., 1912

G. Campbell Morgan Reprint Series

Foreword

If it is true that the measure of a person's greatness is their influence, not only on his own time but on future generations, G. Campbell Morgan must be regarded as a great person. His greatness is seen not only in the wide impact of his ministry on both sides of the Atlantic, but in the fact that his books are still read and studied sixty-five years after his death. Named one of the ten greatest preachers of the twentieth-century by the contributing board of *Preaching* magazine, Morgan made the Bible a new and living book not only to the congregations who listened to him, but the vast multitude of persons who read his books.

Fox sixty-seven years Morgan preached and taught the Scriptures and served churches in England and the United States. What is remarkable is that his commentaries and expositions of the Bible still speak to persons of a new millennium. There have been many changes in the world since he faithfully preached and taught the Scriptures, but the wide appeal of his books testify to the timelessness of his message.

Although he held pastorates in the Congregational and Presbyterian denominations, he had an ecumenical appeal to persons of all denominations and traditions. The mystic

Thomas á Kempis once wrote, "He to whom the eternal word speaks is delivered from many opinions." In one of his sermons, he referred to the words of Amos that there would be a famine for hearing the word of God (Amos 8:11). The timeless work of G. Campbell Morgan addresses that hunger, as his books enable his readers to get beyond opinions to the living Word.

Wipf and Stock Publishers have rendered a great gift to the religious world in reprinting dozens of Morgan's books. This growing collection makes his books more available, so that readers have an option other than searching the internet for used, and often expensive, copies. Among this collection is the classic *The Great Physician* and commentaries on the Gospel of Matthew and John. Persons seeking a living faith and a meaningful encounter with God would profit from reading any of these Morgan books.

Near the end of his ministry, in a sermon entitled "But One Thing," Morgan commented on how Portugal changed the words of a coin after Christopher Columbus discovered America. No longer did the inscription say, *Ne Plus Ultra* (nothing more beyond) but *Plus Ultra* (more beyond). It is the hope of the G. Campbell Morgan Trust that the reprinting of these books will bring readers to the "more beyond," and an even deeper encounter with the Word in Scripture.

THE MORGAN TRUST
Richard L. Morgan
Howard C. Morgan
John C. Morgan

NEW TESTAMENT
BOOK ONE

CONTENTS

THE MESSAGE OF—

MATTHEW 9

MARK 25

LUKE 41

JOHN 57

ACTS 75

ROMANS 93

I. CORINTHIANS 111

CONTENTS

THE MESSAGE OF—

 II. CORINTHIANS 131

 GALATIANS 149

 EPHESIANS 167

 PHILIPPIANS 187

 COLOSSIANS 207

THE MESSAGE OF MATTHEW

A THE ESSENTIAL MESSAGE	B THE APPLICATION

I. The Central Teaching
" The Kingdom of Heaven is at Hand."
i. Proclamation of the Kingdom.
    a. The Fundamental Conception.
        The Kingship of God. Sovereignty.
        The Kingdom of God. Sphere.
    b. The Special Revelation.
        The King revealed.
        The Kingdom revealed.
ii. Interpretation of the Kingdom.
    a. Its Principle. Righteousness.
        The Words of the King.
    b. Its Practice. Peace.
        The Works of the King.
    c. Its Purpose. Joy.
        The Will of the King.
iii. Administration of the Kingdom.
    a. By the King as King.
        His Person.
    b. By the King as Prophet.
        His Propaganda.
    c. By the King as Priest.
        His Passion.
 	
II. The Abiding Appeal
" Repent."
i. The Fundamental Meaning.
        Consideration.
ii. The Inevitable Sequence.
        Conviction.
iii. The Resulting Activity.
        Conversion.
	I. To the Church
	
	i. She is " The Holy Nation."
	    a. Submitted to Christ.
	    b. Realizing the Kingdom.
	    c. Manifesting it to the World.
	
	ii. Repent.
	    a. Submit.
	    b. Realize.
	    c. Manifest.
	
	II. To the World
	
	i. Under the Sovereignty of God.
	    Yet in Anarchy.
	
	ii. Repent.
	    a. Conception.
	    b. Conduct.
	    c. Character.

THE MESSAGE OF MATTHEW

IN seeking for the messages of the books of the New Testament it is necessary to remember the difference between these books and those of the Old Testament. In those we sought amid local conditions and colouring for permanent values, which permanent values create the living and abiding message. In every book of the Old Testament we had to do with an incomplete revelation, for the Old Testament itself does not constitute a complete revelation. It is a library of expectation and of hope.

When we turn to the New Testament we still find ourselves amid local conditions, but we have no longer to deal with an incomplete revelation. We have now to consider the literature of that Christ Who is the final speech of God to the world. The writer of the letter to the Hebrews affirms that "God, having of old time spoken unto the fathers in the prophets by divers portions and in divers manners, hath at the end of these days spoken unto us in His

Son." That message of the Son is God's final message to man. It is for us now to ask what is the essential message of each book, and what is its abiding appeal.

The four gospel narratives constitute the foundation literature of Christianity in that they present the Person of Christ, record His teaching, and give an account of His work on earth in the days of His flesh.

When we turn to the Gospel according to Matthew we find in it the final teaching on the subject with which it deals.

What then is the essential message of Matthew, and what its abiding appeal? Here we are not left to anything in the nature of speculation. The essential message and the abiding appeal are contained in one brief declaration. That declaration is twice uttered. It was first made by the voice of the herald who foretold the coming of the King; it was repeated by the King Himself when He commenced His ministry; "Repent ye, for the Kingdom of heaven is at hand." That is the voice of the herald, and the word of the King. The essential message then is "the Kingdom of heaven is at hand"; and the abiding appeal is "Repent ye."

I recognize that there is a sense in which both the message of the herald and that of the King had immediate and local application. This word was spoken by John the Baptist peculiarly to the Hebrew people. When Jesus commenced His ministry He did so as the Jewish Messiah, and His word was consequently peculiarly to the people of the ancient covenant. While that is admitted it must not be forgotten that in the economy of God the Hebrew people existed not for themselves but for the world at large. This cannot be too often repeated if we are to understand that economy of God, in the case of His people Israel, and as to His perpetual method. Consequently the word of the herald and the word of the King constitute the one great message of this Gospel. This is not the final message of Christ; not that He has changed or altered this by a hair's breadth, but He has a great deal more than this to say. The message of Matthew is not the final Christian message, for just as we need the four Gospels for the presentation of Christ, so we need the four messages for the delivery of the Christian message to the world at the present hour.

First then let us examine the essential message, "The Kingdom of heaven is at hand." Both the herald and the King uttered first the words of appeal, "Repent ye," but that appeal gained its force from the declaration which immediately followed it, "The Kingdom of heaven is at hand." That is the central teaching of the whole Gospel, and in examining it we shall discover three values. It is first the gospel of the proclamation of the Kingdom. It is secondly the gospel of the interpretation of the Kingdom. It is thirdly the gospel of the administration of the Kingdom. It proclaims the fact, explains the meaning, and describes the method of administration.

The abiding appeal of the Gospel is that of its call to repentance in the light of its teaching concerning the Kingdom.

The one theme of the book is that of the Kingdom. The word Kingdom occurs fifty times in the course of the story. There are different phrases of which it forms a part. The one most often recurring is that of "The Kingdom of heaven." This is peculiar to this Gospel according to Matthew, and occurs two-and-thirty times. The phrase "The Kingdom of God" occurs four times. The phrase "The Kingdom," which evidently has reference to the same idea, occurs eight times. The phrase "Thy Kingdom" when the reference is to God Himself is found once, and once when the reference is to Jesus. The phrase " His Kingdom " occurs twice with reference to the Son of Man, and once with reference to God. The last occurrence of the word is in the phrase " My Father's Kingdom."

That is a somewhat mechanical paragraph, but it serves to show that the word Kingdom is stamped upon the page from first to last. As this Gospel presents the King, its message is that of the Kingdom.

This word has two values which are complementary to each other, and both of which we need to recognize. These values may be expressed by the two words Kingship and Kingdom, in the way in which we make use of them to-day in our general conversation. The word Kingship emphasizes the fact that God is King. The word Kingdom refers to the realm over which He reigns. When we speak of the Kingdom of God we most often think only of the latter value, that, namely, of the realm over which He reigns. The fact that He is King is the fundamental message of this book.

Of the phrases to which we have referred "The Kingdom of God" is the greatest, because it at once insists upon the fact that God is King and refers to the realm over which He rules. There are occasions when it is evidently limited by the context, but considered alone it is certainly the greatest of these phrases, being the most spacious in its suggestiveness.

The phrase "The Kingdom of heaven," which as we have said is only used by Matthew, demands our special attention in any consideration of the message of the Gospel. In order to understand it, it is necessary that we should find out what it meant to the men who first heard it. Now it is an interesting fact that Christ never explained the phrase, neither did His forerunner. Simply because all who heard it were perfectly familiar with the one idea for which it stood. In the book of Exodus, which deals with the founding of the nation, we find the declaration "Ye shall be unto Me a kingdom of priests, and an holy nation," and there we discover the idea which the phrase "the Kingdom of heaven" suggested to the Hebrew. The peculiarity of the nation consisted in the fact that it was a Theocracy, a people with no king other than God Himself. It was a nation under the Kingship of God. It was a holy nation, a kingdom of priests, the Kingdom of heaven. When therefore these people heard John the Baptist and Jesus say " Repent ye, for the Kingdom of heaven is at hand " they understood them to mean that they were not living in accord with the underlying principle of their national life, and that it was necessary for them to repent in order to the restoration of the lost ideal.

The simple meaning of the phrase then is that it refers to the establishment in the world of the heavenly order, the submission of every king to God, the overturning of all save that which results from the recognition of the abiding throne of God. The Kingdom of heaven is the establishment of the Divine order on earth, the supremacy of the will of God in the affairs of men. The teaching of this Gospel then is that the only hope of humanity is in the establishment of the Kingdom of heaven, and that this can only be secured by submission to the throne of God. When men talk about the Kingdom of heaven as though it could be set up by human action, by the parliaments of men, or by a godless social propaganda, they are proving their blindness;

and when they attempt the enterprise they are attempting to build without a foundation. The Kingdom of heaven is the reign of God over humanity. This Gospel proclaims that fact.

In the second place this Gospel interprets the Kingdom. It does infinitely more than assert the fact of the Divine Kingship, it explains the order of the Divine Kingdom. It contains a proclamation of the principle of the Kingdom, an explanation of the practice of the Kingdom, and a revelation of the ultimate purpose of the Kingdom. These things may be expressed in three words by quotation from the letter to the Romans in which the apostle declares, "The Kingdom of God is not eating and drinking, but righteousness and peace and joy in the Holy Ghost." Righteousness is the principle, peace the practice, and joy the purpose, of the Divine Kingdom. The words of the King constitute the law of the Kingdom, and proclaim the principle of righteousness. The works of the King exhibit the powers of the Kingdom which operate towards the practice of peace. The will of the King is revealed in the opening word of the Manifesto, "Blessed,"—or perhaps Happy, for happiness is the ultimate purpose of the Kingdom.

Thus the interpretation of the Kingdom is best expressed in the words of the apostle to the Gentiles. The master principle is righteousness, the practice is peace, and its purpose is joy.

Finally, this Gospel reveals the method of the administration of the Kingdom. In the key words to the analysis of the book this method is suggested. In the first division we have the presentation of the Person, and it is that of a King. In the second division we have the Propaganda, in which the King is revealed as Prophet. In the third division we have the Passion, in which He is seen as Priest. He is at once King, Priest, Prophet. The Old Testament asks for this Person. In the law, consisting of the first five books, it demands the Priest. In its historic section it seeks for the King. In its prophetic books it reveals the need of the Prophet. The Gospel of Matthew shows how the whole expectation of the old economy is fulfilled through One Who is Priest and Prophet and King. Through that threefold ministry, the Kingdom of God is to be established, and in no other way. The Gospel presents the One Who as King has all authority; Who as Prophet utters the final words of truth; Who as Priest deals with sin in such a way as to make possible the redemption and renewal of man, and through man of the whole creation. Thus the administration of the Kingdom is accomplished by the King Who is also Prophet and Priest.

In the light of that central teaching we turn to the consideration of the abiding appeal of this Gospel which is expressed in the one word "Repent."

It is necessary that we should first consider the fundamental meaning of this word. We are all familiar with the long continued controversy between the Roman and Protestant theologians as to the nature of repentance. This controversy arises out of the fact that two distinct words in the Greek New Testament are translated in our versions "Repent." One of these lays emphasis upon a change of mental attitude; the other is burdened with a sense of sorrow. Into that discussion we need not enter here. The particular word made use of by the forerunner and by the King is the one which quite literally means, Think again. The fundamental meaning then of the appeal of this book is that it calls men to consideration.

Such consideration will have as its inevitable

THE MESSAGE OF MATTHEW 19

sequence, conviction of sin, and a consequent sense of sorrow. While it is perfectly true that the sense of sin and the sense of sorrow are not suggested by the word, they are involved, for it is impossible for any man honestly to consider his life in the light of what this Gospel reveals without coming to consciousness of his own sin, and sooner or later to the sense of sorrow.

There is, however, yet another and further result involved—that namely of the activity of conversion which will follow. Conversion in itself is not regeneration. Regeneration is the act of God. Conversion is the act of man. Conversion is that turning round from rebellion to submission which results from the conviction of sin which follows repentance as reconsideration. Thus the threefold fact suggested by the word may be expressed as a sequence by the use of these three words, Consideration, Conviction, Conversion.

It must, however, be remembered that this word "Repent" loses its force if it be removed from its immediate connection with the central teaching contained in the words "The Kingdom of heaven is at hand." It is possible for a man to think again, and for his second thinking to be as false as the first. Therefore the Gospel says to man, Behold the King, understand the Kingdom, and think again in the light of these facts. Repentance here then means the submission of the life to the standards of the Kingdom and to the throne of the King. It is possible for men to repent without moral or spiritual result. They can think again, and depart from the old secularism to the new theosophy without being any nearer to realization or establishment of the Kingdom of God. This Gospel proclaims the King, interprets the Kingdom as righteousness, peace and joy; shows that the Kingdom is administered by One Who is perfect King, perfect Prophet, perfect Priest. It then appeals to men in the presence of these facts to repent.

To obey its appeal is inevitably to be brought to a consciousness of sin as coming short of the glory of God, and such consciousness invariably results in sorrow for sin. Repentance has its final value in that turning round, from sin and towards God, which Paul described, when writing to the Thessalonian Christians, in the words, "ye turned unto God from idols."

While therefore the great appeal of this Gospel is Repent, it is useless to take that word and preach it save in connection with the central teaching of the Kingship of God revealed to men in Jesus, and of the Kingdom of God opened to men through the work of Jesus.

There is a twofold application of the message of this book to our own age. Its first application is to the Church because the Church is now the holy nation, the Theocracy, whose function it is to realize and to manifest the principles and practice and purpose of the Kingdom of God. At Cæsarea Philippi Jesus said to Peter, "I will give unto thee the keys of the Kingdom." He also declared to the disciples after instructing them in the mysteries of the Kingdom, that every scribe instructed to the Kingdom of heaven "is like unto a man that is a householder, which bringeth forth out of his treasure things new and old." The world to-day can only understand the meaning of the Kingship and Kingdom of God through the Church. The first application of the message of this Gospel must therefore be to the Church, and this because she is responsible for manifestation.

The measure in which she is failing to reveal these things to the world is the measure in which she should obey its call to repentance. Her membership consists of those who are submitted to Christ, who realize in their own lives the fact of His Kingship and who therefore through their transformed lives manifest to others the grace and glory of His reign. The measure of the failure to reveal is the measure of the failure to obey. To Ephesus, fallen from first love, the word of the King was, "Repent, and do the first works." That is still His word to those who name His name, but fail to reveal Him to others.

The message of Matthew to the world can only be delivered through the Church. Its first note must be that of insistence upon the abiding Kingship of God. No man can escape from that Kingship. It is possible for men to live within the Kingdom of God in such wrong relation to it that it becomes a scorching, destructive fire instead of a beneficent and healing force. God reigns to the uttermost bound of the universe. Nothing escapes His authority. It is our business to proclaim to men the established fact of the Kingdom of God, and the fact that He has anointed His well beloved Son as King over the whole earth.

In the light of that fact, men who are in rebellion against the Divine government are to hear as the first note of the Gospel the word "Repent."

THE MESSAGE OF MARK

A THE ESSENTIAL MESSAGE	B THE APPLICATION

I. The Central Teaching. i. 14, 15.
i. The Nature of the Service.
    Creation of a Gospel.
ii. The Law of the Service.
    a. Sympathy.
    b. Suffering.
    c. Sacrifice.
iii. The Result of the Service.
    a. The Gospel.
        Cf. i. 1, The Person.
          xvi. 15, The Resurrection.
    b. The Opportunity of Salvation.
 	
II. The Abiding Appeal
i. The Perpetual Preliminary.
    "Repent."
ii. The Essential Call.
    "Believe *in*."
	I. To the Church
	i. The Law of its Life.
	    Abiding Confidence in the Servant of God.
	ii. The Law of its Service.
	    Abiding Confidence in the Gospel.
	
	II. To the World
	i. The Gospel.
	    a. A perfect Servant.
	    b. A perfected Service.
	    c. A perfecting Salvation.
	ii. The Condition.
	    a. Repent.
	        Activity of the Mind in the Presence of Sin.
	    b. Believe.
	        Activity of the Mind in the Presence of the Saviour.

THE MESSAGE OF MARK

THE Gospel according to Mark presents Jesus as the Servant of God. Whereas in Matthew He is seen in the purple of His royalty, in Mark He appears girded for service.

The inclusive message of the book is found in ch. i. 14, 15 —

"Now after that John was delivered up, Jesus came into Galilee preaching the gospel of God, and saying, The time is fulfilled, and the Kingdom of God is at hand: repent ye, and believe in the gospel."

As in the first Gospel the inclusive message is contained in the words which record the message which Jesus delivered as He commenced His preaching, so in the same place, in the same relation, we find the message of this Gospel of Mark.

Another verse, central to the Gospel, gives its content in brief outline —

"The Son of Man came not to be ministered

unto, but to minister, and to give His life a ransom for many."

That covers the whole Gospel: the first division, Sanctification, "The Son of Man came"; the second division, Service, "not to be ministered unto, but to minister"; the last division, Sacrifice, "and to give His life a ransom for many."

What then, is the message of that life, of that service, and of that sacrifice?

We shall follow exactly the same method as we adopted in dealing with the message of Matthew; inquiring first what is the essential message, and then noticing the application of that message.

In dealing with the essential message we shall attempt first to state the central teaching, and then to consider its abiding appeal.

We have said that this Gospel presents the Servant of God. When we turn from the study of its content in order to listen to its message, we must pause first to inquire in what sense it is true that Jesus was Servant of God. There are senses in which He never can be described in that way. Indeed, there is only one sense in which the Son of God can be spoken of as the Servant of God. By nature He is Son of God. By nature He is

THE MESSAGE OF MARK 27

equal with God; but for certain purposes, and in certain relationships, He became Servant of God.

This Gospel, standing as it does in the midst of revelation, is intimately related to the prophecies of the past, and has close relationship to the apostolic writings which follow. Isaiah was the prophet of the Servant of God; and Paul was the apostle who most clearly wrote of the Kenosis, or self-emptying, whereby the Son of God became the Servant of God. We have in this Gospel the real portraiture of that Servant. It reveals first, the nature of His service; secondly, the law of His service; and finally, the result of His service.

First then, as to the nature of His service. The introductory word of the Gospel is, "The beginning of the gospel of Jesus Christ, the Son of God." The final command of the Servant of God is, "Go ye into all the kosmos, and herald the gospel to the whole creation."

The Son of God became the Servant of God in order to create a gospel, to provide good news for men. The Servant of God is the Saviour of men. In order to provide salvation for them, He, Who was equal with God, became Servant; and in no other relationship can He be thus described. Wherever in the ancient prophetic writings, or in this Gospel, or in the subsequent apostolic writings, our Lord is referred to under this title of Servant of God, the subject under consideration is that of salvation. Mark commences with citation from the prophecy of Isaiah which is preëminently the prophecy of the Servant of God. The prophet's picture of that Servant was that of One Who comes to accomplish the Divine purpose of salvation. As we study the book we see the growing portrait of Him, line added to line, beauty to beauty, until we reach the mystic teaching of the fifty-third chapter, in which the Servant of God is seen, wounded for our transgressions, bruised for our iniquities, the chastisement of our peace laid upon Him. Thus He is seen fulfilling His service and accomplishing the purpose of God, that of providing a way whereby it is possible, immediately after the record of suffering, to sing the song of redemption, and to tell the story of great and gracious restoration.

Thus at the heart of the prophetic fore-vision of the Servant of God is the picture of the passion through which He is able to provide pardon, purity, peace, and power for humanity.

In the writings of Paul we may confine our attention to one passage in the Philippian letter. The injunction of that passage is, "Have this mind in you, which was also in Christ Jesus." All that follows is argument, but the argument is greater than the injunction. Charging the Philippian Christians to have the mind of Christ, the mind of graciousness, of humility, of love, Paul argued for obedience by showing what that mind really was. In studying the matchless passage we must keep our mind on the Person referred to, Who, in the essential fact of His personality, is the same throughout. This Person is first declared to be One Who, being in the form of God, did not count it a prize to be on an equality with God. It is next affirmed that this same Person emptied Himself. We must remember here that the Person is still the same. He did not empty Himself of Himself. That doctrine of the Kenosis which declares that the Son of God laid aside His Deity is not warranted by New Testament teaching. He emptied Himself as He became Man. That emptying consisted in His taking the form of a Servant. The form chosen was that of Man. Thus He laid aside one form of manifestation and took another. The form laid aside was that of sovereign Deity. The form taken was that of subservient humanity. The form alone changed; the essential Being remained the same.

For what purpose then did He thus empty Himself and take the form of a Servant? In what sense can He be spoken of as Servant?

In order to find the answer to these inquiries let us follow the descending scale. "Being made in the likeness of men; and being found in fashion as a man, He humbled Himself, becoming obedient even unto death, yea, the death of the Cross." That is why He became a Servant, and that is the sense in which He was a Servant. He is revealed in this passage as one Person, emptying Himself of one form of manifestation and taking another for the purpose of the Cross, and the purpose of the Cross is that of the salvation of man.

Thus Isaiah when he presents the great Servant shows that the central meaning of His mission is that of salvation through sacrifice; and Paul in language still more definite even though more mysterious, language which shows a deeper insight into the infinite mystery, presents this same Son of God, equal with God in His nature, partner of His throne, becoming a Servant for the Cross and for salvation. There is no sense in which the Son of God is Servant of God, save that He became such to create a gospel by providing salvation for man who is without salvation, and fast bound in sin and nature's night.

When Jesus began His ministry in Galilee He struck the key-note thereof in the words "The time is fulfilled." I remember hearing Mr. Johnston Ross say that there are some texts in the Bible of which none but an Eastern can appreciate the full meaning. Such a text is this word of Jesus, full of profound significance. "The time is fulfilled." It is the language of One Who in circumstances of lowliness, about to make His home in despised Galilee of the Gentiles, recognized the fact that the ministry He was about to exercise was the fulfillment of eternal purpose. The hour had struck, the time was filled to the full. The statement referred to all the economy which ended with the prophecy of John the Baptist. The last voice of prophecy had been heard, and all that the prophet uttered, together with all that the prophets preceding him had said, was fulfilled. Seers had for ages been looking towards the dawn of a new age, the coming of the Servant-Son, the advent of One Who would be Son by nature, and Servant for the accomplishment of the purpose of salvation and restoration.

When Jesus commenced His ministry He said, "The time is fulfilled." The Kingdom of God is near. God Himself is near. He is here in the form of a Servant, bending toward the Cross, in order that in the mystery of that "death-grapple in the darkness 'twixt old systems and the Word," He may conquer that which has spoiled, ascend the throne of empire, restore the lost and ruined order, and establish the Kingdom of God in all its grace and glory.

Thus the nature of the service is that of providing a gospel of salvation; and that fact is indicated in the opening words, "The beginning of the Gospel"; after which the Person is described by names and titles which perfectly reveal Him. Jesus is the familiar name of His humanity; Christ is the title of His Servanthood; the Son of God is the designation of His nature.

In the second place let us observe what this book teaches concerning the law of His service. This may be expressed in three words intimately related to each other; sympathy, suffering, sacrifice.

THE MESSAGE OF MARK 33

The Servant of God was in sympathy with man even in his sin; not in sympathy with his sin, but in sympathy with the sinner. If this Gospel be carefully considered—indeed if the four of them be examined—no single word of severity can be found which this Servant of God uttered to sinning men and women. His severity was reserved for hypocrisy, and that because it wrought ruin in the lives of others. For the woman taken in the very act of sin; for men steeped in sin, and held in contempt by the religious teachers of their day; He had nothing but tenderness, sympathy, and infinite compassion.

Oh, that all of us who name His name might learn the lesson of this Gospel in that respect! Salvation results from sympathy; sympathy means suffering; and suffering is only dynamic when it becomes sacrifice. If we say to men, Be warmed, and do not clothe them, there is no sympathy in such speech, neither is there any value in it. Let these men be warmed and clothed at cost, that is sacrifice. Whether we make application in the material or spiritual realm the principle is the same. I think that is what the apostle meant in his Galatian letter when he uttered the injunction which seems so commonplace in comparison with the argument which is so profound, "Bear ye one another's burdens, and so fulfill the law of Christ." I do not understand the apostle to mean that we should obey the law that Christ enunciated, but rather that which He Himself obeyed. The law of Christ's life was that of bearing the burdens of others. That is the whole story of the service of the Servant of God. The master law of His life in the presence of human sin and sorrow was that of the bearing of burdens—"Behold, the Lamb of God, which taketh away the sin of the world." Himself took our sins and bare them. The law of His service then was that of sympathy, suffering, and sacrifice.

What then was the result of His service? Its nature was the creation of a gospel; its law was the bearing of burdens; its result is found in the gospel created. The Servant is introduced as "Jesus Christ, the Son of God"; and the last words recorded by Mark as falling from His lips by way of command, are "Go ye into all the kosmos, and herald the gospel to the whole creation."

What did He mean by the Gospel? We have no right to speculate on the matter. The answer is found in the context, which, when we examine, we find that He presenced Himself in the midst of His disciples after the resurrection, and they were filled with doubt and fear. He rebuked their unbelief, and then said, Go, and preach the good news to the whole creation; that is, He commanded them to tell the good news of the resurrection. The good news then is that of the risen Christ. The resurrection is the demonstration of the fact that the Servant has accomplished His work, that He has provided salvation, that He is master over the forces that wreck and ruin and spoil. The result of His service is the provision of that gospel.

If that be the central teaching, what is the abiding appeal? The answer is found in the words of our Lord at the commencement of His ministry, " Repent ye, and believe in the gospel." "Repent ye" is the abiding preliminary. No man is ever ready to believe in the Gospel until he has obeyed the first word. That, however, is not the supreme appeal of this Gospel. The supreme appeal is contained in the words " Believe in the gospel." I know it is unsafe to base a great doctrine on a preposition; but nevertheless there is wonderful value and instruction in the prepositions made use of by the writers of the New Testament. "Believe *in* the gospel," not into it. Whenever the preposition *eis* is used with the accusative it suggests motion into. The preposition *en* used here has quite another significance. It signifies neither motion into, nor nearness to, but rest at the centre of. Jesus said, "Believe in the gospel." The Gospel is the sphere of rest; have confidence in this gospel, put your trust in it, having ventured into it, rest in it. That is the abiding appeal.

What is the application of this message to the Church of God? There is first the application to the life of the Church. This word "Believe" reveals the law of the Church's life. That life is continued and developed as she has abiding confidence in the Gospel of the Servant of God, abiding confidence in its message of pardon and power. Again, the message has yet another emphasis in its application to the Church. Not only is belief in the Gospel the law of the Church's life, it is also the law of her service. When we lose our confidence in this Gospel, then our service becomes weak. If we doubt the Gospel of the Servant of God, then we have no Gospel for the man who is fast bound in sin

THE MESSAGE OF MARK 37

and nature's night. It is in the proportion that we believe in it, are sure of it, know it, that we are able to help our day and generation. The inter-relation between life and service is of the closest. We cannot believe in this Gospel as the result of intellectual argument. We can only believe in it as the result of experience. It is only as we believe into the One it presents and find His power to save, that we believe in it when we are in the presence of other men.

What does this book say to me personally? It first calls me to believe in this Gospel, to rest in it for my life, for pardon and for power. It also calls me to rest in it for my service. The word gospel occurs eight times in the book, and a study of the passages will show the true relation of the Christian to Christ in the matter of service. It is a study for which we cannot take time here, but I suggest it as full of interest and value.

Once again, what is the message of this book to the world? What is its message to London, East End and West End, to rich and poor, to high and low, to man as man, to humanity as humanity? It tells the story, announces the good news, of the perfect Servant of God, of

His perfected service, and of His perfecting salvation. Get men to read this book, help them to understand it, interpret it to them. Sit down by the side of men mastered by sin, and read them this book. Say to them, Behold God's Servant, God's Son become Servant in order to get near to you, to help you, to lift you. Through that perfect Servant's perfected service there is perfecting salvation for you. That is preaching the Gospel.

If that be the essential message of the book to the world, its appeal is first, Repent. That is the necessary activity of the mind in the presence of sin. Its final appeal is, Believe. That is the activity of the mind in the presence of the Saviour.

This Gospel according to Mark begins where that according to Matthew ends. Matthew said, "Repent ye, for the Kingdom of heaven is at hand." As I read his story I see the King and know my own failure; I become conscious that this personality of mine is territory belonging to the King, but waste, spoiled, wilderness without blossom.

I take up the Gospel according to Mark, and it says, Behold the Servant of God. He is the

Saviour of men. I believe into Him. I believe in His Gospel. I risk eternity and my soul upon Him, and thus I am restored to the possibility of the garden, and of all fruitfulness.

THE MESSAGE OF LUKE

A THE ESSENTIAL MESSAGE	B THE APPLICATION

I. The Central Teaching
i. The Presentation of the Saviour. "The Son of Man."
   a. The racial First-born.
      1. The Fact. { Hebrew merged in humanity.
                  Humanity springing from God.
      2. The Method. { Immaculate Conception.
                      The sinless Man.
   b. The representative Brother.
      1. The Negation of Distinctions.
      2. The Realization of Essentials.
   c. The Redeeming Kinsman.
      1. The Right.
      2. The Accomplishment.
ii. The Proclamation of Salvation. "To seek and to save that which was lost."
   a. Through Redemption, Regeneration.
   b. Through Regeneration, Relationship.
   c. Through Relationship, Realization.
 	
II. The Abiding Appeal
i. The Attraction of the Personality. { *a.* The Identity.
                                             b. The Distance.
                                             c. The Sympathy.
ii. The Terms of Discipleship.
   a. Negation of old relationships and Choice of new. xiv. 26.
   b. Acceptance of Law of new Relationships. xiv. 27.
   c. Renunciation of all in order to the Reception of all. xiv. 33.
	I. To the Church
	"Witnesses."
	i. In the Power of Relationship with the Son of Man.
	   a. Fulfillment of Terms.
	      Redemption.
	   b. Realization of Results.
	      Fellowship.
	   c. Demonstration of Truth.
	      Manifestation.
	ii. For the Sake of the Lost.
	   a. Revelation.
	   b. Conviction.
	   c. Persuasion.
	
	II. To the World
	"The Son of Man came to seek and to save that which was lost."

THE MESSAGE OF LUKE

THIS third Gospel presents Jesus of Nazareth to us in the grace and glory of His perfect Manhood.

Its essential message is crystallized in the declaration of the Lord Himself in answer to the persistent criticism of the Pharisees; "The Son of Man came to seek and to save that which was lost."

The message of this Gospel is not a simple message. The more carefully we study this book the more are we impressed with its profundity, with the wonder and spaciousness of the thing it has to say to us concerning Christ. It first presents the Saviour, the Son of Man; it secondly, and consequently, proclaims the possibility of salvation for the sons of men.

Let us then first consider the Saviour that this book presents to us. There are three things to be noted. Luke is careful, in his introductory section, to show us the nature of this Person. He presents to us the racial First-born; the *second* man; the *last* Adam. The first man appears upon the page of the Old Testament, and he fails. The second Man appears upon the page of the New Testament, and He realizes all the Divine intention for humanity. The first Adam, the head of the race, from whom the race has proceeded, is presented to us in the Old Testament. The last Adam, the Head of a new race, is presented in the New Testament. There will be no other. The ultimate, the final race, is to spring from this second Man, Who is the last Adam.

He is then presented as the representative Brother, not Brother of the race that is fallen, but Brother of the race that is to be made—a distinction which we need to make very carefully. There is a sense in which He took on Him the very nature of Adam; but He did not share his sinful nature, although eventually He bore his sin in the mystery of His dying. We look first of all, not at the Saviour Who in the mystery of His passion wrought out human redemption; we look at a Man, the second Man, the last Adam, the racial First-born, and therefore the representative Brother of all such as are to follow, of all such as are to spring from Him, as surely as the race sprang from Adam.

THE MESSAGE OF LUKE 43

Finally, and let us mark the sequence, He is presented as the redeeming Kinsman, or, to borrow the old Hebrew word, the *Goel*.

The experimental process is in the reverse order. We come to the redeeming Kinsman; and receiving the redemption which the Kinsman provides, enter into fellowship with the representative Brother; until at last we are made perfect partakers of that life which makes us one with the racial First-born.

In presenting the First-born of the new race, Luke is careful to show how the Hebrew was merged in humanity, and how humanity sprang from Deity. That is the suggestiveness of the genealogy which he gives. Notice the difference between that of Matthew and that of Luke. Matthew, who was presenting the King, was careful to set Him in relation to David, as of the royal line, and to Abraham, as of the Hebrew people. Luke sweeps back through everything that is purely Hebrew, until he comes to the fountainhead of humanity, Adam; of whom, in a word that would astonish us if we were not so perfectly familiar with it, he says, "the Son of God." Thus he presents Jesus as human, of our very nature, human as we are human, but he puts Him even in that nature into immediate relationship with God.

Luke then tells us the mystery of how this second Man came into human life. He declares that the conception of this Man was immaculate. The Roman dogma of the immaculate conception has nothing to do with the phrase in the sense in which I use it. That dogma was promulgated in 1854, and was never held before. There had been long arguments from the twelfth century, not as to the sinlessness of Jesus, but as to the sinlessness of Mary, which is a very different thing. When the Roman speaks of the immaculate conception, he means that Mary was sinless in being, because sinless in the mystery of conception, which is the Roman theologians' way of attempting to account for the sinlessness of Jesus. To say the least that is but to put the difficulty one stage further back, namely, to the mother of Mary, and then to fail to solve it. With fine delicacy of touch Luke declared that in the mystery of the conception of this new Man there was a process by which He was sinlessly conceived—" That which is to be born shall be called holy." In the mystery of that Divine activity of the overshadowing of the Virgin, she was cleansed from all sin, so that the Man Who appears before us is immaculately conceived, and therefore is a sinless Man.

In the Biblical account of creation we have an ascending scale. Day one; light and darkness, day and night. Day two; the dividing of waters. Day three; land, and vegetable life. Day four; signs and seasons, days and years. Day five; sentient life. Then what? Man, the result of all the upward processes from chaos and darkness, the crowning glory of all that which constitutes the lower side of his being. But how? Mark this most carefully; there was now a new activity, not part of the process that had preceded, but distinct from it; God "breathed into his breathing places the breath of lives," and man appeared. The processes did not create man, they only contributed towards the material fact of his human nature. Human nature is not animal nature. All the processes did but produce the temporary tabernacle, that which is to pass and perish. The Divine in-breathing produced the man.

The next picture is that of an assault upon man by the powers of darkness, of man yielding to those powers, and of his consequent descent or fall. The process runs on through history.

From that man sprang the race, inheriting and sharing the results of that man's loss of the sceptre, because of his rebellion against the throne of God.

Now behold the second Man, the last Adam. As the first man was, as to his material nature, taken out of the dust through the processes of ascent, and then by the final act of Divine breathing was made man, who never had been man before, and never could be man but by that mystery; so now in the fullness of time God again took hold of dust, only beginning this time not away back where we cannot trace the workings, but beginning at the point where He ended before. This second Man was taken out of humanity, inheriting all its essential qualities, but distinct from it; like in all things to His brethren, unlike all those from whom He is taken, because of immaculate conception, and therefore sinless. This is a new beginning, a new start in the history of the race. From that moment I read on, and the Gospel reveals this Man as the First-born of the race, as the representative Brother of the whole family.

When we look at this Man we see the negation of all distinctions. I quote from Paul in the

THE MESSAGE OF LUKE 47

Galatian letter for the sake of conciseness and brevity: "There can be neither Jew nor Greek, there can be neither bond nor free, there can be no male and female: for ye all are one in Christ Jesus." Mark the divisions. How is humanity divided to-day? By race, by caste, and by sex. In Christ there is neither race, nor caste, nor sex. Think in the presence of Paul's word of this Man presented in the Gospel, and see how He represents every type, every class, every possibility, every phase. Jesus was not a poet. You cannot place Him in the Poets' Corner; but more poetry has come out of the things He said than from any other fountainhead in the history of literature. Jesus was no philosopher. He enunciated no system of philosophy; yet the great philosophies all owe something to His inspiration and suggestion. Jesus was not a Man of science; but all scientific investigation has had its chance as the result of His opening the way and making possible the investigations of the centuries. The Easterner is at home in the presence of Christ with all his mystic dreaming; and so also is the Westerner, with his ceaseless, practical, determined endeavour. Whatever the type or class may be, both men and women find in Him the inspiration of noblest things, the crown and glory of all that which is peculiar to them. There He stands upon the page of the Gospel, the Representative Brother. Whether men dwell North, South, East or West, they touch Him and feel the answering thrill of His Brotherhood. He is the Head of the race, and therefore the Representative Brother.

If in Him I find the negation of distinctions, in Him I also find the realization of the essentials of human nature as I know it.

Finally, He is the redeeming Kinsman. What was the right of the *Goel*, according to Hebrew law and practice? Nearness of kin was the fundamental right. It was the next-of-kin that must redeem his brother. So He came, the next-of-kin to humanity. But the redeemer must accept responsibility. He came accepting responsibility. The redeemer must overcome those who are against his brother. He overcame all the forces against humanity. The redeemer must create the opportunity for his brother's reinstatement; the work of the *Goel* was the redemption of the person and the inheritance. All these things are fulfilled in this Man. Luke the Greek, writing

THE MESSAGE OF LUKE 49

to Theophilus the Greek, declared that in this Man he had found the fulfillment of the Greek ideal: being and birth, childhood and confirmation, development and anointing; physical, mental, spiritual perfection. In the next section he showed how this perfect Being was perfected, demonstrated perfect through processes of temptation, teaching, and transfiguration. That was the filling to the full of the Greek ideal. They never saw any further than the possibility of perfecting the individual.

The final section of the Gospel, the greatest section of all, shows that this Man not only fulfilled the Greek ideal of personal perfection, but He broke it into a thousand fragments, seeing it was too small to hold Him, as He turned His back upon His personal rights, that He might die and liberate His life, and so make it dynamic for others.

This Gospel of Luke says, Behold the Man; the racial First-born; the representative Brother; the redeeming Kinsman. So it presents the Saviour.

Then it makes proclamation of salvation. "The Son of man"; that is the Saviour presented; "Came to seek and to save that which was lost"; that is salvation proclaimed.

Through His redemption, He regenerates men who have fallen; and through that regeneration, He brings them into living relationship with Himself as the new Head of the new race; and through that relationship with Himself, makes them members of the new race. That is salvation.

He came "to seek and to save that which was lost." By the mystery of His death He put sin away, and liberated His life, placing it at the disposal of those who have lost their own. When they receive His life, it is His life they live. Through regeneration He brings them into living relationship with Himself. By that relationship He makes possible their realization of the same nature. Christ is more than human. Every Christian becomes more than human. Christians are made "partakers of the Divine nature."

What then is the abiding appeal of this Gospel? Its first note is that of the attraction of the Personality. First because of the identity between men and Himself. His familiarity with men was born of His conception of the dignity of humanity. If we feel that there are people we hold in contempt, it is because we have a low estimate of humanity.

People were attracted to Christ also by the sense of distance. They said, He is so near us, and yet is so different. He sits down to eat with us, and yet all the while He is saying things we have never heard before.

The final reason of His attractiveness was that of His sympathy. Give that Gospel of Luke to some man who has never read it, who is an honest man; let him sit down and read it, and I venture to affirm he will feel the same charm that men of old felt, the humanness of this Man, the identity with our own life, His distance from it, and the tender sympathy breathing through everything He does and says. That is the first appeal of this Gospel.

The appeal is more than that. It is not only the attraction of Personality. It is that of the terms of discipleship. It is in this Gospel that I find the passage which I never read without trembling. Just before the parable of lost things occur the most severe and appalling words that ever fell from His lips, "If any man cometh unto Me, and hateth not his own father and mother, and wife, and children, and brethren, and sisters, yea, and his own life also, he cannot be My disciple. Whosoever doth not bear his own cross,

and come after me, cannot be My disciple
. . . Whosoever he be of you that renounceth not all that he hath, he cannot be My disciple." That is the appeal of the Gospel.

These three conditions correspond to the three facts we have considered. Racial First-born, He says to men, You must sever connection with the old race entirely if you are coming after Me; if there is any love in your heart for father, mother, wife, child, brother, sister, which is going to interfere with your loyalty to Me, you must crucify it. I am the First-born of a new race, and you must come after Me by severing your connection with the old race.

Representative Brother of the new race, He says that we must accept the new responsibility. If you are coming after Me you must take up the cross! You cannot find your way into the brotherhood with all its benefits, if you are not fulfilling the conditions.

Redeeming Kinsman, He declares that He can only redeem us, as we give up everything for Him. If you are going to have the benefit of redemption, you must renounce all that you have! There must be mutual sacrifice. It is upon the plane, where He is stripped of dignity, and I am stripped of everything, that we meet.

That is the appeal of the Gospel according to Luke. The attraction of Personality and the terms of discipleship.

In a word, let me make the twofold application. I find the application to the Church in the words of the risen Lord, "Ye shall be My witnesses." In the power of the relationship with the Son of Man, I am to become His witness, His defense, His evidence! His witness, fulfilling the terms we have considered. His witness, realizing the results of the fulfillment of those terms in actual fellowship with Himself. His witness, demonstrating His power because I who was ruined am now redeemed. I who had lost my sense of the infinite and my love of the pure have been brought into fellowship with God, and have purity as the passion of my heart.

Then, because He came to seek and to save the lost, this Gospel calls the Church into fellowship with Him for the sake of the lost; by revelation of what He is able to do in our transformed lives, by conviction so produced in the minds of those who observe, and then by persuasion of such as are convinced towards the selfsame Saviour.

What is the message of this Gospel to the world? Carry it to the ends of the earth, let it speak its own truth to the men who are lost, and it tells them of a Kinsman Who, to borrow the old Hebrew figure, is able to discharge their debt, destroy their enemies, make possible the redemption of their persons and the redemption of their inheritance, as offspring of God.

Behold the Man, but do not try to place Him on a level with yourself. He is intimately near; all the essential things of my humanity are in Him! He is infinitely far; all the incidentals of my sin and pollution are not in Him! Because of His purity, in the mystery of His death, He becomes the Son of man seeking and saving the lost.

THE MESSAGE OF JOHN

A THE ESSENTIAL MESSAGE	B THE APPLICATION

I. The Central Teaching—God
i. Full of Grace.
    a. The Fact.
        1. Love the Divine Consciousness.
        2. Love the Inspiration of the Divine Activity.
        3. Love the Law of the Divine Government.
    b. The Illustrations.   Works.
        1. Water to Wine.   The Joy of Life. Marriage.
        2. Nobleman's Son.   Family Life.
        3. Bethesda Man.   Sin and Suffering.
        4. Feeding Five Thousand.   The Support of Life.
        5. Walking on Sea.   The Succour of Life.
        6. Blind Man.   The Light of Life.
        7. Lazarus.   Redemption.
    c. The equal Fullness of Truth.
    Passion governed by Principle.
ii. Full of Truth.
    a. The Fact.
        1. Light the Divine Consciousness.
        2. Light the Inspiration of the Divine Activity.
        3. Light the Law of the Divine Government.
    b. The Illustrations.   Words.
        1. "I am the Bread of Life."   Sustenance by Holiness.
        2. "I am the Light of the World."   Illumination by Holiness.
        3. "I am the Door."   Safety by Holiness.
        4. "I am the Good Shepherd."   Supply by Holiness.
        5. "I am the Resurrection and the Life."   Triumph by Holiness.
        6. "I am the Way, the Truth, and the Life."   Progress by Holiness.
        7. "I am the Vine."   Fellowship by Holiness.
    c. The equal Fullness of Grace.
    Principle suffused with Passion.
II. The Abiding Appeal
i. The Call to Worship.
    a. The Tabernacle—the Flesh.
    b. The Glory. Full of Grace and Truth.
ii. The Call to Service. "As the Father hath sent Me . . ."
	I. To the Church
	i. Intellectual.
	    Give the Lord Jesus Christ His true Place.
	ii. Spiritual.
	    Believing ye have Life.
	    Grace.
	    Love the Motive.
	    Truth.
	    Light the Method.
	
	II. To the World
	i. No man hath seen God.
	ii. The Only-born hath declared Him.
	To the satisfaction of
	The Intellect.
	The Conscience.
	The Heart.

THE MESSAGE OF JOHN

IT is sometimes affirmed that the synoptic Gospels are simple and easy of understanding, and that the Gospel according to John is profound, full of mystery, and difficult of interpretation. There is a sense in which all this is true. There is another sense in which the first three are books of mystery, while the last is the book of revelation, of unveiling. In John we find the solution of the mysteries of which we are inevitably conscious in studying Matthew, Mark, and Luke.

The Gospel according to Matthew presents Jesus as King, and it is impossible to read it without being brought to consciousness of His authority, even though we may not yield thereto. We are convinced of His kingliness, but are unable to account for that tone of authority which distinguishes His teaching from that of all others. In the Gospel according to Mark we find the picture of the Servant of God, eager, full of ceaseless activity, accomplishing His service and crowning it by sacrifice. We cannot read it, however, without feeling that there are depths to the consecration, and sublimities in the sacrifice, for which we cannot account. In the Gospel according to Luke we find a Man of our own humanity, but are conscious that while He is in many senses near, in others He is far away, and the contemplation fills us with awe and wonder.

These three stories demand another, or else they remain full of beauty, but inexplicable, for the Person presented as King, as Servant, as Man, possesses in all these aspects some qualities or quantities which lack explanation. In the Gospel according to John we find the answer to the riddle, the solution of the enigma, the unveiling of the mystery. This Gospel is as certainly an apocalypse as is the book which bears that name. This is unveiling. Here we meet exactly the same King we met and crowned in Matthew; the same Servant we saw and trusted in Mark; the same Man we observed and longed to be like in Luke. It is indeed the same Person; the same face, the same love-lit eyes and awful purity; the same regal authority; the same unobtrusive humility. Sometimes I think in reading this Gospel that I feel the touch of the flesh of Jesus more really than in Matthew, Mark, or Luke; yet from the first and sublime words with which it opens, to the simple and wonderful declarations with which it closes, I know that I am in the presence of an unveiled Person. The mystery of Matthew, Mark, and Luke is solved for me when I read John. This Gospel accounts for that note of authority which sounded in the Manifesto, and which breathed in power through the invitation, "Come unto Me all ye that labour . . . and I will give you rest." When I see Him in the Gospel of John I understand the secret of His sublime service. Here I have the explanation of the spaciousness and wonder of His humanity. In this Gospel the Person comes not from Abraham through the royal line of David; not from Nazareth; without genealogy; not from Adam, without a father; but from eternity and from God, as the Only-born of God.

The essential message of this Gospel is found in the closing declaration of the prologue. "No man hath seen God at any time; the only begotten Son, which is in the bosom of the Father, He hath declared Him." First, a recognition of limitation and need, "No man hath seen God at any time"; then the essential affirmation, "God only-born which is in the bosom of the Father, He hath declared Him." There is diversity of opinion concerning the actual form of the phrase translated in our English versions, "only begotten Son," resulting from the fact that the manuscripts are not in agreement. It is difficult, therefore, to be dogmatic. I do not think the meaning is materially changed whichever form we take, as either phrase suggests the same thought of relationship between the Son and the Father.

This "only begotten Son," or "God only-born of the Father," has declared God. The Greek word translated declared is that from which we have obtained our word exegesis, and means the leading-out of something that is hidden, in order that it may be seen. The Son, therefore, is declared to be—I use the word, knowing the difficulty of it—the exegesis of God; that is, the interpretation of God, the explanation of God. That is also the teaching of the principal statement of the prologue. "In the beginning was the Word, and the Word was with God, and the Word was God. . . . And the Word became flesh, and dwelt among us (and we beheld His glory, glory as of the only begotten from the Father), full of grace and truth." That is the value of this book. It presents the Person Who is the exegesis of God, that is, the manifestation of God.

Consequently the central teaching of the book is that it reveals the truth about God. If we would know the truth concerning His nature, we must study this Gospel. If we would know the laws which govern His activity, we discover them here. All that man needs to know about God is contained in this Gospel according to John. It is the final document of revealed religion concerning God. It is the story of the Son as the Revealer of the Father; the presentation of the One Who unveiled the face of God, Who told us the deepest secrets about His nature, Who revealed to men the laws of His activity.

> "Would we see God's brightest glory,
> We must look in Jesu's face."

Man is forever attempting to represent God in some way. That is the meaning of all idolatry, and of every idol. In the intention of those who made it, the golden calf was a likeness of God; for when they erected it they worshipped Jehovah. The golden calf was the golden ox, the symbol of service and sacrifice, and these people were attempting to express certain truths in some way which would appeal to the senses. Their action was the result of hunger for manifestation. God had said, "Thou shalt not make unto thee a graven image, nor the likeness of any form that is in heaven above, or that is in the earth beneath, or that is in the water under the earth; thou shalt not bow down thyself unto them, nor serve them," because that which man makes as a likeness of God can only libel God. The highest forms of man's attempts to give expression to the facts concerning the nature of God consist in the projection of human personality into immensity. The trouble with all false religion is that man has projected himself into immensity with all his faults and failure, and the deity so imagined is a magnified sinner, and men worshipping that, become more and more like that which they have made.

Man is ever seeking a manifestation, and the incarnation was God's answer to that need of humanity. He came into human nature, and through the Manhood of Jesus manifested Himself, in order that men seeking for manifestation which should enable them to know Him might find it. He was of our humanity, not by will or act of humanity, as we have seen in Matthew, and in Luke; but by the overshadowing and mystery of the Divine power, and by the activity of His own Holy Spirit, grasping our humanity, grafting Himself upon it in order that man seeking for manifestation might find One Who is at once of his own nature and of the nature of God. In the Gospel of John we look at Jesus, but at the same moment we see God. In the tears of Jesus we see the tears of God. In the pain of Jesus we see the passion of God. That is the value of this book, and that is why it is not easy to deal with. We touch and handle a Man; He is the Word of life; a word cannot be touched, and life cannot be handled; yet through this Man we do touch and handle life, age-abiding life, for in Him the Word is become flesh. To use the daring declaration of Charles Wesley, " God is contracted to a span " in order that men may see Him.

What then is the central teaching of this book concerning God? What do we know of God through Jesus? In the prologue we have a comprehensive answer which is dealt with more particularly, subsequently by illustration, "We beheld His glory, glory as of the only begotten from the Father, full of grace and truth." When we have uttered those two words, grace and truth, we have uttered all the truth about God. In the subsequent part of the book these words are illustrated; but the inclusive fact of grace may be revealed in a threefold affirmation concerning love. Love is the Divine consciousness. Love is the inspiration of the Divine activity. Love is the law of the Divine government. The result is grace.

Love is the Divine consciousness. When we speak of our own mind we speak of consciousness and subconsciousness. The fact of subconsciousness results from our finite and limited nature. With God there is no subconsciousness. He has perfect consciousness, and that is love. If it would be right to speak of God in the terms which we use about ourselves we might ask, What is the experience, the consciousness of God underlying all His action? There can be but one answer, and that is Love. That is the profoundest truth.

Therefore all the activity of God is love in-

THE MESSAGE OF JOHN 65

spired, and the law of His government is love. That is the truth which is revealed concerning God through His Son.

For illustration of that we may take out of the mass of material the great signs. Sign is John's word for the wonders of Jesus. He never speaks of a parable. The word parable as we find it in the other Gospels does not occur in this one. We do find it in our English versions, but the margin suggests proverb, which is perhaps a more insufficient translation than parable. The Greek word of which John makes use would be better translated in our language, allegory, for it has a much wider meaning than parable. The miracles which John records are chosen with evident intention of teaching larger truths; they are signs. Every one is an activity of love. The first was that of turning the water into wine. Right on the threshold of the revelation of God, this Man went to a marriage feast and ministered to the joy of life. The next sign was the restoration of the nobleman's son to health. Love recognized the sorrow in the family circle through sickness, and the fact that death was threatening; and acted to end the sorrow by healing the sickness, and defeating death. The next sign was that of the healing of the man in the Bethesda porches. Love suffering in the presence of sin, as seen in its result, acted for the sake of the sinner. Love entered into suffering, and breaking the power of sin ended it, and so gave deliverance to the sinner. The next sign was that of the feeding of the five thousand. Love, recognizing man's need of actual support, provided it. The next sign was that of the walking on the sea. Love, coming to troubled souls, tempest-tossed, bewildered, walking in infinite dignity over the waters that threatened to engulf them, and through the wind which impeded their progress, coming on board produced a great calm. The next sign was that of the blind man. Love opened his eyes and, claiming to be the Light of the world, gave spiritual teaching. Love is the illumination of all life. The last sign was the raising of Lazarus. Love groaned in spirit and was troubled and wept; and in that groaning we hear the distress of God, in those tears we behold the grief of Deity. Love was troubled in the presence of death, and through the mystery of its own trouble and pain broke the bands of death.

There is equal fullness of truth wherever we

THE MESSAGE OF JOHN 67

look upon the fullness of grace. Love breathes through every one of the signs, but light shines also. Grace is there, but so also is truth. There was no shadow, no duplicity, no turning aside from the master principle of holiness which rests at the heart of the universe, no deflection from the straight line of righteousness. Love and light, grace and truth, passion governed by principle.

What we have said of grace when interpreting it as love, we can with equal accuracy affirm of truth when interpreting it as light. Light is the Divine consciousness. Light is the inspiration of the Divine activity. Light is the law of the Divine government. As we took the great works to illustrate grace we may take the outstanding words to illustrate truth.

"I am the Bread of life"; sustenance by holiness.

"I am the Light of the world"; illumination by holiness.

"I am the Door"; safety by holiness.

"I am the good Shepherd"; supply by holiness.

"I am the Resurrection and the Life"; triumph by holiness.

"I am the Way, the Truth, and the Life"; progress by holiness.

"I am the Vine"; fellowship and identity with holiness.

From out of the resplendent glory of the revelation of God in the bush, burnt but not consumed, Moses heard the Divine affirmation, "I AM"; and then, as though there could be no unveiling, the declaration turned back upon itself in majestic mystery, and ended with the affirmation "THAT I AM."

"The law was given by Moses; grace and truth came by Jesus Christ." He took up the same great revealing name "I am," and linking it to simple symbols, enabled men to understand in fuller measure the being of God. In connection with the communication of the name to Moses the supreme fact insisted upon was that of the holiness of Jehovah, as he had been commanded "Put off thy shoes from off thy feet, for the place whereon thou standest is holy ground"; that same fact of holiness is always present in the use of the title by Christ, and as we have seen, He revealed the relation of holiness to all the facts of life already suggested.

When we study these words revealing the

truth, the light, we must not forget the equal fullness of grace. As when speaking of grace we insisted upon the equal fullness of truth, so while we are conscious of the awful purity of holiness in the shining of the light, we are nevertheless conscious that the light is suffused by a great love. If when considering grace we declared that therein we saw passion governed by principle, in this consideration of truth we may declare with equal accuracy that we have principle suffused with passion. John saw in the Man upon Whom he looked grace and truth, and thus saw the glory of the Father.

The abiding appeal of this is first that of the call to worship. "The Word became flesh and tabernacled among us," that is, pitched His tent among us. John, a Hebrew, used language which would be perfectly familiar to his own people. He was thinking of the tabernacle in the wilderness, the tent pitched in the midst of the people, the centre of their life, and the appointed place of their worship, and he said, "The Word . . . pitched His tent among us." His flesh became the tent; but as in the ancient tabernacle the central fact was the glory of the Shekinah, so in this new tent of the flesh of the Man of Nazareth, the central fact was the glory of the Only begotten of the Father, full of grace and truth. When the tabernacle was finished according to pattern, the glory of the Lord filled it, and it became the place of worship. In the new covenant we find the fulfillment of the olden symbolism. The Word is incarnate and through the eyes of the Son of man we see the light of God; and in His voice we hear the accents of the love of God; in Him we see God full of grace and truth, and the unveiling cries to us, "O worship the Lord in the beauty of holiness."

The appeal is a call to service as well as a call to worship. The tabernacle being erected, the nation was completed by worship, and so prepared for witness. When we stand in the presence of this Man and see through the veil of His flesh Divine "the light that were else too bright for the feebleness of a sinner's sight" we worship, and we are also compelled to serve. When Isaiah beheld the temple full of the glory of the Lord, and cried out because of the uncleanness of his lips, and when the seraph had cleansed those lips with the live coal from off the altar, then the voice of God was heard, " Whom shall

THE MESSAGE OF JOHN

I send, and who will go for Us?" the answer of the prophet was immediate, "Here am I; send me." When we stand in the presence of this unveiling and see the glory of God in this tabernacle; when we worship in response to that revelation, then we hear out of the tabernacle the word "As the Father hath sent Me, even so send I you," and we shall be ready individually to respond, "Here am I; send me."

There is intellectual and spiritual application of this message of John to the Church of God. The intellectual application is that the Church must give to the Lord Jesus Christ His true place, and His true place is that which is here revealed. In this Gospel we see Him perfectly, finally. To speak of Him as Jesus of Nazareth only is to degrade Him, and the moment we do so we fail to find God, and sooner or later our conception of God will be false. There will be denial of essential truth, and excuse made for sin. There will be denial of essential grace, and all the springs of service will be dried up. It is only when the Church of God sees this Man at the centre of her life, and He is recognized as being the tabernacle in which essential God is resident for purpose of revelation, that she can realize her own life, or fulfill her service.

The spiritual application is that in believing we have life, and that such life will manifest itself in grace and truth. Grace will be the motive, and truth the method of all our acts. The proportion in which we have seen and believed and become what He would make us, is the proportion in which we manifest His life in grace and truth.

There is an application of this message of John to the wider world. "No man hath seen God at any time," yet man needs God, and subconsciously is aware of his need, and is groping after a god, trying to find a centre for his worship, something to which he can bow himself down. All the result of such groping is deeper darkness and more disastrous failure. Let man take the Person of this Gospel and consider Him well, and he will find God to the satisfaction of his intellect, to the satisfaction of his conscience, to the satisfaction of his heart.

The final appeal is to the will of man. This God satisfies my intellect, my emotion, and appeals to my will. I can still rebel. This Man stood in the midst of His own age and said, "Ye will not come to Me, that ye may have life." May that lament of Jesus not be true of us, but may we come to Him, and find our life, as we find our God.

THE MESSAGE OF ACTS

A THE ESSENTIAL MESSAGE	B THE APPLICATION

I. The Central Teaching. Concerning the Church
i. The abiding Principles.
    a. Origin. Created by the Son.
    b. Nature. "Many Sons unto Glory."
    c. Function. The Work of the Son.
ii. The revealed Perils.
    a. Prejudice. The Grip of the Past.
                       { Judaism.
                       { Lack of Confidence in the Spirit.
    b. Passion. The power of the Flesh.
                       { Carnality.
                       { Lack of Yielding to the Spirit.
    c. Pride. The Lure of the World.
                       { Apostasy.
                       { Lack of Obedience to the Spirit.
	I. To the Church
	i. A Question of Motive. The Glory of God.
	
	ii. A Question of Method. The Work of the Son by the Spirit.

II. The Abiding Appeal
i. The master Passion of the Church is that of the Glory of God.
        { The unveiling of Himself.
        { The Establishment of His Kingdom.
ii. The inclusive Principle of the Church is that of Loyalty to the Lord.
        { Realization of His Life.
        { Prosecution of His Work.
iii. The sufficient Power of the Church is that of the Holy Spirit.
        { Likeness to the Lord for the Revelation of God.
        { Direction in His Work for the Glory of God.
	II. To the World
	This Book, as a Book, has no application to the World.

THE MESSAGE OF ACTS

THIS book is of great importance to the students of the New Testament. It is the link of continuity, binding together into one great whole the historic records of the life of our Lord, and the didactic and devotional writings of the apostolic period. In the gospel narratives, as the writer of this book reminds us, we have the story of beginnings; the beginnings of the doing and teaching of Jesus; and this is the only historic record upon which we can depend, as to those events which immediately followed His death and resurrection and ascension.

Turning to the other part of the New Testament, I find constant references to churches. The word church has no full and final explanation in the four gospel stories. Thirteen of the pamphlets in that which remains of the New Testament were written by a man whose name was Paul. He is never mentioned in the four Gospels. In order to understand the continuity of the story commenced in the Gospels we need this book. In order to an interpretation of all that follows in the great didactic and devotional writings we need this book. It is the link between the first four books and all that remains, binding them together. It is the bridge over which we cross from the story of the beginning of the doing and teaching of Jesus, to those writings which are the result of the fulfillment of the promise He made to His people that, after He had left them as to bodily presence, they should have full and spacious teaching for all life and service. He said that it was better for them that He should go away. He declared that when He went away the Spirit should be given, Who would bring to their remembrance the things He had said to them, guide them into all truth, and teach them concerning things to come. In the epistles and devotional literature we have the fulfillment of these promises in interpretations of the Christ, and in teaching concerning things to come. How the promise was fulfilled we find in the book of the Acts of the Apostles, in the account of the coming of the Spirit, and in the record of that Spirit's ministry in and through the disciples of Jesus.

In our study of the content we laid great

THE MESSAGE OF ACTS 77

emphasis upon the one word "began"; and in our analysis of the book we devoted a section of the first division to one verse, because the light from it flashes back upon the story of the Gospel, and forward upon the story of this book, and upon all the writings that follow.

That word "began" gives the true value to the gospel story, showing that it is not the account of consummated work, but the story of the initiation of work. It also flings its light upon the book of the Acts of the Apostles, suggesting that it is the story of the things He continued to do and to teach. One Christ is presented to our view both in the Gospels and in the Acts. In the Gospels we see Him in limited, localized, and straitened circumstances; the limitation, localization, and straitening necessary in order to completion of the initial, preparatory work. In Acts we see the same Christ, no longer limited, no longer localized, no longer straitened; the unlimited nature of His work, the universal application of His power, and the unstraitened operation thereof, all resulting from the mystery of the things He began to do and to teach in circumstances of localized limitation.

Now when we begin to seek for the message,

there is another word upon which we must lay equal emphasis. It is the first word of the second verse; "*until* the day in which He was received up, after that He had given commandment through the Holy Ghost unto the apostles whom He had chosen." In the former treatise we have the account of the things He *began* to do *until*. That word "until" carries over the force of the word "began" into the new book. In the first book we have the things He *began* to do and to teach *until* He was received up. In the book of the Acts we have the things He *began* to do *after* He was received up. This book is also the story of beginnings. Nothing is finished. That quality creates its value. When we discover it, and remember it, and depend upon it, we are very near to the discovery of its message. It is not the story of a completed movement. It is the story of all He began to do after He was received up. He has never ceased the doing until now. The work is going forward. He is still doing. He is still teaching. The risen, ascended Lord is the living centre of His Church.

The beginnings of Divine activities are always ideally and potentially perfect; but they are always actually and effectively imperfect. I turn

THE MESSAGE OF ACTS

to the first book of the Bible and read, "In the beginning God created." That was the beginning of Divine activity in creation. In the Gospel of John I read, "In the beginning was the Word, and the Word was with God, and the Word was God"; and that declaration prepares the way for the teaching concerning the beginning of the Divine activity of redemption in human history when the Word became flesh. The third new beginning is in this book of the Acts of the Apostles. The beginning in creation; the beginning of the new departure in incarnation; the beginning of the new departure in the Church; these are the three great beginnings of Divine activity which our Bible reveals to us, and in each case we see beginnings ideally and potentially perfect; and actually and effectively imperfect.

As we look at the creation as it is revealed in the poetic, majestic, true story of Genesis, it is ideally, potentially perfect. The morning stars sang together over that first creation, and I think I know the burden of their song; The whole earth is full of the glory of God. In the midst of the earth is man, made as the psalmist long afterwards sang, "but little lower than

God," crowned with glory and honour that he might have dominion over the whole creation. That is creation ideally, potentially perfect! But actually, effectively it is imperfect, in that it is waiting for development. The perfect earth needs cultivation, development; needs that man, its king, shall discover its secrets and obey its laws, in order to the discovery of its hidden mysteries and wonders. Man to-day is standing in the presence of the wonders and hidden forces of the earth saying: We have but scratched the surface, and have hardly begun to understand the depths. But all the forces and all the glories and all the beauties were resident in the earth on that morning flushed with beauty when the sons of God sang together over creation. The Divine beginnings are always ideally, potentially perfect; and actually, effectively imperfect.

If with profounder reverence we look upon the mystery of the incarnation we find the same facts. Mark the perfection of it; "We beheld His glory, glory as of the only begotten from the Father, full of grace and truth." That was the beginning, ideally, potentially perfect; but actually and effectively the beginning was imperfect. The life must be consummated;

THE MESSAGE OF ACTS

and the death must be accomplished. The beginning of the Divine activity was perfect, ideally and potentially, "It was the good pleasure of the Father that in Him should all the fullness dwell . . . in Him dwelleth all the fullness of the Godhead bodily." But there was work to be done; through the processes of passion, death, and resurrection the work must be accomplished; actually and effectively the beginning of the incarnation was imperfect.

Now we come to the beginning described in the book of the Acts. "Having received of the Father the promise of the Holy Ghost, He hath poured forth this, which ye see and hear." That statement is full of suggestiveness. That was the new beginning; the dawn of a new day; as wonderful a thing, a more wonderful thing, than the dawn of creation long ago.

It was a new beginning, ideally and potentially perfect. The risen and ascended Lord, in His own Person, by virtue of the victory of the purity of His life, and the passion of His death, had received the plenitude of the Spirit of God as a deposit for all for whom He lived and died. This gift He poured out upon His waiting disciples, and in the upper room there was the dawn of a new creation, the break of a new day, the initiation of a new movement.

It was a new beginning, actually and effectively imperfect. These waiting men in the upper room received the Holy Spirit, but they had to learn the law of the Spirit, to discover the method of the guidance of the Spirit; through long processes they had to learn the meaning of the power that had come to them through Christ. This book gives us the picture of the new beginnings. That is its value. A note of warning is immediately necessary. We must not go back to the Acts of the Apostles and try to imitate the incidentals. We must go back to it to discover its essentials, and these essentials are not nineteen centuries away from us; they are with us perpetually. This book then is of supreme value because it reveals the principles and the perils of the age of Pentecost. These constitute the message of the book, and create its abiding appeal.

The central teaching of this book concerns the Christian Church, and deals with fundamental matters. Through the incidentals we see the essentials.

First, it is a revelation of the abiding principles

of the Church of God. For purposes of conciseness and brevity I want to group these under three heads; the origin of the Church of God; the nature of the Church of God; the function of the Church of God. The revelation is all the more wonderful, and all the more valuable, and all the more perpetual, because it is not formulated. I know that some would be far more comfortable if they could have a book with a formulated system of Church government; but spiritual intelligence thanks God for atmosphere.

As to origin, the Christian Church is the creation of the Son. He prepared, during the three years of His public ministry, a little group of men and women; stored their minds with truth, which they did not then understand; impressed upon them the fact of His personality, which they did not then apprehend. Then He left them, prepared for something larger and greater, yet unable to move forward until they should be "clothed with power from on high."

Then having risen from the dead and ascended to the right hand of the Father, He received the fullness of the Holy Spirit and poured it out; "There came from heaven a sound as of the rushing of a mighty wind, and it filled all the house where they were sitting. And there appeared unto them tongues parting asunder, like as of fire; and it sat upon each one of them. And they were all filled with the Holy Ghost." That is the Christian Church; created by His humiliation, by the perfection of His human life, by the mystery of His passion, by His victory over sin and death and all the enemies of the race, by His triumphant resurrection, by His ascension, by the Spirit bestowed as the result of His own accomplished victory. When He poured the Spirit out upon that handful of people, the Church was born. The Church consists then of all those men and women who are made one Spirit with the Lord, who share His very life by the coming of the Spirit, who are united to Him, no longer upon the basis of human sentiment, no longer by the limitation of geographical situation, but because the one Spirit of God that fills the risen Man in glory, perfectly fills men and women who trust Him in the world. The unity of the Church is not ecclesiastical; it is not based upon uniformity. I could hold a brief for Presbyterianism, Episcopalianism, or any other form of ecclesiastical polity upon the basis of this book. The underlying unity of the Church is that of the baptism by the Spirit into union with the risen Lord of all such as believe on Him. Thus is created and constituted the Church.

As to nature, the Church is of one life with the risen Lord. In the Gospel accorded to Luke, we saw Jesus as the racial First-born, the second Man, the last Adam, the Head of the new race; the representative Brother of all such as are in the new race; the Goel, or redeeming Kinsman. In this book we see the race springing from the racial First-born; the brotherhood resulting from the representative Brother; the redeemed kinsmen resulting from the redeeming Kinsman. The Church is the fulfillment of that which He uttered prophetically when His mother after the flesh, in anxiety because He was overworking, came to persuade Him to go home; "Who is My mother? and who are My brethren? . . . Whosoever shall do the will of My Father which is in heaven, he is My brother, and sister, and mother." That was a great prophetic word, into the meaning of which the little band of disciples could not enter at the time, declaring that there is an affinity nearer and dearer than that of flesh and blood. We behold in the Acts of the Apostles that new race; very foolish, very feeble, very faulty, but brothers of the Lord, kinsmen of the Kinsman Redeemer. Christ is repeating Himself in redeemed men and women. That is the nature of the Church. Through nineteen centuries she has been upon her march, growing ever, faulty, failing, trembling, but her life is ever His life.

As to function, the Church is the instrument of the risen Lord for carrying on His doing and His teaching. He came to perfect and bring to glory many sons; every son incorporated in the family by the communication of the life of the Son carries on that work. Life in the Spirit is the life of Christ communicated by the Spirit. Therefore it is life like the life of Christ; and consequently it is life for Christ. That is the story of the men revealed in this book. Its greatest interest centres in Paul and his missionary journeyings. In all kinds of peril he pressed forward, the regions beyond his perpetual watchword. That is the function of the Church. The life of Christ repeated in the power of the Spirit. So she marches, enlarging the opportunity of Christ, by multiplying the members of His holy and sacred body.

THE MESSAGE OF ACTS 87

Life in the Spirit is also light in the Spirit. The Spirit chooses persons, indicates places, initiates practices. Choosing persons; Saul of Tarsus to the Gentiles; Philip the deacon to go to Samaria; nameless men, "Men of Cyprus and Cyrene, to Antioch, preaching the Lord Jesus." Indicating places; the strategic centres, Jerusalem, the city of Judaism; Antioch, the gateway to the Gentiles; Corinth, the market of Greece; Ephesus, the centre of pro-consular Asia; Rome, the metropolis of the world. The centres occupied, and so the villages and hamlets evangelized. Initiating practices; we cannot read the Acts of the Apostles without seeing that where the Spirit of God is, there is liberty. The moment men try to cramp the Church's operations within rules and regulations they cripple and spoil her.

Not only life and light in the Spirit; but also and supremely, love in the Spirit. Love of the Lord, that is the master passion of this Church; and out of it grows love of the brethren, and love of the whole world. That is the function of the Church, life, light, and love, in the Spirit; or in other words, Christ's work continued.

The revealed perils may be grouped under

three heads. There is first the peril of prejudice; the grip of the past, Judaism. It is manifest all the way through. The bondage of the past is always the result of lack of confidence in the Spirit in the present. How these things continue! There is no need to make application. How constantly the Church of God is hindered in her work because the grip of prejudice is upon her. "As it was in the beginning, is now, and ever shall be." That is not a Biblical quotation. The Spirit of God forevermore will break down traditions by doing new things.

Another peril is the mastery of Christian men and women by unholy passion. That was a peril of the Church at the beginning. It is a peril of the Church to-day. If prejudice is the result of lack of confidence in the Spirit; unholy passion is the result of lack of yielding to the Spirit.

The final peril is pride; the pride of the eye, the vainglory of life, the lure of the present world. Demas forsook Paul. Demas is a type. This results from lack of obedience to the Spirit; or lack of attention to the Spirit's teaching; or both. When we cease to listen to the Spirit's interpretation of the spiritual and eternal things, then the lure of the present world is upon us.

The abiding appeal of this book consists in the fact that it teaches us that the master passion of the Church must be that of the glory of God. She goes, as her Master went, to unveil God to the world, and to establish the Kingdom of God upon the earth. That must be the master passion of the Church. It is not that of the amelioration of human suffering. God is glorified by the amelioration of human suffering; but our passion is that of the glory of God. It is not the bettering of human conditions. The best conditions of human life are in the purpose of God for humanity; but we are to seek them because they are in harmony with the will of God. The great discourses of the Acts of the Apostles were all delivered to the outside world, except the one Paul addressed to the elders of Ephesus. Read those discourses, and find that their purpose was always the glory of God.

The inclusive principle of the Church's activity is that of loyalty to the Lord Christ, Whose passion is that of the glory of God. The Church is to prove that loyalty by realization of His life and prosecution of His work.

Finally, the sufficient power of the Church is that of the Holy Spirit; sufficient for the life of likeness to the Lord in order to the revelation of God; sufficient for direction in work for the glory of God.

What then does this pamphlet say to the Church of God to-day? It institutes investigation along two lines. It asks the Church first, what is the *motive* of all its activity? It asks secondly, what is the *method* of all its activity?

The motive of the Church ought to be the glory of God, nothing less, nothing more, nothing else; and that means devotion to the Lord Jesus Christ. The method of the Church ought to be the work of the Son, seeking and saving the lost by the Holy Spirit; and that means fellowship in the cross and resurrection and ascension of Christ.

This book, as a book, has no application to the world. Only as the Spirit-filled race continues the ministry revealed here will like results follow in the world. It is not by this book I make my appeal to the world; but it is by the Church living and serving according to the pattern revealed in this book that she makes her appeal to the world. It is only thus that similar effects in the world will be produced; the arrest of cities; the adding to the Lord of men and women; the abandonment of idols. When the Church is true to the principles revealed in this book she will arrest the attention of cities again; she will always be adding men and women to the Lord; in the wake of her triumphant march idols will be destroyed.

When we are in this succession we shall set forth the God, ignorantly worshipped by the Athenians; we shall proclaim the evangel to the uttermost part of the earth; we shall win territory for the King; and hasten the coming of His final victory.

THE MESSAGE OF ROMANS

A THE ESSENTIAL MESSAGE	B THE APPLICATION

I. The Central Teaching
i. The awful Helplessness of the sinful Race.
   a. The Light of Nature.   Failure.
   b. The Light of Revelation.   Failure.
ii. The absolute Perfection of the Divine Salvation.
   a. The Provision in Christ, the Son of God.
      1. Manifestation.
      2. Propitiation.
   b. The Relation to God.
      1. The Activity of His Love in Holiness.
      2. The Vindication of His Holiness by Love.
   c. The Provision for Man.
      1. Justification.
      2. Sanctification.
      3. Glorification.
   d. The Relation to Creation.
      1. The Restoration of its King.
      2. The Realization of its Possibilities.
	I. To the Church
	i. The ultimate Value, the Glory of God.
	
	ii. The supreme Responsibility, communication to others.
	
	iii. The personal Necessity, full Realization in Character and Conduct.

II. The Abiding Appeal
i. The Revelation of the true Sanctions and final Standards of Life.
   The Divine Throne and Government.
ii. The Call to Faith as the Faculty to apprehend the Unseen.
   The Divine Provision for Sight. "The Son of God . . ."
   The Call for Faith in all that which the Manifestation declares.
iii. The Call to Dedication, the Attitude which is the only Evidence of Faith.
	II. To the World
	i. "All have sinned." iii. 23.
	ii. God "the Justifier of him that hath faith in Jesus," iii. 26.

THE MESSAGE OF ROMANS

IN this letter we are dealing with one of the greatest writings of the New Testament; greatest, that is, in its setting forth of the foundation facts of our most holy faith. It was Martin Luther who said of it, "It is the chief part of the New Testament and the perfect gospel"; Coleridge the poet declared it to be "the most profound work in existence"; and Godet described it as "the cathedral of the Christian faith."

In order to a clear and sharp apprehension of the message of this letter, we need to recognize the assumptions of the writer, for these constitute the sanctions of his teaching. In the background of this letter there is evident a definite cosmology; and an equally definite conception of history.

The cosmology and history are those of the Old Testament. If we have lost the book of Genesis, and the history of the Old Testament, this is a foolish and meaningless document.

First, there is on the part of the writer a very clear recognition of the one God. He never attempts to demonstrate the existence of God ; nor does he argue for the unity of Deity ; he takes these things for granted ; and in many references we find evidences of this fact.

Moreover he assumes that this God is in character holy and just. Again he never argues for either of these things ; but takes them both for granted. He argues of other matters, assuming this twofold fact of the holiness and justice of God. If this man, living in the midst of sin, iniquity, and difficulty is conscious of the problem of human redemption, that problem is as to how God can be just and the Justifier.

It is further taken for granted that this one God, Who is holy and just, is the Creator, Sustainer, and Governor of the universe. He never admits for a single moment in the process of his argument concerning human salvation, that any part of the universe has escaped or can escape the government of God. He never admits that man can escape from the government of God. He does admit that man may give himself up to material wrong-doing, mental depravity, and spiritual death; but he affirms that if man does give himself up to these things, then God gives him up to the issues of them; and thus he reveals the supreme fact, that even a sinning man is still held in the grip of the Divine government; and shows that if a man will not submit to the infinite love and mercy of God by falling into line with the provision of His grace, that man must endure the unutterable penalty of his sin.

Man by nature, by first creation, by Divine intention, by the possibilities and potentialities of his own being, stands in the universe, subject to the throne of God, and reigning over all the creation beneath him.

Creation then, according to the cosmology of Paul, is subject to man, beneath his control, dependent upon him for realization and fulfillment of its hidden potentialities; and consequently sharing man's experiences. If man be noble, the nobility in creation is manifested. If man be debased, creation is debased. If man shall through sin groan and travail in pain, the whole creation groaneth and travaileth in pain beneath him. If man shall be manifested in the midst of creation as the son of God, the sighing and groaning of creation shall cease, and it shall be lifted to the level of the man who is over it. Such, in brief, is the cosmology behind the letter; this man's conception of things as they are, as to origin, nature, and government.

Now observe history as this man sees it. It is interesting how very few references there are in the writings of Paul to what we call profane history, to events that stand out upon the page of human history. Human history is set entirely in the light of the Divine. History for Paul begins with Adam, the first man, the head of the race. That man is seen in rebellion against the Throne, —disobedient, is Paul's word. One man's disobedience produces one result in human history; the dethronement of God from the actuality of human consciousness, the degradation of man immediately following the dethronement of God, and the consequent degradation and spoiling of all creation beneath him. Paul did not look upon all the groaning and pain of creation as a process that was tending to upward development. The first man disobeying loses his sceptre because he ceases to bow to the sceptre of God; losing his sceptre, the kingdom beneath him suffers, he is unable to realize it, unable to lead out its hidden potentialities into fulfillment.

Creation groans and travails in pain because its king has lost his sceptre, because he has ceased to kiss the sceptre of God, or to bow to His throne.

After long centuries, Paul recognizes another point of departure; a man, Abraham, and a people, called out into separation from all that order of things which has resulted from the sin of the first man; and this man and this people called out for the sake of all the rest, that by the life of faith, which is a life of submission to the throne of God, they might reveal to men the breadth, the beauty, and the beneficence of the Divine government. And again there follows the story of failure; failure of faith and consequently failure of testimony. The next point of departure is that of the advent of a second Man, the last Adam, the Head of a new race; with the result of the enthronement of God in human consciousness and in human life. This restoration of man to the image and likeness of God results ultimately in the restoration of the whole creation.

One man failing and falling, the whole creation failing and falling with him; groaning, travailing, sighing, sobbing. One Man victorious and realizing, and by the mystery of death bringing every man into fellowship with Himself; and creation by the manifestation of the sons of God restored to the true order of the universe. In the midst of the darkness and sorrow and sin, Paul sings, "Let us rejoice in hope of the glory of God."

Upon these assumptions Paul bases the arguments of his teaching; and they constitute the sanctions of his system of human salvation. That teaching has to do specially and definitely with the gospel of the second Man, the last Adam. It is the statement in order and sequence of the method by which God, Who has never vacated His throne, never given up the reins of government, comes into the midst of all the failure resulting from the sin of the first man, in order to restore, and heal, and realize His own high and gracious purpose.

This letter is not a tract to be put into the hands of the sinning man in order that, believing what it says, he may be saved. It is rather a treatise to be put into the hands of Christian men in order that they may understand the method of their salvation.

The central teaching is first that of the awful helplessness of the sinful race; and secondly that of the absolute perfection of the Divine salvation. There is no book in the New Testament, there is no book in the Bible, that so fearlessly looks into the abysmal depth of the degradation resulting from human sin. Read the third chapter of this book, and read no more, and you will say that it is the most pessimistic page of literature upon which your eyes ever rested. Read that which immediately follows it, and follow the argument to the end, and you will say that it is the most optimistic poem to which your ears ever listened. These are the two qualities of this book. A straight, fearless, daring look at the human heart, and at human sin; and then a clear look at the Divine heart, and the perfection of the Divine salvation. Ruin and redemption; these were the words of our fathers; we use them much less than they did, and the loss is ours. Absolute ruin and helplessness, that is the apostolic outlook upon man; plenteous redemption and perfect salvation, that is the apostolic outlook upon God.

In dealing with the ruin and helplessness of the human race, Paul divides that race into two parts. He speaks of the Gentiles, who have had the light of nature; and he speaks of the Jews, who have had the light of revelation.

In dealing with the Gentile he does not admit that God has left men anywhere without light. Those who have had the light of nature have at least had the opportunity of discovering two things about God, His wisdom and His Divinity. These are the things which men will always find in nature, and never anything beyond. It is a remarkable fact that this apostolic declaration harmonizes with the most recent findings of men of science who have turned away from revelation. Huxley,, Darwin, Tyndall, Spencer, and Bayne, all admitted the evidences of force and intelligence in nature. The admission was most forcibly put by Bayne when he declared that the varied phenomena of nature revealed the activity of a double-faced somewhat ; double-faced in that it had these two qualities of force and intelligence, working in harmony. That is exactly what Paul says. The men who walk in the light of nature can and will discover the Divine wisdom and power; that is, force and intelligence. The apostle then described the state of those who had the light of nature, in character and conduct. Let me take out some of the descriptive phrases : " vain reasonings . . . senseless hearts . . . fools ; . . . vile passions

... unseemliness ... reprobate mind; .. unrighteousness, wickedness, covetousness, maliciousness; envy, murder, strife, deceit, malignity; whisperers, backbiters, ... insolent, haughty, boastful, inventors of evil things, disobedient to parents, without understanding, covenant-breakers, without natural affection, unmerciful." If any are inclined to make a protest against that description as being unfair, let them walk through the streets of London, where men have turned from the light of revelation, and turned from the faith of Christianity, and are walking only in the light of nature; and they will find that this is still an accurate description.

The writer then turns to those who have had the light of revelation. The Jew, judging the Gentile, called him heathen. Now what does Paul say of the men who have had the light of revelation? He declares that they do the same things. Read again the dark and awful list of the things done by men who have the light of nature. Men who have the light of revelation do the same things; and worse, because they have named the name of God, and profess to be teachers, the name of God is blasphemed among the heathen through them.

Therefore Paul expressed his conviction of the appalling helplessness and hopelessness of humanity; "There is none righteous, no, not one"; "All have sinned, and fall short of the glory of God." It is the most terrible indictment of humanity that was ever penned. Thank God there is something more in the letter than that.

The second message is that of the absolute perfection of the Divine salvation provided in Christ the Son of God. Paul introduces Christ in the very first page of the letter, declaring that He was Son of David according to the flesh; and that He "was declared to be the Son of God with power according to the spirit of holiness, by the resurrection of the dead." I never can quote that passage without desiring to anglicize the Greek word which is there translated "declared to be"; "Who was *horizoned* the Son of God with power, according to the spirit of holiness, by the resurrection of the dead." He appeared on the horizon as the Son of God by the resurrection. We must start the Roman letter there; for unless we do so, we have lost the key. The Person presented to men, upon Whom they may believe; the Person from Whom comes the new life, creating the members of the new race; the

Person Who is the second Man, the last Adam, the First-born of the new creation; is the Son of God; and He was declared to be the Son of God, horizoned as the Son of God, by the resurrection. Deny the resurrection, and we may tear up the Roman letter. Admit the resurrection, then at once the Jesus of the gospel stories is the Son of God, demonstrated such, definitely revealed as such, so that there can be no doubt about it.

Two words tell the story of the office of this Person: Manifestation, and Propitiation. The righteousness manifested in Him is righteousness at the disposal of every man through the mystery of propitiation wrought out in His death. That is the perfection of salvation. In that Person there is righteousness at the disposal of every man, because in Him there is propitiation for every soul that believeth.

The relation of this salvation to God is that it results from the activity of His love in holiness; and is the vindication of His holiness by the activity of His love.

The result to man is threefold; that of justification, sanctification, and glorification.

Justification; that is infinitely more than human

forgiveness can ever be, infinitely more than a promise to pass over, and never mention again, the sin committed; justification is the reinstatement of the soul of man in such relationship and actual fellowship with God, as that soul would have occupied had there never been any sin, had there never been any guilt.

Sanctification; all the forces of the life of the Son of God, Head of the new race, are communicated to the members of the new race, so that they may live as He lived; growing up into Him in all things which is the Head.

Glorification; man resuming finally his true place in the universe of God, lifts again, to the place from which it has fallen, groaning, sighing, sobbing creation.

The relation therefore of creation to the work of salvation is that of the restoration of its king, the manifestation of the sons of God, and the realization of its possibilities.

Paul looks at human history and sees two or three outstanding facts; the original creation, and man; man rebelling and falling, and following that fall, the fall and sob of creation; the new daybreak, when the Head of the new race stands horizoned by resurrection; all men believing in Him, receiving righteousness, not merely imputed but imparted also; and he watches the process on and ever on, until the groaning creation ceases its groaning, and its sob and its sigh merge into the song of a great triumph. That is the march of history.

If that be the central teaching of the letter, what is its abiding appeal? It first recalls men to the true sanctions and the final standards of human life, those of the Divine throne and government. This book calls men to measure themselves no longer by the standards of their own aspirations or ideals, but by the standards of Divine requirement.

If any man will obey the call which demands that he shall abandon the standards of his own age, the measurements of his own imagination, the ideals of his own heart; and presenting himself to the throne of God, accept the purposes of God, what is the result? It is always the same. Every mouth must be stopped; all the world must become guilty before God. If we measure ourselves as among ourselves many of us will find a good deal to satisfy ourselves in the exercise. If we measure ourselves by our own ideals and aspirations we shall not be quite so satisfied, but we shall think that we are doing fairly well. But if we have done with false measurements, and stand in the light of the Throne of holiness and purity, and are measured there, we shall lay our hand upon our lip as surely as did the leper, and cry unclean, unclean; guilty before God.

This letter calls men to the exercise of the only faculty which can apprehend the unseen; that is the faculty of faith. That is what submission to the throne of God means; it is remitting all the life to the unseen; and the only faculty which can do that is faith. God in great grace has stooped to the human level and has presented Himself to the human mind, in order that faith may repose upon that manifestation, and make connection with the infinite forces that lie behind the manifestation. That is the meaning of the incarnation. By incarnation God did not come any nearer to humanity, but He came into observation. He was as near to humanity before the mystery of the appearing in Judæa, as then and since. But He then came into visibility. He has given men a vision in the Son of God, horizoned by resurrection. This letter says belief in Him, faith in Him, the Son of God, is the starting-point of the new life. If you ask me to discuss the reason, I reply that it is not upon the basis of reason that man finds his way into life. This is God's appointment, God's provision; that when a man shall rest upon this Jesus, believe into Him, venture everything on Him, risk eternity and heaven upon Him, then by that act of faith, that man takes hold of all the forces of the spiritual and unseen, and receives in answer the value and dynamic of righteousness.

This letter calls men also to the attitude which alone is evidence of faith, that of dedication, " I beseech you therefore, brethren, by the mercies of God, to present your bodies." If a man shall say he have faith, and there be no works giving evidence of his faith, then his declaration that he has faith is not true. Faith in the death of Jesus is expressed in consent to die to everything that caused His death. Do I trust in His death for my salvation? Then I am to show my trust by reckoning myself to be dead to the things that caused His death. If I simply consent to trust in His death, and there be no corresponding consent to death in my own life, then my profession of consenting is blasphemy and impertinence. Faith in the life of the Son of God is to be expressed in the habits of the life of that same Lord Whom we trust. We are to present our bodies as alive from the dead; and it is in the activities of life, harmonizing with the life of Jesus, that we give evidence of our faith.

The present application of this letter to the Church of God is that the ultimate value of the salvation which God has provided is the glory of God; and the supreme responsibility resting upon those who share this life is that of communicating to other people the great evangel.

On the first page he writes it, "I am debtor . . . I am ready . . . I am not ashamed of the gospel." Do we feel we are in debt to every man we meet, that he may know our salvation and share it? That is the great responsibility, and in it is involved that of the personal necessity for the full realization in character and conduct of all God has provided for us, not merely that we should be beautiful in character; but in order that through our conformity to our Lord, men may see Him and be attracted to Him. In order that men may share the virtue of His dying, He calls us to fellowship with His sufferings. Do we rejoice in the plenteous salvation? Then let us remember

THE MESSAGE OF ROMANS 109

that it lays upon us these tremendous responsibilities.

What does this letter say to the men and women who are outside, who are still living as members of the lost race? Two things, First, all have sinned, all are guilty. Then what? God is "just and the Justifier of him that hath faith in Jesus." Come with all your weakness and pollution, your inability, the awful helplessness of your own nature; and put your confidence in this Christ; and He will blot out your sins through the mystery of the shedding of His blood; and by the gift of His life communicated, He will negative the poison, quench the fires, break the chains; and lifting you into fellowship with Himself, make you a channel through whom His virtue shall flow to creation for its healing and its lifting.

THE MESSAGE OF I. CORINTHIANS

A THE ESSENTIAL MESSAGE	B THE TWOFOLD APPLICATION

I. The Central Teaching
i. The Causes of Failure.
    a. The Spirit of the City had invaded the Church.
        1. Religious Licence.
        2. Moral Laxity.
        3. Social Disorder.
    b. The Failure of the Church to realize its own Life.
        1. The Word of the Cross.
        2. The Purity of the Christ.
        3. The Law of His Love.
ii. The Secrets of Success.
    a. The Realization by the Church of its own Life.
        1. The Organism. { One Lord. One Spirit. One God.
        2. The Law. Love.
        3. The supernatural Secret. The Resurrection of Christ.
    b. The Spirit of the Church invading the City.
        1. Proclaiming the Lord.
        2. Rebuking Immorality.
        3. Cancelling Selfishness.
II. The Abiding Appeal
i. To a Recognition of Responsibility.
ii. To a complete Separation in order to a Fulfillment of Responsibility.
iii. To a Fulfillment of her own Powers.
	I. To the Church
	i. The Influence of a Church is the Influence of her Members.
	ii. The Conflict between the City and the Church.
	iii. Certain Questions.
	    a. What is our Influence?
	    b. Is there a Conflict?
	    c. If not, why not?
	
	II. To the World
	i. The Church is against the City as it is, in order to make the City what it ought to be.
	ii. Our central Message is that of the Resurrection.

THE MESSAGE OF I. CORINTHIANS

IN attempting to discover the message of this letter a phrase in the introduction, "The church of God which is at Corinth," is of great value. It immediately suggests the theme of the letter, because in it two pictures are presented to the mind; first, that of the church of God, and secondly that of the city of Corinth; the church of God being a community sharing the life of God, governed by the will of God, cooperating in the work of God; Corinth being a city of the world, ignorant of God, self-governed, antagonistic to the purposes of God. The two pictures stand opposite each other in striking and vivid contrast.

Of course the phrase "The church of God" here had reference not to the whole Catholic Church, but to the local church in the city of Corinth. Nevertheless, because the local church is a microcosm of the Catholic Church, each local church embodying the principles and methods of the whole Church, being an assembly of men and women united in the bonds of the life of the Lord Christ, the very fact of their churchmanship consisting in their relation to Him and in the real presence in the midst of them of this Christ, the things said of the Church are most evidently true of the church at Corinth. It consisted of a community of people sharing the life of God, made partakers of the Divine nature; a community of people therefore governed by God; a theocracy, a holy nation; and consequently a people in fellowship with Him, in coöperation with Him in Corinth for the accomplishment of His work. All that is included in the first picture suggested by the phrase "The church of God which is at Corinth."

The city of Corinth was at the time a centre of learning and luxury. The name Corinth was a synonym for profligacy and vice. There was a proverb extant, "They live as they live at Corinth," which suggested life in lust, lasciviousness, and luxury. Corinth as a city was ignorant of the one true God, and entirely self-governed. Individual life in Corinth was self-centred, and consequently social life was self-governed. Therefore, unconsciously perhaps, but quite definitely, Corinth was a city antagonistic to God. It is impossible to have two things more entirely opposed brought close together into one brief phrase, than these two facts of the church of God, and the city of Corinth.

The atmosphere of this letter is that of Paul's conception of the responsibilities of the church for the city. In the Acts of the Apostles we have the account of the presence of this man in Athens in one brief declaration, "While he waited for them at Athens, his spirit was provoked within him, as he beheld the city full of idols." He left Athens and came to Corinth, and during that visit the foundations of the church were laid. Now, after some years had passed, he wrote a letter to the church there, and evidently his conception of the responsibility of the church concerning the city harmonizes with his own consciousness when in the city of Athens. At the commencement of the letter in the fundamental proposition he said, "God is faithful, through Whom ye were called into the fellowship of His Son Jesus Christ our Lord," and in these words we at once discover his conception of the responsibility of the church for the city. The word "fellowship" means a great deal more than privilege; it includes responsibility. Fellowship with Jesus Christ does not merely mean that all His resources are at our disposal; it means that all our resources are, or ought to be, at His disposal. The church in Corinth was in fellowship with Jesus Christ. All the resources of Christ were at her disposal, and all the resources of the church were properly at the disposal of Christ, and that in order to the accomplishment in Corinth of the work of God. Three sentences at the portal of the Roman letter indicate the apostolic sense of responsibility, "I am debtor . . . I am ready . . . I am not ashamed." Whereas in that case the note is personal, that sense, multiplied, reveals the apostolic conception of the responsibility of the church of God in any given city. The church of God in Corinth is in debt to Corinth, because the truth which the church holds as a deposit and has realized in her own life, is the very truth that Corinth needs. When Paul said, "I am ready to preach the gospel to you also that are in Rome," he expressed the true attitude of the church in every city. The church should be ready to declare to the city in its godlessness and its resulting lust, lasciviousness, and luxury, the same great evangel. When he said, "I am not ashamed of the gospel," he indicated what should be the attitude of the church in the midst of the city. This whole letter to the Corinthian church was written out of this overwhelming sense of the responsibility of the church for the city in which it exists.

The church at Corinth had failed to discharge its debt to Corinth; failed in readiness to declare the evangel; failed in courage and conviction concerning her own gospel. That was the trouble which filled the heart of the apostle. It was not merely that the church was in itself carnal; it was rather that the carnal church in Corinth was unable to deliver the spiritual message to Corinth.

In this letter we discover the causes of the church's failure and the secret of her success. In dealing with the content we divided the letter into two sections: Corrective—of the carnalities; Constructive—of the spiritualities. The carnalities prevented the church bearing spiritual witness in Corinth; the spiritualities were for the correction of the carnalities, that the church might be enabled to deliver her message.

In dealing with the central teaching of the

letter we notice first the causes of failure, and secondly the secrets of success.

Now, again if we fix our attention upon the two thoughts suggested by the phrases the church of God and the city of Corinth; if imaginatively we look back through the centuries to Corinth, and see the church of God in the centre of its life, we shall understand the causes of the failure of the church there.

The first cause was that the spirit of the city had invaded the church. Every evil thing with which Paul dealt in his letter was an evil thing which had come into the church from the city. There was first religious licence; secondly, moral laxity; and thirdly, social disorder.

Look at Corinth alone and it will be seen full of religious licence. Intellectually, it was the centre of divers opinions, for the hour was one of intellectual strife, and in that strife the city was finding amusement. It was an hour of superb rhetoric and eloquence; "Corinthian words" was another of the phrases of the times, a synonym for rhetoric. In the schools of Corinth men were debating, and rejoicing in the wisdom of words; all sorts of opinions were rife, and men were gathered into small sections

THE MESSAGE OF I. CORINTHIANS 117

defending those varied opinions. The city of Corinth religiously was characterized by diversities, differences; great dialectical skill; an infinite variety of opinions; perpetual arguments in the schools, and among the religious leaders. That was the spirit of the city. That spirit had invaded the church. Men and women within the fellowship had caught the intellectual restlessness of the religious life of the city, with the result that some said, We are of Paul, others, We are of Apollos, others, We are of Cephas; while yet others said, We are of Christ. The diversities of opinions expressed within the church were the results of the differing emphases in the preaching of these men, Paul, Apollos, and Cephas. All this was due to the invasion of the church by the intellectual restlessness of the outside world.

The city was also characterized by moral laxity. The effect of the diffusion of devotion was the lowering of the moral standard. For example, the nature of the worship of Aphrodite is a story too vile for telling in the assembly of the saints. That moral laxity had invaded the church. Many of these Christian people were lax in their own moral life, and there was one case so flagrant and so terrible, that Paul declared that those outside the church would have been ashamed of it.

Finally, in the city self was supreme; there was no conscious responsibility for others. Each was for himself, and selfishnesss was the basis of all endeavour, the method of all government. This spirit also had invaded the church, and relative obligations were unrecognized.

Beneath all this there was something profounder. These were really effects, rather than causes. While Paul saw and corrected disorder in detail in the early part of this letter—and indeed throughout it, for even in the constructive part he perpetually returned to correction—he did so consistently by showing that the reason of the disorder was that the church had forgotten the central, unifying word of the Cross.

She had been invaded by the spirit of division from the city, and had created her own sects out of divisions and differences concerning doctrine, because she failed to respond to the word of the Cross in her own life. She had been invaded by the moral laxity of the city, because seeing that she had not lived according to the word of the Cross, neither had she lived in the power of the resurrection, which is the power of the infinite purity of Christ. The church had been invaded by the selfishness of the ideals of the city, because unyielded to the Cross; and devoid of the power of the resurrection, she had failed to be impulsed by the abiding law of love.

The two central truths which this letter teaches are first that the church fails to fulfill her function in the city when she is invaded by the spirit of the city; secondly, that the church allows the spirit of the city to invade her when she is untrue to the central facts of her own life, when she does not realize in actual experience what she is potentially in the economy of God.

These facts account for the perpetual method of the apostolic writers and teachers; that method which Paul adopted when in effect more than once in the course of his writings he said, You are saints, be saints; you have put off the old man, put off the old man; you have put on the new man, put on the new man; be what you are; realize your own life; be true to the great word of the Cross by which you have become redeemed, ransomed people; let the word which is in you, dwell in you richly.

Here are laid bare the secrets of the Church's

failure whenever the Church fails to deliver the message of God to the age. This is the secret of her failure through the centuries. The measure of failure on the part of the Church is the measure in which she has allowed herself to be influenced by the spirit of the age, because she has been untrue to the facts of her own life. We are sometimes told to-day that what the Church supremely needs is that she should catch the spirit of the age. A thousand times no. What the Church supremely needs is to correct the spirit of the age. The church in Corinth catching the spirit of Corinth became anæmic, weak, and failed to deliver the message of God to Corinth. The church of God in London, invaded by the spirit of London, the materialism, militarism, sordidness, and selfishness of London, is too weak to save London.

When the Church of God is invaded by the spirit of the age or of the city, it is because the forces equal to repelling the invasion of that destructive spirit are neglected. The Church of God needs no new visitation of power from God. She needs the realization of the power she already has, the appropriation of the forces already resident within her.

The word of the Cross, the Corinthians had heard it, they knew it; the purity of Christ had touched them in regenerative miracle; the love of God was already shed abroad in their hearts; but they had not abandoned themselves to the claim of the word of the Cross; they had not yielded themselves in entirety to the impulse of His purity; they had not responded to the clamant cry of the love of Christ. The forces of their own preservation being weakened within themselves, the spirit of the city swept in, and the church in Corinth failed because she was invaded by the spirit of the city which she ought to have saved.

Thus we learn what are the secrets of success. The church can only be successful in fulfilling her function in the city by realization of her own life in Christ, that life which is revealed as an organism; one Lord, she shares the life of her Lord; one Spirit, she is under the government of that Spirit Who communicates gifts severally as He will, blessing each member of the body in order to the fulfillment of the function of the whole body; one God, she makes His glory the supreme and ultimate fact. The realization of these facts is the secret of success. Let the

Church of God share the life of the Lord, obey the government of the Spirit, and seek the glory of God; and by that separation from the city, she prepares herself for the work of helping and lifting the city.

The law of the Church is the law of love, severest of sentinels as it watches the activity of men, mightiest of all motives as it impels life and service. At the centre of the classic passage on love which we know so well by letter is the declaration "Love never faileth." That is the law of the Church's life.

The supernatural secret of the Church is that of resurrection. The Church of God is a community of people related to the historic resurrection of Christ, and to the coming resurrection of the saints. Between these the Church must fulfill her function in immediate relation to both. Her life is life won out of death, and communicated by the resurrection of Christ. Her life is life tending to consummation and perfection in the resurrection of the saints at the second Advent. The Church is supernatural, mystical, separated in the very nature of her life from all the men of the age. The secret of the fulfillment by the church of her function in the city is her realization of these facts. She is an organism; she has one law, that of love; the supernatural secret of her life is that of resurrection.

The exercise of function is that of the Spirit of the church invading the city. If the Church's failure is due to the fact that the spirit of the city has invaded the church; the Church's success is due to the fact that the Spirit of the church invades the city, proclaiming the Lordship of Christ based upon His resurrection; rebuking the immorality of the city by the revelation of His purity; cancelling the selfishness of the city by her own example, and by insistence that all men shall have granted to them an opportunity to live.

The Church of God always fails when she becomes conformed to the methods, maxims, and manners of the city. The Church of God always succeeds when, true to the supernatural nature of her life, she stands in perfect separation from the city. Only thus is she able to touch and help the city.

Consequently the abiding appeal of the letter is patent. It calls the Church of God in every age to recognition of responsibility concerning the city. The church is responsible for the religious life of the city, for the moral standards of the city, for the social order of the city.

If you can persuade me that we have no responsibilities, that the Church exists merely for the conserving of the life of her own members, then I will leave the Church, and join with others who have a keener sense of moral and religious responsibility; but it is impossible to persuade me to that conclusion in the light of New Testament teaching. The Church is responsible for the religious life of the city, for the affirmation and revelation of God therein. There never was a time when the fulfillment of that function was more necessary than now. We are no longer face to face with old-fashioned antagonism. A time there was when blatant infidelity had its halls in all our great towns, and in them made attack upon the very idea of the existence of God. There may be such halls of assembly still; but they lurk in hidden corners. The infidelity of the hour is the infidelity of indifference; and the business of the Church is to arrest the indifferent, to arouse the conscience, to affirm God, to compel men to the consideration of the infinite, eternal, and abiding things.

The religious effect must first be produced. Then resulting from it there must be the erection of moral standards. The Church is to deny that there can be lasting and final morality unless it is homed in spirituality of conception. In the teaching of the Lord Jesus Christ there was always the closest connection between spiritual conception and moral standard; so with the Church, she is to stand in every age affirming that the only sufficient moral standard is that of right relationship to God and eternity.

Consequently the Church is responsible for the social order of the city. She cannot, if she be true to her own life, be silent and careless while there are in the city men, women, and little children without the opportunity of finding and worshipping God, living and working in such conditions that culture of the essential spiritual life is impossible.

The call of this letter in the second place is a call to complete separation in order to the fulfillment of responsibility. Separation, first, from all licence in religious thinking. There is a toleration which is of the very essence of destruction. If we admit for a single moment that all these differing opinions outside the Church concerning matters of religion may lead ultimately to true religion, apart from the word of the Cross, that will presently make us untrue ourselves to the word of the Cross, which word declares all men guilty, and all human wisdom foolishness, and demands that men shall find their way into true wisdom and true life through, and only through, the surrender of the life to the Lord Christ.

We are called also to complete separation from all laxity in dealing with immorality. While the outside world is declaring to-day, for instance, that it is time we faced again the problem of the marriage relationship and made easier divorce laws, it is for the Church of God to abide in the name of Christ by the great ideal of the Bible, and whatever personal suffering may be entailed, insist upon it that men and women must be true to the marriage relationship in the interests of the family and the national life. That is only a passing illustration of the principle. The Church must never give countenance to the lax conceptions of morality which abound in the life of the city. The Church must be free from carelessness about social iniquities.

This letter calls us supremely therefore to the

fulfillment of the powers of our own being; the life of the Lord in the Spirit; love supreme; the power of the resurrection, His resurrection from among the dead operating in victory in our own lives, our coming resurrection at the second Advent flashing like a beacon light upon all the pathway and calling us to purity.

The application of this great appeal to the Church of God may thus be stated. The influence of the Church is the influence of her members. The sum total of the membership in any church is the sum total of that church's influence. Thus ultimately the great truth about the Church is reduced to the point of personal application. Each one in the measure of personality is responsible for the influence of the church in the city.

There is a perpetual conflict between the city and the church; the city that is godless and the church which is God-centred. By way of application let one question be asked and answered alone. What is our influence in the life of the city? Is there any conflict between the Church of God and the city? If not, is it not because the spirit of the city has invaded the church until it has become difficult to discover where the city ends and the church begins; sometimes almost impossible to distinguish between the man actuated by the godlessness of the city, and the man who, calling himself by the name of Christ, is yet not living the life God-centred and God-governed.

In some senses this letter has no message to the world. Inferentially it declares that the church is against the city as it is, in order to make the city what it ought to be. The Church lifts her voice in protest against iniquity in the city or nation, because her business is to make the city and the nation what God would have them be. Our central message to the world, according to the teaching of this letter, is that of the resurrection of the Lord. That resurrection unifies religious truth. Every doctrine is centred therein. That resurrection is the standard of morality, for in that stupendous mystery God did accept the Man of Nazareth as the type and pattern of humanity. That resurrection is the declaration of power at the disposal of all men, for in the mystery of His resurrection the Lord placed His life at the disposal of others.

Inclusively and finally, the appeal of the letter to the Church is contained in the actual words of the apostle, "Be ye steadfast, unmovable, always abounding in the work of the Lord."

THE MESSAGE OF II. CORINTHIANS

A THE ESSENTIAL MESSAGE	B THE APPLICATION

I. The Central Teaching
i. The Ministry within the Church.
    a. Its Authority.   Divine Appointment.
    b. Its Message. { The Word.
                      The unveiled Glory.
    c. Its Resources. { The Comfort of God.
                      Visions and Revelations.
                      The Prayers of the Saints.
    d. Its Experiences. { Tribulation.
                      Hope.
                      Triumph.
    e. Its Aim.   The Perfecting of the Saints.
ii. The Ministry of the Church.
    a. Its Equipment. { Obedience to the Word.
                      Separation from the World.
                      Conformity to the Will.
    b. Its Exercise. { Discipline to Restoration.
                      "No occasion of stumbling."
                      The Grace of Giving.
 	
II. The Abiding Appeal
i. To the Ministry Within.
    a. Loyalty to the Message of the Word of Reconciliation.
    b. Absolute Rest is the Sufficiency of God.
    c. Acceptance of the Principle of the Cross.
    d. The Relationship of the Minister to the People.
ii. To the Church as to its own Ministry.
    a. "Be ye reconciled to God."
    b. "Receive not the grace of God in vain."
	I. To the Church
	i. A Recognition of the Sacredness of the Ministry.
	    a. By the Ministers.
	    b. By the Church.
	ii. An Acceptation of the Responsibilities of Reconciliation and Grace.
	    a. Purity. Discipline in Love.
	    b. Unity. The Collection for the Saints.
	    c. Testimony. To the World.
	
	II. To the World
	". . . That the Life also of Jesus may be manifested in our mortal flesh."
	
	"We are Witnesses."

THE MESSAGE OF II. CORINTHIANS

IT is quite evident that the second letter to the Corinthians is a sequel to the first. There is a marked difference between the two. The first is systematic; corrective and constructive. The second seems to be characterized by lack of system; it is largely personal, and emotional; it throbs with a sense of anguish, and yet perpetually rises to the height of great and gracious song. The matters dealt with were of an immediate and local kind. The writer was suffering from personal misunderstanding, resulting from personal misinterpretation; and evidently wrote to set himself right with those who had misunderstood him because of this misinterpretation. The letter was also concerned with a certain collection which was being made; and with the apostle's proposal to visit Corinth.

All this is not to undervalue this letter, for it is impossible to read it without feeling that in some senses, perhaps a little difficult to explain, there is in it a note and a quality of intense spirituality almost beyond that of the first letter. This note of intense spirituality results from the fact that the matter of his own personal misunderstanding and misinterpretation; the matter of the collection in Corinth on behalf of the poor saints in Jerusalem; and the matter of his proposal to visit them, and his reasons for not visiting them when they expected he would; are all set in the light of the great Christian conceptions.

The essential message of this letter is discovered as we recognize these great conceptions. We find in it the recognition and revelation of certain truths that are of vital importance to the Christian Church.

In our consideration of the message of the first letter we found that the spirit of the city had invaded the Church; and by that invasion the Church had become unfitted for fulfilling its true functions of ministry in the city. The message of the letter, therefore, was one of warning against the perils of the city to the Church; and one calling the Church to fulfill its function in the city.

In this second letter we have the same two pictures. Again Paul wrote to the Church of God in the city of Corinth. As in his first letter

THE MESSAGE OF II. CORINTHIANS 133

he called the Church to fulfillment of its ministry in the city; in his second he dealt with the ministry within the Church, by which the Church is to be perfected, in order to the fulfillment of its ministry in the city. This is peculiarly, therefore, the letter of the ministry, taking that word in its fullest sense. Whenever ministry is dealt with in the New Testament, the ultimate thought is not that of the ministry of the men we call ministers to-day, but that of the ministry of the whole Church. That is not to undervalue the sacredness of the ministerial calling within the Church; but to reveal its deepest meaning. Within the Church there are ministers, created by gifts bestowed by the Holy Ghost; and the business of such ministers is that of the perfecting of the saints, in order that the Church may fulfill its ministry in the city.

With that key to the situation, I understand the passion in the heart of Paul; the reason of his trouble, the reason of his tears, the reason of his anxiety. He knew that the Church at Corinth was failing to understand the true function of the ministers of Jesus Christ, and was failing to obey the teaching of those ministers; and therefore was failing to fulfill its own ministry in Corinth.

He was not fighting for official recognition. He was not angry because some did not think as highly of him as of Apollos or Cephas.

In this letter then we have a picture, for all time, of what the ministry within the Church is; and of what the ministry of the whole Church ought to be. Therefore the central teaching has to do, first, with the ministry within the Church; and secondly, with the ministry of the Church; principally with the ministry within, for the ministry of the Church had been dealt with in the first letter, and appears here again only incidentally, though quite clearly.

Dealing first then with the ministry within the Church: we notice in the first place the apostle's teaching concerning the authority thereof, in his opening words; "Paul, an apostle of Christ Jesus through the will of God, and Timothy our brother." Carefully notice how he brings into association with himself a man who is not an apostle. He had to fight for his own apostleship as against the misunderstanding and misinterpretation even of some who were apostles; but Timothy was not an apostle; he was an evangelist certainly, and in all probability ultimately a pastor and teacher. Thus two men were associated in the writing of the letter, and presently Paul referred to Silvanus, and also to Titus. All these were in the ministry by Divine appointment. That is the New Testament conception of the authority of the Christian ministry. I am not now discussing the methods by which the Church of God recognizes the gift bestowed, prepares for the exercise of it, and solemnly ordains to work within the Church. All these are necessary and important matters, but the form which these arrangements of the Church may take is of minor importance. The supreme value of this letter, in the matter of the authority of the Christian ministry, is its revelation of the fact that a man is in the ministry, whether it be as apostle, prophet, evangelist, or pastor or teacher, by the appointment of God. That fact creates his authority, and consequently the authority he exercises must be the authority of the One Who appoints him, and the authority of the One Who appoints him is always the authority of His Word spoken. The authority of Jesus was the authority of His teaching. The multitudes heard Him utter His Manifesto, and they were astonished because He taught as One having authority. It was the authority of inherent and essential truth which captured them. The authority of God is always the authority of His Word, the authority of essential Truth. The authority of the minister is not the authority of an office conferred; it is the authority of the Word that is committed to him to preach; that great and sacred deposit which he holds on trust for the Church, and by exposition of which he perfects the Church for its work of ministry.

This leads us naturally to what this letter teaches concerning the message of the minister. The apostle says, "We are not as the many, corrupting the Word of God: but as of sincerity, but as of God, in the sight of God, speak we in Christ"; and later, "Therefore seeing we have this ministry, even as we obtained mercy, we faint not: but we have renounced the hidden things of shame, not walking in craftiness, nor handling the Word of God deceitfully; but by the manifestation of the truth commending ourselves to every man's conscience in the sight of God." The message then of the apostle, prophet, evangelist, pastor, and teacher, is the Word of God, which must not be corrupted, not handled deceitfully.

Between these essential declarations, the supreme glory of the Word to be preached is revealed; it is that of the unveiled glory. There was a ministration of death in the case of Moses. The ministration of life and the Spirit came through Jesus Christ. The apostle claimed that the same results follow the preaching of the Word by Christian ministers of the Word as followed the ministry of the Lord Himself. Therefore that Word is the burden of the message of every Christian minister. The difference between the apostle, the prophet, the evangelist, and the pastor and teacher, is not a difference of message, but a difference of emphasis and application. Whether the work be apostolic, pioneer work, in exposition of the doctrine; or prophetic, which makes application of the truth of God to the age; or evangelistic, which repeats the message, and woos men to allegiance to Christ; or pastoral and didactic, which feeds and instructs the flock; the message is always the Word of God, the Word of this unveiled glory in the face of Jesus Christ, the Word of Spirit and life.

Next in order we have in this letter a revelation of the resources of the Christian minister. Of these there are three, and the first is dealt with at length in the first chapter; it is that of the comfort of God. This becomes more wonderful as, reading on through the letter, we see the experiences through which the apostle had passed, and what he had proved of that comfort in circumstances of testing and trouble and trial. The first resource of the Christian minister is always that of the comfort of God.

As we get to the end of the letter, we find him making his boast in visions and revelations; that is, in the fact of personal, first-hand, direct, immediate speech of God to his own soul. It is to be observed that these visions and revelations were not for publication. In all probability fourteen years had passed before he made any reference to these visions and revelations; and then he declared they were not lawful to be uttered; but they completely captured his life, and kept it bent in the true direction, so that there was no possibility of doubt or fear. I believe that men still have visions and revelations; but I am always suspicious that a man who is anxious to talk of visions is suffering from nightmare. The true vision and revelation cannot be talked about. Even when at last, compelled by the misunderstanding of this Corinthian Church, to refer to them, the apostle apologized, saying:

You have compelled me, I am bound to boast now. He could not, however, explain the experience. I may have been in the body or out of it, I know not, God knows; I saw things and heard things that I cannot tell.

Let any man in the ministry feel that there is something lacking, unless in the hour of lonely communion with God there flame before him such visions, that he never can tell, but which, abiding with him, create the note of his confidence and authority, and inspire his determination to prosecute the work of his ministry to the end.

The final resource of the minister is that of the prayers of the saints; and the apostle declared that, not only by this exceeding comfort of God, and not only by visions and revelations; but also by the prayers of the saints had he been delivered. The value of such prayers cannot be overestimated; and those who are in the ministry know them to be among the most powerful and prevailing sources of strength.

Again the letter is a remarkable revelation of the experiences of the Christian ministry. These are described in three notable passages which are so graphic that they need little exposition. Let us read them.

"We have this treasure in earthen vessels, that the exceeding greatness of the power may be of God, and not from ourselves; we are pressed on every side, yet not straitened; perplexed, yet not unto despair; pursued, yet not forsaken; smitten down, yet not destroyed; always bearing about in the body the dying of Jesus, that the life also of Jesus may be manifested in our body."

"In everything commending ourselves, as ministers of God, in much patience, in afflictions, in necessities, in distresses, in stripes, in imprisonments, in tumults, in labours, in watchings, in fastings; in pureness, in knowledge, in long-suffering, in kindness, in the Holy Ghost, in love unfeigned, in the word of truth, in the power of God; by the armour of righteousness on the right hand and on the left, by glory and dishonour, by evil report and good report; as deceivers, and yet true; as unknown, and yet well known; as dying, and behold, we live; as chastened, and not killed; as sorrowful, yet alway rejoicing; as poor, yet making many rich; as having nothing, and yet possessing all things."

"I take pleasure in weaknesses, in injuries,

THE MESSAGE OF II. CORINTHIANS

in necessities, in persecutions, in distresses, for Christ's sake; for when I am weak, then am I strong."

These are the experiences of the Christian ministry. There is experience of tribulation. That is a subject not perhaps to be dealt with in detail in the great assembly; yet one which we all need to face. Is it not true that the Word of God only becomes truly quick and powerful, full of solace and help, when spoken by such as have suffered? I say this, not that any should seek the pathway of suffering, but that the man to whom is committed the preaching of the Word, and who is in the midst of buffeting and bruising and suffering, may know that by such processes the Word of God from his lips will become quick and powerful. I had a young friend who was brought to God, through His good grace, by my ministry. He devoted himself to the ministry. I never heard him preach until his college days were over. Then his sermon was wonderful, brilliant, sparkling in eloquence. When it was over and we were in the private seclusion of home, I asked my wife what she thought of the sermon. Her reply was: It was wonderful; but it will be better when he has had some trouble. I never heard him again until he had stood by the side of a grave, and his heart had been smitten; and oh, the difference! It is through tribulation that the Word of God becomes powerful. I think I would hardly dare to write that, but it may be that some brother in the ministry may read this, who is in trouble. God help you, my brother! It is by the pressure on the earthen vessel that the light flames through. It is by the hour of sorrow that we become instruments able to convey to the people of God the message that heals and helps.

Tribulation is not all of the experience of the minister of the Word. He has an experience of hope; of perfect confidence; there is always a song in his heart if he preach the Word of God; and he has also an experience of triumph, for He leadeth us everywhere in triumph.

With the aim of the Christian minister we need not tarry, having already seen in another connection that it is that of the perfecting of the saints, unto the work of ministering. We are only successful in the measure in which the result of our ministry is the larger ministry of the Church in the city.

Neither need we stay to consider at any length

the ministry of the Church, that having been the burden of the first letter. We need only stay to remind ourselves of our responsibilities as to equipment and exercise.

The Church's equipment for its ministry is that of obedience to the Word which is preached; separation from the world which is to be saved; and conformity to the will of the Lord which is revealed.

The Church is to exercise its ministry by seeing to it that it puts no occasion of stumbling in the way of the Word; by seeing to it that it is living a life of reconciliation to God; by seeing to it that it does not receive the grace of God in vain.

Or to summarize the whole suggestiveness of this letter in this respect, the Church of God fulfills its ministry when it incarnates the truth to which it listens. The responsibility of the Church towards the minister is not that of obedience to an official; but of obedience to the Word of God which he proclaims.

The abiding appeal of the letter is patent. It appeals to those of us who are in the ministry within the Church, to be loyal to the message of the Word of reconciliation. "All things are of

God, Who reconciled us to Himself through Christ, and gave unto us the ministry of reconciliation; to wit, that God was in Christ reconciling the world unto Himself." That is the all-inclusive harmony of the evangel. It has many notes, many tones, many emphases, many applications; but that is our message; and this letter calls us to be faithful to it.

It calls us also to absolute rest in the sufficiency of God, and to acceptation of the principle of the Cross. "We have this treasure in earthen vessels," and the measure in which the treasure in the earthen vessel is communicated to those who need it is the measure of the pressure on the vessel. The sacrificial note must be in the life of the preacher, or his preaching is in vain.

Finally, this letter teaches us that the true relationship of the minister to his people is first that of disinterested independence; and secondly, that of dependent interest.

The final appeal of this letter is to the Church as to its own ministry; and that is crystallized in the words, "Be ye reconciled to God." The measure in which the Church is composed of men and women who are living the life of reconciliation, is the measure in which the Church

THE MESSAGE OF II. CORINTHIANS

is declaring the evangel of reconciliation to the world. Are we reconciled to God? Fundamentally, as to standing, if we are Christian men and women we are reconciled; but experimentally, as to state, are we reconciled? Is there controversy between us and God, something that breaks in upon the experience of reconciliation? By that controversy we are rendered unable to proclaim the evangel of reconciliation in the city. The Church reconciled experimentally, living in fellowship with God, is the Church that preaches the gospel of reconciliation. Therefore the final word of appeal is, "Receive not the grace of God in vain."

There is a twofold application needed at the present hour. First to the Church. The Church needs a return to recognition of the sacredness of the ministry. I use the word ministry now in its more restricted sense. There has been an appalling tendency amongst us to degrade and forget the sanctity of the office of the minister of the Word of God. We serve tables altogether too much; and are unable to give ourselves to the proper ministry of the Word. We allow ourselves all too constantly to be deflected from the main line of our endeavour; and find that we have been so busy doing excellent nothings that we have been able to do nothing excellently.

The minister of the Word needs to get back to the fact that his burden is the Word, and his business is to preach it. His toil is to know it, and he cannot trifle with it without degrading the sacredness of his office. Oh, for the tears and the travail of Paul! As I look at him, my soul is often ashamed, because I seem to lack the brands of Jesus.

There must be return to recognition of the sanctity of the ministerial position by the Church itself. She must come to understand that those whom God has appointed to this ministry have a responsibility to Him, and that the Church has a tremendous responsibility of obedience, not to the minister as an official, but to the Word of which he is the messenger, the expositor.

There must therefore be acceptation of the responsibilities of reconciliation and of grace. There must be discipline of the sinning brother, but there must be his restoration after he has repented. There must be recognition of unity, and if the poor saints in Jerusalem are suffering for lack of material things, then the grace of giving must be exercised by the wealthy church at

Corinth, and she must give, not as though the giving were a charitable addition to her activities, but out of a heart of love.

Is there any application of this letter to the world? None; save that if the Church of God, and the ministry within the Church, are not true to the ideals, they had better hide this letter from the world; because if the worldly man shall read this letter, and then look for the marks and the signs, what an appalling disaster if he do not find them!

So may we all in this ministry learn its secrets, obey its call, and fulfill the purposes of our Lord.

THE MESSAGE OF GALATIANS

A THE ESSENTIAL MESSAGE	B THE APPLICATION

I. The Central Teaching. A Proclamation
i. Life. The Root. The Supply of the Spirit. iii. 5.
    a. The Way of Life is Faith.
    b. Nothing else necessary to Salvation.
    c. To add is to deny Faith and to destroy Life.
ii. Law. The Culture. The Lust of the Spirit. v. 17.
    a. Liberty is not Licence.
    b. It is Capture and Constraint by the Spirit.
    c. Ability to obey.
iii. Love. The Fruit. The Triumph of the Spirit. v. 22.
    a. The Mastery of Love. Fruit.
    b. The Mastery of Selfishness impossible. Works.
    c. Results. Works issue from Ritualism.
               Fruit results from Life.
 	
II. The Abiding Appeal. A Protest
i. The Preachers of another Gospel. Accursed. i. 8, 9.
    Anathema. (Cf. 1 Cor. xvi. 22.)
    That is the Condition. Suicide.
    Let those loyal to the one Gospel agree.
ii. The Receivers of another Message. Severed from Christ. v. 4.
    To trust in Ceremony is to deny Christ.
    To deny Christ is to be severed from Christ.
    To be severed from Christ is to fall from Grace.
iii. The Practicers of resulting Deeds. Excluded from Kingdom of God. v. 21.
    The Works of the Flesh. Sensual.
                              Spiritual.
                              Social.
    Resulting from Lack of Life.
    Resulting in Exclusion.
	I. To the Church
	To superimpose on faith, any rite or ceremony or observance as necessary to salvation, is to sever from Christ; both in the case of the individual and the Church.
	Those guilty of so doing are Anathema; whether individuals, or councils, or churches.
	
	II. To the World
	The Way of Life. Faith in Christ. Any other Way is the Way of Death.
	
	To believe in Him is to need no other; and to find deliverance from all bondage.

THE MESSAGE OF GALATIANS

IT is impossible to read this letter without being impressed by the severity of its note. It is evident that the writer was dealing with matters which, from his standpoint at least, were of vital importance. The letter is vibrant with passion, and yet consistent with principle. From the introductory sentences to the final words, it is quite evident that the apostle was profoundly moved; but it is equally evident that he never allowed emotion to carry him away from the line of a clearly defined system of thought and teaching. Whereas, as our analysis of the content reveals, personal matters largely enter into the letter, yet the supreme concern of the writer is for truth, and its bearing upon human life, in view of the perils which threaten men when truth is in any way violated or changed. There is an entirely different note running through this letter to that which characterized the Corinthian letters. This also is corrective; but as we turn over from the Corinthian letters we find a tone entirely different. Note the omissions from the salutation. Paul makes no reference to their standing in Christ. There is no single word of commendation. These two things mark this letter as peculiar from all others in the Pauline writings to the churches. The introduction is almost prosaic, "the churches in Galatia," not "them that are sanctified in Christ Jesus, called saints," and such rich phrases as mark the beginnings of other letters; no word of thankfulness for their state. After a few brief words of introduction, he commences, "I marvel," and immediately he proceeds to deal with them in terms of great severity.

Notice the specially declamatory passage of this letter in chapter one, and mark the severity of it;—

"I marvel that ye are so quickly removing from Him that called you in the grace of Christ unto a different gospel; which is not another gospel: only there are some that trouble you, and would pervert the gospel of Christ. But though we, or an angel from heaven, should preach unto you any gospel other than that which we preached unto you, let him be anathema. As we have said before, so say I now again, If any man preacheth unto you any gospel other than that which ye received, let him be anathema."

Turn to another declamatory passage, in the third chapter, and again note the intense severity ;—

"O foolish Galatians, who did bewitch you, before whose eyes Jesus Christ was openly set forth crucified? This only would I learn from you, Received ye the Spirit by the works of the law, or by the hearing of faith? Are ye so foolish? Having begun in the Spirit, are ye now perfected in the flesh? Did ye suffer so many things in vain? if it be indeed in vain. He therefore that supplieth to you the Spirit, and worketh miracles among you, doeth he it by the works of the law, or by the hearing of faith?"

Turn over yet once more to chapter four, and the same severe note is found ;—

"Howbeit at that time, not knowing God, ye were in bondage to them which by nature are no gods: but now that ye have come to know God, or rather to be known of God, how turn ye back again to the weak and beggarly rudiments, whereunto ye desire to be in bondage over again? Ye observe days, and months, and seasons, and years. I am afraid of you, lest by any means I have bestowed labour upon you in vain."

Or take the one tender outburst of the letter:

"My little children, of whom I am again in travail until Christ be formed in you, yea, I could wish to be present with you now, and to change my voice; for I am perplexed about you."

This passage thrills with the pain of a troubled heart; concern fills the mind of the writer.

I lay emphasis at such length upon these matters in order that we may come with solemnity to the letter, in our attempt to discover its message. Evidently the matter of which the apostle wrote was, in his estimation, of supreme importance. He was not writing to people who had failed in behaviour. The peril was of the gravest; the foundations were threatened, and consequently the whole superstructure was in danger.

This letter has been called the Magna Charta of the early Church. It is the Manifesto of Christian liberty, explaining the nature of that

THE MESSAGE OF GALATIANS 153

liberty, applying the laws of that liberty, and cursing the enemies of that liberty. It is of perpetual value from that standpoint, and more than once in the history of the Christian Church this little pamphlet has sounded the clarion call of return to freedom. Take one flaming illustration of the truth of what I now declare. This was Luther's letter, the letter that found him, and revealed to him the true meaning of Christianity, and made him the flaming prophet of liberty, breaking the chains of cruel oppression from the captive people of God. Godet says with reference to Luther and this letter, "This was the pebble from the brook with which, like another David, he went forth to meet the papal giant and smite him in the forehead." Whenever the Church of God bends to a bondage which results from denial of the foundation principles of her life, we find in this letter to the Galatians the corrective for such apostasy.

In seeking for the message we must begin at the right point. We are perhaps a little prone to be occupied only with the denunciations which the letter contains. As a matter of fact, the profoundest value of this letter is not to be discovered in the denunciations. The profoundest value of the letter is discovered in its enunciations. To discover these is not to weaken the denunciations, but to understand their force. We read the declamatory passages; they must be read, and ought to be read; but we must understand what Paul meant when he said, "If any man preacheth unto you any gospel other than that which ye received, let him be anathema"; we ought to understand what he meant when he declared that to produce works of the flesh which result from ritualism is to be excluded from the Kingdom of God. We do not understand the force of the denunciations save as we are conscious of the enunciations of truth which lie behind them. The truths constitute the dynamic. The teaching causes the explosion. We are often more occupied with the explosion than with the dynamic when we read this letter; more interested in the way in which Paul dealt with Peter when he came to Antioch, than with the reason of Paul's so dealing with Peter. If I am to discover and interpret in any sense intelligently the message of this letter I am compelled to lay my emphasis, not principally upon the denunciation, but upon the enunciation of principle; not upon

THE MESSAGE OF GALATIANS 155

the protest, but upon the proclamation that lies behind the protest.

The essential message of this letter has to do then with liberty. Its central teaching is a proclamation or enunciation of truth, concerning liberty. Its abiding appeal is a protest or denunciation of everything which contradicts that truth.

First, then, as to the central teaching. In the proclamation of Galatians the epistle to the Romans is found in essence. Here we have in unified form, in germ and potentiality, the great doctrines which are elaborated and systematically stated in the larger epistle. It is perfectly evident that this letter was written in the light, and under the impulse, of that great controversy which broke out at Antioch after the first missionary journey, and which resulted in the Council at Jerusalem. The apostle, in correcting error, did not go into any detailed statement of truth; but the truth is recognized.

The proclamation of this letter may be gathered round three words—life, law, love; and the teaching is condensed in three principal statements.

The fact of Life is recognized in the words,

"He therefore that supplieth to you the Spirit." That is not to take a text out of its context; it is rather to discover within a text the supreme thought which inspired the teaching. The whole paragraph gives the apostolic conception of Christianity. Life is supplied in the supply of the Spirit. That is the root of Christianity in individual experience.

The fact of Law is recognized in the words, "The flesh lusteth against the Spirit, and the Spirit against the flesh; for these are contrary the one to the other; that ye may not do the things that ye would." The doctrine involved is that the Christian life is not a life of licence; it is under law, but it is a new law, that of the lust of the Spirit. I retain the word lust, using it in its true sense of desire. As the root principle of the Christian life is the supply of the Spirit, the culture of this life is the result of obedience to the lust of the Spirit.

The fact of Love is recognized in the words, "The fruit of the Spirit is love." That is the final word, fruit, the triumph of the Spirit.

In these statements we have the doctrines of this letter revealed. Christianity is a life; its root principle is the supply of the Spirit. No man is a Christian unless he have the Spirit of God. But Christianity does not set a man free to go where he likes, or to do what he pleases. There is a law for the culture of the life received, and it is that of the lust of the Spirit within the man; the Spirit desiring in him, correcting his desires. As man yields to the lust of the Spirit, he is master over the lust of the flesh. The outcome of such life, yielded to such law, will be love, which is the fruit, the triumph of the Spirit.

Let us pass over that ground again for it is fundamental. First, as to Life. Life is received by receiving the supply of the Spirit. The Spirit is received in answer to the exercise of faith. That is the master thought of the letter. The deduction from that is that nothing other than faith is necessary to salvation. Therefore to affirm that men must be circumcised or baptized in order to salvation is to proclaim the most deadly heresies that can possibly be taught. To superadd anything to faith is to destroy the foundations of Christianity. Life is by faith.

Secondly, as to Law. Liberty is not licence. When a man has life by faith he is thereby set free from all other bondage. He is set free from the bondage of the flesh, because he has the power that masters it and brings it into subjection. He is set free from the bondage of rites and ceremonies, because he has found life apart from rite, and without ceremony; and he is henceforward, so far as life is concerned, independent of all ceremony and of every rite. He is set free from bondage by life; but that liberty is not licence. The liberty of this life is that of the capture and constraint of the spirit of man, by the Spirit of God. The capture of the spirit of man by the Spirit of God means that man is made able to obey, and no man was made able to obey by circumcision or by baptism. Man is made able to obey when that life becomes law, and he yields to it. The lust of the Spirit within is the law of the new-found life.

Finally, as to Love. The fruit of this life, obedient to this law, is love; the whole life under the dominion of love, bondage to self is therefore no longer possible. When we read the fifth chapter, whatever wider application we may make of it, we must be true to the first line of its argument. I know there are more spacious applications of these Bible truths than were made by the writers. They dealt with great principles, the ultimate applications of which are far wider than the one the writers indicated at the moment. But when we read of "the works of the flesh," and "the fruit of the Spirit," we must remember that the passage is part of one great argument. "The works of the flesh" are things which result from a religion which is not a religion of faith unto life. Works of the flesh are the activities of godless and irreligious men; but primarily, in the apostolic argument, the phrase refers to things resulting from the observance of rites and ceremonies as though such observance constituted religion. Works of the flesh are things which result from ritualism which becomes an evasion of righteousness.

Here we touch the real reason of the vehemence of the apostle's anger. Superadd to faith anything else, as necessary to salvation, and inevitably the outcome is that faith is neglected. The moment we make anything other than faith supreme, we establish a rite—whether it be this, that, or the other, I care nothing—and men will say, If we fulfill this rite, then are we religious, and religion will be divorced from morality, religion will have lost the inspiration of righteousness. That is what is wrong with all false religion. That is the supreme difference between

Christianity and every other religion. All the great systems of religion have rites, and ceremonies, and creeds, but no life. Consequently there is not the remotest connection between religion and morality. That is what the apostle saw was the supreme danger of these Judaizing teachers. They were adding to faith, which is the only way into life, with the inevitable result that presently men would say, We have observed this rite, now we can do what we like. All forms of sensuality and spiritual sin result from the tragedy of superadding something to the one law of faith.

Therefore the abiding appeal of this letter is of the nature of a protest. Its first note is a denunciation of the preachers of another gospel;—"If any man preacheth unto you any gospel other than that which ye received, let him be anathema." That is not an episcopal curse; it is not an apostolic malediction. It is the statement of the case as it is. "Let him be anathema." The word anathema, which means accursed, occurs in only one other passage in the New Testament, in the letter of Paul to the Corinthians, "If any man loveth not the Lord, let him be anathema." That is not a curse pronounced as by ecclesiastical authority; it is a declaration of truth concerning the condition of any man who loves not the Lord Jesus Christ; he is anathema; therefore let him be anathema. And so with the use of the word in this letter;— "If any man preacheth unto you any gospel other than that which ye received, let him be anathema"; the man who preaches another gospel, by such preaching substitutes the false which issues finally in the works of the flesh, for the true which issues in the fruit of the Spirit.

Not only the preacher, but the receiver of the other gospel is severed from Christ. To trust in ceremony is to deny Christ; and to deny Christ is to be severed from Christ; and to be severed from Christ is to fall from grace. To add to faith in Christ as the foundation of religious life, either rite or ceremony, as necessary to salvation, is to deny Christ and to be severed from Christ, and fallen from grace.

I am not dealing with rites and ceremonies save as rites and ceremonies are made essential to salvation. Baptism has its place in the Christian Church. The observance of the Lord's Supper has its place in the Christian Church. The assembling of men and women for worship has its place in the Christian Church. But to make baptism, or the Lord's Supper, or the assembling, necessary to salvation, is to deny Christ.

There is only one way in which a man can be a Christian, and it is the way of honestly and sincerely saying,

> "Nothing in my hand I bring,
> Simply to Thy Cross I cling."

If I come to the Cross and say, By that and by my baptism I will become a Christian, I deny Christ.

The last note of the appeal is the solemn declaration that the practicers of the deeds resulting from a false gospel, the deeds of the flesh, are excluded from the Kingdom of God. With what great and grave sense of responsibility the apostle wrote these words.

These were the terrible possibilities which Paul saw. These were the things that made his words vibrant with passion. His profound understanding of the peril of the Christian Church, through the influence of Judaizing teachers, called forth this letter.

In a closing word let us make a twofold application of the teaching of the letter. This Galatian letter warns the Church that to superimpose upon men any rite or ceremony or observance, as necessary to salvation, is to sever from Christ both in the case of the individual and in the case of the Church. I care not what the Church may be as to ecclesiastical conviction. I have less and less concern for such things. I am growingly convinced that ecclesiastical matters are not essential matters. There is room for every form of Church government within the economy of the Spirit of God. I decline controversy over ecclesiastical convictions. But whatever Church adds to faith in Christ, any rite or ceremony or observance of any kind, as essential to salvation, that Church is severed from Christ.

We need to get back to these fundamental documents, to these tremendous revelations of the apostolic writings; to the sense of the importance of things, which, if we are not very careful, we are allowing to appear as though they were unimportant. You began in the Spirit, will you attempt to gain perfection by the flesh? That is the great question of the letter. We need to-day to understand that in our preaching and in our teaching, and in order to strength of Church life for the accomplishment of the Divine purpose in the world, the one condition of salvation is that of faith in Christ, and the reception of life from Christ; not because of our observance of rite or ceremony, but simply and solely and wholly by His great unmerited grace in response to faith. That is fundamental to personal Christianity and to Church life. Those guilty of superimposing upon faith any rite or ceremony or observance, as necessary to salvation, are anathema; whether they be individuals, or councils, or churches.

If I am emphatic about this, it is because the letter is emphatic about it. Where there is faith unto life, the life becomes a law, and there result no works of the flesh, neither sensual things, fornications, uncleanness, and lasciviousness; nor spiritual things, idolatry, sorcery, and the like.

The freedom of the Church is not political. It is spiritual or nothing. The only freedom that comes from absolute unbending loyalty to the will of God is bondage to the law of life, interpreted by the Spirit of God. Let us make our protest, and let it be vehement, against all bondage; but let us see to it that behind the denunciation is the enunciation of principle. It is only as we live in the power of that dynamic, that we shall be strong enough to burst all bonds, and fling off all yokes, and live in the spaciousness of spiritual freedom. May we learn the lesson and live the life.

THE MESSAGE OF EPHESIANS

A THE ESSENTIAL MESSAGE	B THE APPLICATION

I. The Central Teaching. " The Saints . . . in Christ Jesus "
i. The eternal Character of the Church.
    a. The Conception. The Plan of God from Eternity.
    b. The Construction. The Power of God in Time.
    c. The Consummation. The Purpose of God to Eternity.
ii. The temporal Conduct of the Church.
    a. The Construction. Conformity to the Unity.
    b. The Confession. Sanctification of all Life.
    c. The Conflict. To stand, To withstand, To stand.
 	
II. The Abiding Appeal. " Walk worthily. . . ."
i. According to the eternal Plan.
    " Grow up into Him . . . the Increase of the Body."
ii. Appropriating the eternal Power.
    " Understand the Will of the Lord . . . filled with the Spirit."
iii. Approaching the eternal Purpose.
    " Against " . . . " The whole Armour of God."
	I. To the Church
	i. The Measure of the Church's Power to help this World is the Measure of her Other-worldliness.
	ii. The Test of the Otherworldliness of the Church is the Measure of her Influence in this World.
	
	II. To the World
	i. The Church of God is the Instrument of God for the Establishment of His Kingdom.
	ii. The Way into the Church is through the One Lord, One Faith, One Baptism.

THE MESSAGE OF EPHESIANS

THIS letter leads us to the high places of vision, and to awe-inspiring sublimities; it leads us there, and then leaves us in amazed and wondering adoration in the presence of the truths revealed. There is a sense in which an attempt to declare its message is easy. There is a sense in which it is difficult. It is easy because the whole letter is a message. It is difficult because the letter is a message, and therefore, having studied the content we have already heard the message. Yet with the consciousness of that content in our minds, we may reverently inquire what is its essential message, and what its persistent application.

Let us then consider, first, in broad outline the essential message, as to its central teaching, and its abiding appeal; and secondly, give attention to its application.

We are immediately arrested by the fact that there are no salutations in this letter, in the ordinary sense of the word; and as we proceed through the argument we are impressed by the fact that there is very little local colouring. It stands alone, a great message of truth. It is quite evident that more than one particular church was in the mind of the apostle. Even if he wrote it to one, it is a message preëminently to the whole Church, the Catholic Church of Jesus Christ.

The teaching of this letter has to do entirely with the Church. It is the final word of the New Testament concerning the Church. It is the last exposition of the words of Jesus Christ at Cæsarea Philippi, "Upon this rock I will build My Church; and the gates of Hades shall not prevail against it. I will give unto thee the keys of the Kingdom." In that declaration we have the full and final truth concerning the Church. For its exposition we need the whole of the Petrine and Pauline teachings; but especially the Pauline, because Paul was the steward of the mystery of the Church. In this letter, then, we have the last exposition of the meaning of Christ. To study it in the light of that statement at Cæsarea Philippi is at once to discover the connections. The Lord said, "I will build My Church," and the figure of building is here employed by the apostle. The Lord said, "The gates of Hades shall not prevail against it," and the apostle deals with the conflict very fully. Finally the Lord said, "I will give unto thee the keys of the Kingdom"; that is, the standards of moral and ethical interpretation; and in the heart of this letter we find the application of the ethic of Jesus, to all the details of every-day life.

The central teaching of this whole letter is suggested by words taken from its opening address, "The saints . . . in Christ Jesus," as they describe the composition of the Church of God.

The phrase "in Christ Jesus" following the words "the saints" indicates the unification of the units into the unity of the Church. The word "saints" suggests diversities, differences; the phrase, "in Christ Jesus," reveals the fact that all are one; and thus there breaks upon the mind the vision of the whole Church, that Church being Christ and all those who are united to Him.

The central teaching deals with the Church, and falls into two parts; that first, of the eternal character of the Church; and that secondly, of the temporal conduct of the Church.

And first as to the eternal character of the Church, the letter teaches us three things as it deals with the conception, construction, and consummation thereof; showing that it was in the plan of God from eternity, is being realized by the power of God in time, and will fulfill the purpose of God in eternity.

The conception of the Church comes up out of the past eternity. It is almost impossible to use such words with absolute accuracy. I have spoken of eternity past; there is a sense in which that is a contradiction in terms. Eternity is eternity; it is an ever-present now. With God there is neither past nor future. His is age-abiding life; a great and infinite mystery which our finite minds cannot fully grasp. Consequently we are bound to think of these things by the dimensions with which we are familiar, and we speak, therefore, of the past, present, and future. A fine attempt to give expression to these truths is found in Hebrew literature in the declaration, "From everlasting to everlasting Thou art God." If we translate the Hebrew word rendered "everlasting" in our versions,

THE MESSAGE OF EPHESIANS 171

according to its first significance, the statement will read, "From the vanishing-point to the vanishing-point Thou art God." That is to say, the writer was conscious that there is a limit to human understanding, and a limit to the stretch and sweep of the human mind, both backward and forward. There is a vanishing-point. Some men have seen further than others because they have climbed higher than others; but there always has been, and still is, a vanishing-point. We find it in Genesis, as we step out of the unseen into the seen; "In the beginning," that is the vanishing-point. John climbed far higher up the mount than Moses, and he also said, "In the beginning," but his "beginning" was further back than that of Moses, for Moses referred to the period immediately preceding creation; but John referred to the essential fact of eternity, that timeless, limitless fact ere time or creation in any form existed.

To-day we are looking on. How far can we see? As far as the second Advent? Yes, and beyond it. To the millennial reign? Much further! To the Kingdom of the Son? Yes, and beyond. To the generation, that is to the new birth, of the age of the ages. There again we come to the vanishing-point. "From the vanishing-point to the vanishing-point, Thou art God."

Turning our thoughts back again to what we thus speak of as eternity past, this letter teaches us that the plan of the Church was formulated there; it is eternal. It comes up out of these vast distances, out of the eternities, the ages that we cannot comprehend, and of which the utmost we can say is that they are beyond the vanishing-point.

May God deliver us from taking so great, so stupendous and sublime and far-reaching a vision of the wisdom which transcends our finite theory, in order to formulate a doctrine that God has chosen a few people to be saved and left the rest to be damned. That is an unwarranted deduction.

The plan of the Church existed in the mind of God from eternity. He predestined the Church that it should be conformed to the image of His Son. Paul peered into the deep things, the infinite mysteries, until somewhere back in those past eternities he saw in the mind of God, the Son of His love, the archetypal pattern of all perfection, and he declared that He predestined

THE MESSAGE OF EPHESIANS 173

men and women that they should be conformed to that likeness. The Church then is not an experiment in human history. It is part of the plan of God. Let no member of the Church be anxious as to whether it is going to be destroyed or not. Let us not be filled with panic because the Church of God is being criticized by men who know neither the Church nor God. It is eternal because it is the conception, the plan of God, from eternity.

It is eternal in another sense. If the conception is the plan of God from eternity, the construction is by the power of God operating in time; that is eternal power; it is power coming from eternity past, and continuing to eternity future. The power which, operating in Christ, raised Him from the dead, is the power by which He builds His Church. In Christ, men and women are quickened, raised, and seated in the heavenlies. That is the operation of the power of God in time, and that is the whole story of the construction of the Church.

And finally the Church is eternal in yet another sense. The consummation is eternal, for the Church is to serve the purpose of God in the coming eternity. Through the Church in its union with Jesus Christ there will be revealed to the ages to come "the exceeding riches of His grace"; and there will be unveiled before the angels "the manifold wisdom of God."

That is the first note of the central teaching of this letter. The Church of God is eternal. Its conception in the past eternity was the plan of God. Its construction in time is by the power of God. Its consummation in the coming eternity will be for the fulfillment of the purposes of God. Are we of this Church? Then we were in the heart and mind and plan of God in the ages gone; we are to fulfill the purposes of God in the ages to come; and the plan of the past, and the purpose of the future, are linked by the power of the present; for plan, and power, purpose are alike eternal.

From these stupendous declarations the apostle turned to the subject of the temporal conduct of the Church. When that great vision has broken upon the life, and its virtue has empowered it, what will be the result in conduct? With the winds of the past eternity blowing across her, and the light of the coming eternity streaming upon her path, what manner of people will the members of this Church be?

The apostle describes that conduct as having relation to the construction of the Church; as constituting a confession before the world; and as being a conflict against all opposing forces.

Concerning the construction of the Church, he appeals to the members thereof; "I therefore . . . beseech you to walk worthily of the calling wherewith ye were called." This he shows they will do by "giving diligence to keep the unity of the Spirit in the bond of peace." This is followed by a picture of the Church, being built up, growing up, " in all things into Him." The first responsibility of churchmanship then is the maintenance of the Spirit of unity. Can such a word be uttered without shame, without a sense of disappointment and of failure?

In the next place the apostle shows that the Church is to make a great confession in time concerning God; the mind of God, the purpose of God, the will of God. This she will do by the sanctification of life. Not by creeds written or recited; but by life, true to the heavenly standard and the eternal measurement in the details of every-day experience; husbands and wives, parents and children, masters and servants. The sanctification of all life in the power of the heavenly conception is the confession which the Church makes to the world.

The result of such a confession must inevitably be that of conflict with the forces which are opposed to the purpose of God. The Church must be armed, and at war with these forces. In that conflict she is to stand, to withstand, and having done all, to stand.

Once again, if that be the picture of the temporal conduct of the Church, we cannot fail to notice how it coincides with the word of Christ at Cæsarea Philippi. He declared, "I will build My Church." The first responsibility of the Church is that she obtain and maintain the view of the unity of that Church and "grow up in all things into Him, which is the Head, even Christ . . . unto the building up of itself in love." Building according to the pattern is our first responsibility.

His final word was, "I will give unto thee the keys," that is, the insignia of the office of ethical teaching. The Church is to fulfill that responsibility by the sanctification of life.

Between that first proclamation and that final commission He said "the gates of Hades shall not prevail against it." In order to fulfill the responsibility suggested by that declaration the Church must obey the apostolic injunction : "Put on the whole armour of God, that ye may be able to stand against the wiles of the devil . . . take up the whole armour of God, that ye may be able to withstand in the evil day, and, having done all, to stand."

The Church of God is eternal in character; the plan of God in the past; the power of God today; the purpose of God in the future. Therefore in temporal conduct she must coöperate with God in His building by growing up into the Head; deliver the message of God's purity and holiness to the world by her sanctified life; fight the foes of God by putting on the whole armour of God.

If the central teaching of this letter is unified in that opening phrase, "The saints in Christ Jesus," its abiding appeal is focussed in the injunction, "Walk worthily of the vocation."

First, the members of the Church are to walk according to the eternal plan, to behave in time according to God's purpose from eternity. He predestined us that we should be conformed to the image of His Son. We are therefore to "grow up in all things into Him, which is the

Head, even Christ." That is the standard. The measure in which we are living in holiness and in love, is the measure in which we are conforming to the eternal plan. We are not to be holy because decency demands it; we are not to be righteous because the policeman may arrest us if we are not; these are not our motives. We are to walk according to the eternal plan, remembering that our individual life was in the thought of God, and of it He has revealed the pattern in His Son, and He calls us to be true to the plan that has come up out of the past eternity by conforming to that pattern.

If we are to walk according to the eternal plan we must do it by appropriating the eternal power. When we read this letter we are amazed at its height, and the glory of its suggestion, and we are inclined to say, Who is sufficient for these things? Then we come to the great word in which the apostle says, "Now unto Him that is able to do exceeding abundantly above all that we ask or think, according to the power that worketh in us." Am I a Christian man? Then I am such because I share the life of Christ, and if I share the life of Christ, I have resident within me power enough to make me all that

THE MESSAGE OF EPHESIANS 179

God meant me to be from eternity. The eternal power is within the Christly soul, and we walk worthily as we appropriate it, and make use of it, understanding what the will of the Lord is, being filled with the Spirit, that so we may walk in harmony with the will of God.

The appeal of the letter is finally that we walk not only according to the eternal plan, not only appropriating the eternal power, but approaching the eternal purpose.

That walk will mean a fight against the forces that are attempting to hinder us, spiritual antagonisms, intelligences from the upper spaces who occupy lower places, who inhabit the heavenlies where the saints walk, that they may attack them. The devil's masterstroke to-day is that he has so largely succeeded in hiding himself, while still hard at work. It is quite time the saints awoke to recognition of these principalities and powers. They are manifested in many ways. We read of spiritualistic séances and bureaus; and the tragic thing is that the Church of God is laughing at these things, and saying there is no reality in these doings. It is certain that messages from the spirit-world are being actually received by men to-day; but they are messages of demons. If we are living the age-abiding life, if the plan of our life comes out of eternity, and its purpose runs into eternity, then false spirits will impede our progress, and attempt to seduce us from loyalty to the one Spirit of God; "Our wrestling is not against flesh and blood, but against the principalities, against the powers, against the world-rulers of this darkness, against the spiritual hosts of wickedness in the heavenly places." We are to keep our eye upon the consummation, and "put on the panoply of God," and fight.

So may we walk worthily of the vocation, according to the eternal plan, appropriating the eternal power, and approaching the eternal purpose. Such is the abiding appeal of the letter.

Finally let us briefly make an application of the message of this letter to our own age.

Its message to the Church is, first, that the measure of her power to help this world is the measure of her other-worldliness. I use that phrase because it is being used as a term of reproach. There are men who tell us that the Church has been other-worldly, and therefore has failed. The measure in which she has failed is the measure in which she has ceased to be other-worldly. The darkest day in the history of the Church was the day when Constantine patronized her. Then she ceased to be other-worldly, and instead of leaning wholly and solely upon God, and upon the presence of the Spirit of God, she leaned on the arm of flesh, and by doing so lost her power. That is going far back, but we may make a present application. The measure of the Church's power to help the world is still the measure of her other-worldliness. Only as the Church remembers her heavenly, her Divine calling, can she set up the standards of life, and supply the sufficient dynamic thereof.

This letter further teaches that the test of the Church's other-worldliness is the measure of her influence in this world. If she is so other-worldly that she has no care for the condition of this world ; if she is so other-worldly that she is unconscious of its sigh and sob and sorrow ; if she does not care anything about the slums, then she is other-worldly, but the world she is of is the other world of the devil, which is selfish and un-Christlike. That is the tragic mistake we have too often made. We have sung songs of heaven, and have forgotten this poor sinning, suffering earth ; and so have demonstrated our ignorance of heaven, for it is in heaven that earth's sorrows are most keenly felt, and it is upon the heart of God that earth's wrongs lie most heavily. The measure in which the Church of God is other-worldly in the true sense is the measure in which she is putting her life against the sins and sorrows of the world, to sympathize, to shepherd, and to save. It is not possible to do that unless we are other-worldly. Unless we can bring into the slums of London the light and life of the city of God, we had better leave it alone; it will only degrade us, and we shall not help it. Socialism that begins by telling men that man is in process of evolution, and that sin is an incident, is a cruel lie; such socialism was born in the pit. But the socialism that sees the city of God, the Kingdom of God established in the world, and then lives in the midst of human sorrow and sin to bring to it redemption by blood, and regeneration by life, is the socialism of Christianity.

I take up this epistle to the Ephesians and climb the heights and scale the mountains and gaze upon the far-flung splendours of the eternal vision; and then I climb down and live at home, and in my relation to wife and child, to servant and master, my confession is to be made. The Church of God can never help God when she ceases to be other-worldly. When she is other-worldly she helps the world; and cannot avoid doing so.

This letter declares to the world that the Church of God is the instrument of God for the establishment of His Kingdom; and it teaches that if any man would help to the establishment of His Kingdom, there is one way into the Church; he may enter through the one Lord, by one faith, and one baptism.

While this plan comes out of eternity, while this purpose lies in the distant eternity, and while this power is operating in time, there is no man or woman who may not come into the plan and into the purpose by coming into contact with the power. One Lord, the Lord Christ; Child of the eternities; Master of the ages; the Glory of the coming eternity. One faith; the simple abandonment of the needy soul who says:

> "Just as I am, without one plea,
> But that Thy blood was shed for me,
> And that Thou bid'st me come to Thee,
> O Lamb of God, I come."

One baptism; the baptism of the Holy Ghost, whereby that trusting soul is made a member of Christ, a member of the Church; and enters the plan of the eternities, and travels towards the purpose of the eternities, by appropriating the power of the eternities.

THE MESSAGE OF PHILIPPIANS

A THE ESSENTIAL MESSAGE	B THE APPLICATION

I. The Central Teaching. The Mind of Christ
i. Of Christ Jesus.
   a. The mental Attitude.
        "Counted it not a prize . . ."
   b. The consequent Activity.
        "Emptied Himself . . ."
   c. The resultant Crowning.
        "God highly exalted Him."
ii. Of the Saints in Christ Jesus.
   a. The mental Attitude.
      1. Love abounding more and more.
      2. Sincere and void of Offence.
   b. The consequent Activity.
      1. Manner of Life worthy of the Gospel.
      2. Children of God blameless . . . harmless.
   c. The resultant Crowning.
      1. Present Victory over Circumstances.
      2. Ultimate Realization of Divine Purpose.
	I. To the Church
	The Measure of the Church's Authority is the Measure of her Conformity to the Mind of Christ.
	That Mind is Love.
	Its Consciousness is Joy.
	Its Expression is Sacrifice.

II. The Abiding Appeal. "Have this mind in you"
i. The Resource. "To me to live is Christ."
ii. The Responsibility. "Work out . . ."
iii. The Rules.
   a. Rejoice in the Lord.
   b. Forbearance towards Men.
   c. The Life of Prayer.
   d. The Life of Thought.
	II. To the Individual Believer
	The Mastery of Christ.
	Individual Capture by Christ.
	The one Desire for others.

THE MESSAGE OF PHILIPPIANS

THE Philippian letter is a revelation of the Christian mind. It is largely without system, and extremely difficult to analyze. Who can analyze a love-letter, and that is what this letter is, which Paul wrote to his children at Philippi; and whereas in the deepest fact of his spiritual love this great apostle had no favourites, in the affections of his emotional nature, his children at Philippi were certainly his chiefly loved children. He had come to Philippi in answer to the call of the man of Macedonia. When, crossing over the Ægean Sea, he reached that city and began his work by the riverside, there almost immediately followed that wonderful experience in the prison. With feet fast in the stocks through the brutality of the jailer, at midnight Paul and Silas had sung praises to God. This letter to these Philippian Christians was written in prison, and it seems to me as I read that Philippi was always to Paul the place of prison and the place of song. These children at

188 THE MESSAGE OF PHILIPPIANS

Philippi were near and dear to his heart. They ministered to his need, as he says, once and again; and the letter which he wrote to them from prison is a letter brimming over with love.

If there be no definite system in the letter, some of the profoundest and most wonderful things that ever came from his pen are to be found therein. That marvellous and matchless passage describing the whole mission of the Son of God, from His Self-emptying, through all the experience of His sorrows, back to the throne of heavenly empire, is in this letter. That autobiographical passage is here also, in which Paul gives us the story of his own life in brief sentences, every one of which is full of light and full of colour; so that if we want to know the truth about Paul we turn to this wonderful piece of self-revelation.

The supreme value of the letter is that of its revelation of the true Christian consciousness. Notice the recurrence of the word *mind*, or of cognate words. "To be thus *minded* " i. 7; "Be of the same *mind*" ii. 2; "Lowliness of *mind*" ii. 3; "Have this *mind*" ii. 5; "Let us . . . be thus *minded*" iii. 15; "Who *mind* earthly things" iii. 19; "Of the same *mind*" iv. 2;

"Your *mind* of me" iv. 10;—though our translation, neither Authorized nor Revised, shows the fact, when the apostle spoke of their care for him he used the same word, *mind*. That of course is a grouping of phrases with no apparent connection; and there are some senses in which there is no connection between them. Our only purpose in thus grouping them is that we may notice how the word repeats itself. The fact that these words do not form a key to the analysis is all the more remarkable. They are incidental words arising out of an attitude of mind, and revealing that attitude, as the apostle wrote from his prison-house to his children at Philippi. In every chapter, and in every division, the word is to be found.

The Greek word so translated is one which signifies consciousness, either as the cognitive faculties, or as impression made on the mind. In the Thessalonian letter, we find an analysis of personality by this same apostle,—spirit, soul, and body. Spirit is the essential fact in a man's life; the body is the probationary dwelling-place of the spirit, the instrument through which the spirit communicates with others, and receives communications from others; the soul, or mind is the consciousness; and it is fleshly, or spiritual, according to whether the flesh or the spirit is dominant in the life.

The central teaching of this letter is suggested by the phrase "the mind of Christ." It reveals the mind of Christ. First the mind of Christ personally; and secondly the mind of Christ in the saints. The supreme appeal of the letter is that of the apostle's injunction, "Have this mind in you, which was also in Christ Jesus." Thus if we are to understand the message of the letter we must first discover what it reveals to us of the mind of Christ Himself; then what it reveals to us of the mind of Christian men and women. The appeal of the letter will then be seen to be patent, and necessary; "Have this mind in you, which was also in Christ Jesus."

When we attempt to examine this unveiled mind of our Lord, we are at once brought into the presence of light and glory that surprise, and arrest us, in adoring wonder. The gospel stories tell us of His words and His works, reveal to us His character, and the influence produced upon men by that character; but when we want to see the mind of Christ we turn to the Philippian letter. Herein is revealed that conception, that consciousness, of the Christ of God which lay behind all His words and works, inspiring them.

In the contemplation we first discover His mental attitude, that which caused everything else; then we see the activity springing out of that attitude; and finally we see the victory and crowning following that activity.

The attitude of mind is described in these words; "Being in the form of God, counted it not a prize to be on an equality with God." That is the mind of Christ. Then follows a statement of the activity resulting from that attitude of mind; "emptied Himself, taking the form of a servant, being made in the likeness of men; and being found in fashion as a man, He humbled Himself, becoming obedient even unto death, yea, the death of the Cross." Finally the issue of the activity is declared; "Wherefore also God highly exalted Him, and gave unto Him the name which is above every name; that in the name of Jesus every knee should bow, of things in heaven and things on earth and things under the earth, and that every tongue should confess that Jesus Christ is Lord, to the glory of God the Father."

The crowning of Christ proceeded from the

activity of Christ. The activity of Christ was the result of the mind of Christ. To know the mind of Christ then we must observe His activity. First He emptied Himself. To understand that we must watch the steps that follow. Every sentence tells of a downward movement. He emptied Himself in the infinite heights; and took the form of a Servant in the universe in which He had been Sovereign. He might have taken the form of the highest Servant in the universe, angel, archangel, seraph, or cherub; but He was made a little lower than the angels, and was made in the likeness of men. He might have come into human life at its highest and best, in the midst of ease and comfort; but "being found in fashion as a man, He humbled Himself, becoming obedient even unto death." As a man He might have died, surrounded by those who loved Him, ministering to Him to the last, and helping Him through the hour of weakness; but He died the death of the Cross.

Whence sprang such activity? The first words tell the story, "Being in the form of God, counted it not a prize to be on an equality with God." That is the mind of Christ; it is the mind of lowliness; it is the mind of pure and absolute love. "Love vaunteth not itself." The thirteenth chapter of Corinthians in its description of love is but the description of the mind of the Master. Though in the form of God, of the nature of God, on an equality with God, He had no conception of such a position as to make Him value the position for the sake of the position. When there was a race to be redeemed, the position must be laid aside in order that the Person of such mind might stoop to unutterable depths in order to lift out of ruin those who had been involved therein. That is the mind of Christ.

I am quite well aware that these words of mine are of the poorest, for what expositor can help men to understand this thing? We can only understand it when we have done listening to men and reading books, and when we sit in solemn loneliness in the presence of the unveiled glory of the mind of Christ. I take up this little New Testament, every book of it precious, every page of it invaluable, every pamphlet having some message; but not from Matthew to Revelation have I anywhere else such an unveiling of the mind of Christ, as I have in this one short paragraph, over which we have passed with almost rude footsteps in our attempt to understand it.

This letter reveals also the mind of the saints who are in Christ Jesus. We will take the same three divisions; the mental attitude, the consequent activity, and the resultant crowning; for as these are the great things revealed concerning the mind of Christ, all its preciousness, its values, its virtues, its victories, are at the disposal of the children of God. Even though we descend from the height of ineffable glory and splendour to the level of our own halting and failing experience, nevertheless we find that the true mind of the saint is the mind of the Lord.

What then is the true mental attitude of the Christian man? At the beginning of the letter, Paul prayed for his Philippian children that their "love may abound yet more and more," not emotionally merely, and certainly not ignorantly, but "in knowledge and all discernment." Then he prayed that they "may be sincere and void of offence." I lift my eyes amazed, to the wonder and glory of the mind of Christ; and with all reverence, for one is almost reluctant to do this, I say that His love is the revelation of our love. Being in the form of God He did not

THE MESSAGE OF PHILIPPIANS 195

count such relation a prize to be snatched at for Himself and His own enrichment, though it was already His. That is love abounding, love sincere, love void of offence. That mental attitude of Christ is to be the mental attitude of the saints. Consequently the saint will be mastered by love, and therefore, although we are so far from the heights we must take the measurement of the heights, for whatever position of privilege the child of God occupies within the economy of God, it must not be held as a prize to be snatched at for self-glorification. That is the mind of Christ.

Had Paul the mind of Christ? I affirm that he had. We see it supremely manifest when he wrote these words, "I say the truth in Christ, I lie not, my conscience bearing witness with me in the Holy Ghost, that I have great sorrow and unceasing pain in my heart. For I could wish that I myself were anathema from Christ for my brethren's sake, my kinsmen according to the flesh." That is the mind of Christ; the mind of the man made one with Christ. He had written immediately before, Nothing can separate me from the love of God which is in Christ Jesus; but he did not count that as a prize to be snatched at for his own enrichment, but could wish that he were anathema from Christ for his brethren's sake. That is the mind of Christ.

What then is the consequent activity? Following still the method of examination afforded by the unveiling of the mind of Christ, I take two of Paul's descriptions; "Let your manner of life be worthy of the gospel of Christ"; and "blameless and harmless, children of God without blemish in the midst of a crooked and perverse generation, among whom ye are seen as lights in the world." That is the activity growing out of the mind. The manner of life worthy of the Gospel is that of holiness, purity, truth; but these words do not touch the deepest note. The life must be worthy of the Gospel. The Gospel is the good news of God's grace bringing salvation to all men. Life is worthy of that when it suffers to carry that news, when it enters into travail and pain in order to bring men under the sound of it, and under the power of it, that they may be saved by it. That is the manner of life worthy of the Gospel. It is not merely rectitude of conduct or of character, it is not merely personal; the manner of life worthy of the Gospel is life driven by the Gospel in order to make it known, to proclaim it. That is the activity resulting from the mind.

Again, Children of God, blameless and harmless; blameless, that is the relationship to God; harmless, that is the consequent relationship to men. Once again I lift my eyes to the splendour of the unveiled activity of Jesus resulting from His mental attitude, and I see Him emptying Himself, taking the form of a servant, made in the likeness of man, humbling Himself, becoming obedient to death, the death of the Cross. That is the meaning of life worthy of the Gospel; that is the Son of God blameless and harmless. The mind that was in Christ is to be in the saint; and the mind that was in Christ being in the saint, is to produce in the saint the activity which was produced in Christ. How much do we know about emptying ourselves? How much do we know about humbling ourselves, about being obedient unto death, even the death of the Cross?

Looking thus at the mind of the saints, let us observe, not only the attitude, and the consequent activity, but also the resultant crowning. Of Christ it is said, "Wherefore also God highly exalted Him, and gave unto Him the name which is above every name." So also with the saint. Whenever we find this mind and this activity resulting, we find triumph. This whole letter is a triumph; triumph over circumstances calculated to make Paul feel he was being defeated; the intrepid missionary, the pioneer evangelist; the regions beyond, the perpetual watchword of his strong endeavour; was now in prison and everything was against him; circumstances were combining to crush him. Nothing of the kind. He sang in prison in Philippi long ago; he will sing in a letter to Philippi out of the Roman prison now; that is triumph over circumstances. That is not seen in this letter only, but also in all the letters. This man never called himself a prisoner of anybody save Jesus Christ, he said he was His prisoner; he did not consent to refer to Nero; Nero was out of sight entirely. He had no thought for the jailer by his side, except one of compassion and endeavour to bring him into that bondage to Christ which meant real liberty. He did once say in human weakness, "Remember my bonds"; but he also said that his bonds "have fallen out rather unto the progress of the gospel." Where there is the mind of love, and the consequent activity of self-emptying service, there is perpetual and glorious triumph over circumstances. Any man can sing when he escapes from prison; but this man sang in prison. God has highly exalted Paul and given him a throne of power because of the activity growing out of the mind of love. He triumphed over all circumstances and lifted his eyes, not doubtingly, but courageously, to the ultimate realization of the Divine purpose, so that he said in this same letter, "Not that I have already obtained, or am already made perfect: . . . but one thing I do, forgetting the things which are behind, and stretching forward to the things which are before, I press on towards the goal"; that goal is the hour in which He "shall fashion anew the body of our humiliation, that it may be conformed to the body of His glory." The mind of Christ in the saint is the mind of royalty, of authority, of power.

In the light of that attempt to understand this unveiling of the mind of Christ, we hear the abiding appeal, "Have this mind in you." If that is the abiding appeal, think what this letter teaches us concerning the resources, responsibilities, and rules of the Christian life.

What are the resources? Why should I use the plural form? I will give you the whole story in one little word, "To me to live is Christ." "Have this mind in you." How can I? By imitating it? Surely not. By endeavouring to cultivate it? Certainly not. How then? By entering into the meaning of that "To me to live is Christ." This man said, I only have one life, and that is Christ. As he said in another epistle, "That life which I now live in the flesh I live in faith, the faith which is in the Son of God, Who loved me, and gave Himself up for me." "To me to live is Christ."

> "Christ! I am Christ's! and let the name suffice you;
>   Ay, for me too He greatly hath sufficed :
>
> .   .   .   .   .
>
> Christ is the end, for Christ was the beginning,
>   Christ the beginning, for the end is Christ."

Christ's vision; Christ's virtue. This man saw God as Christ saw God. This man saw man as Christ saw man. This man saw ruin as Christ saw ruin. This man saw God's purpose as Christ saw God's purpose. Christ's outlook, Christ's vision! But more, Christ's virtue, Christ's strength, Christ's ability in the presence of the difficulty. These are the resources. If we would have the mind of Christ, we must have the life of Christ, not by imitation, not by cultivation, but by identification. That is the secret of having the mind of Christ.

What is our responsibility if we have this life and so have this mind? "Work out your own salvation with fear and trembling; for it is God which worketh in you." Our business is to work out what God works in. The apostle shows us how to work out, not in immediate teaching, but in illustration, the illustration of his own life in the autobiographical chapter. How did he work out the salvation which God wrought in him? First by keeping clearly before him the vision of the ultimate. With that vision of the ultimate before him what were his attitudes? Towards the past, abandonment; "I count not myself yet to have apprehended: but one thing I do, *forgetting the things which are behind*, and stretching forward." Towards the present, effort: "I press on towards the goal." "I press," the Greek word so translated might be rendered I persecute, for the word is exactly the same as that used of this same man when he was persecuting the Christians. The significance of this is that it shows us that into this business of pressing towards the goal Paul put all the passion and fervour which, in the olden days, he had employed in his determined effort to stamp out the name of Jesus Christ. That is the kind of loyalty we need. Why is it that when a man steps over the line and finds Christ he so often leaves his passion, a good deal of his common sense, and much of his business ability behind him ? When Christ arrests a man, He wants the whole man, every part of him, every ability he has. Our responsibility is that of absolute dedication and unfailing endeavour.

What are the rules ? At the end of the letter we find them. First, " Rejoice in the Lord." Is that a rule ? I maintain that it is. Paul does not speak of joy as a privilege but as a duty. It is our duty to rejoice ; we ought to sing, we ought to be glad. We owe it to our Lord to go through the streets of London on a foggy day with a smiling face. We ought to be the most cheerful people in the world. There ought to be in our very attitude the manifestation of perennial gladness. That is the rule, and Paul knew that all down the centuries there would be people who would forget, so he added " again I will say, Rejoice."

The other rules all follow; "Let your forbearance be known unto all men"; "In nothing be anxious; but in everything by prayer and supplication with thanksgiving let your requests be made known unto God"; "Think on these things."

The application of this message to the Church to-day is that the measure of the Church's authority is the measure of her conformity to the mind of Christ. The Church of God is authoritative in proportion as the Church of God has the mind of Christ. We depend on all sorts of things to give us authority. The mind of Christ is the only thing that makes us truly royal. Of the mind of Christ the essence is love, the consciousness is joy, the expression is sacrifice. Let the Church of God be mastered by love, filled with singing and with joy, perpetually serving, and she rises to a throne of power and authority in this, and in every age.

If that be the application of the message to the Church, what is the application to the individual? The supreme thing is that we should be wholly, absolutely mastered by Christ, that we should be captives of the Lord. That is the ideal. The ideal of the Son should be our only ideal. The resources of His power should be all we ask in order to fulfillment of the ideal. The certainty of His ultimate victory, in us and everywhere, should be the inspiration of our unceasing, undying song. The present joy of life should be that of constant and immediate comradeship with Him. If I can once learn this secret I shall learn how to sing, and how to smile ; how to love, and how to serve.

THE MESSAGE OF COLOSSIANS

A THE ESSENTIAL MESSAGE	B THE APPLICATION
I. The Central Teaching. ii. 9, 10*a*. i. The Fullness of the Godhead in Christ. 　*a.* Creation.　　The Origin of Life. 　*b.* Resurrection.　The Mastery of Death. 　*c.* Peace.　　　The Reconciliation of all. ii. The Filling of the Saints in Christ. 　*a.* Restored to their Place in Creation. 　　Kingship. 　*b.* Restored to their Relation to God. 　　Subject. 　*c.* Restored to their Fellowship with God. 　　Coöperation.	**I. To the Church** i. The Matter of supreme Import to the Church of Christ for her Life and Service is that of her Doctrine of Christ. ii. To hold fast the Head as He is revealed in this Letter will make impossible the Failures here also revealed.
II. The Abiding Appeal. ii. 6. i. False Philosophy. " Take heed . . ." ii. 8. 　The Tradition of Men.　　Speculation. 　The Rudiments of the World.　Materialism. ii. False Mediation. " Let no man . . ." ii. 16–18. 　Ceremonialism. 　Spiritualism. ii. False Confidence. " Why . . ." ii. 20–23. 　Submission to human Opinion. 　Ascetic Practices.	**II. To the Individual** i. A Christless Philosophy ends in Animalism. ii. A Religion of added Intermediation despoils of the Prize. iii. Asceticism is of no Value against the Flesh.

THE MESSAGE OF COLOSSIANS

WE must necessarily remind ourselves of the connection between this letter and that to the Ephesians. They have been spoken of as twin epistles, and that is a perfectly accurate description with regard to the positive doctrines with which they deal. They are complementary the one to the other, so much so that it is almost impossible to study one without studying the other. As in the Ephesian letter, the theme is that of the glory of the Church in her relation with Christ; in the Colossian letter, the theme is that of the glory of Christ as at the disposal of the Church. In the Ephesian letter we are led to the supreme height, from which it is possible to view the Church in its eternal character, and so to understand what its immediate conduct ought to be. In the Colossian letter the resources of the Church are revealed, and they are all centred in Christ.

While that is true there are differences between the two letters. I propose to refer to one of them only, by way of introduction. This letter to the Colossians cannot be read without a sense of argument, of conflict, of dangers, and of difficulties. All that was absent from the Ephesian letter; it was constructive, preëminently a document of teaching. By that I do not mean to say that the Colossian letter is not constructive; it is distinctly so, but we shall miss the complete message unless we recognize that it is corrective also. Through the letter we have a vision of the Church at Colossæ, and are made conscious of the perils threatening it in the very subtle and insidious dangers which the apostle most evidently had in mind as he wrote. I am not proposing to deal with these in detail, for I do not think an explanation of the dangers constitutes the living message of the letter. We shall, however, be compelled to recognize them, because one vital value of the letter is that it is a corrective for certain perils which threatened the Church at Colossæ, and which threaten the Church to-day. We may forget the local colouring, we may recognize that some of the matters dealt with have passed away; but the essential doctrines abide; and the perils still abide, and can only be corrected by these selfsame doctrines.

Let us first consider the essential message of the letter, as to its central teaching, and as to its abiding appeal.

The whole teaching of the Colossian letter is gathered up in the few brief words, "In Him dwelleth all the fullness of the Godhead bodily; and in Him ye are made full." (Col. ii. 9, 10.) That is a composite sentence, having within it two supreme declarations. The first declaration is that "In Him dwelleth all the fullness of the Godhead bodily;" and the second is that "In Him ye are made full."

The fullness of the Godhead is in Christ; that is the Christian doctrine of the Person of the Lord Jesus Christ. The saints are filled in Christ; that is the Christian doctrine of saintship. The facts are correlative and may thus be stated, The fullness of the Godhead is in Christ; The filling of the saints is in Christ; making a distinction between *fullness* and *filling*. The fullness of the Godhead is an eternal fact, and the apostle made use of, what I would term for the moment, the ever-present tense, when he wrote that the fullness of the Godhead bodily, not dwelt, or will dwell, but dwelleth. That is the constant present tense of essential

Deity. God knows nothing of the limitation of time. When the apostle referred to the saints he used another word, filling. The fullness dwells in Him; but the saints are made full. He is not made full, He is full. The saints are not full, they are made full. Thus we have in two brief sentences the whole of the Christian doctrine with regard to Christ, and with regard to the Church of Christ. Consequently, the central teaching of the letter has to do with the fullness of the Godhead in Christ, and with the filling of the saints in Him.

In dealing with the first of these facts it is a matter, somewhat technical, yet full of interest, that the Greek word here translated "*Godhead*" occurs nowhere else in the New Testament. The word rendered Divinity in the Roman letter is radically different, and signifies an attribute of Deity which may be discovered in nature. This word refers not to an attribute, but to the essential fact of Deity. According to Augustine, Thayer also agreeing, the Latin Fathers had to create a word to convey the thought of the Greek word. The Latin word *Divinitas* did not meet the suggestiveness of the Greek word, and they made the word *Deitas*. That is a distinctively

THE MESSAGE OF COLOSSIANS

Christian word, unknown prior to Christianity. This word Deity best conveys the thought of the word translated Godhead.

That is a distinction which we must be very careful to make. It is not enough to say that Christ was Divine, to affirm belief in the Divinity of Christ. There is a sense in which every man is Divine; but it cannot be said of every man that he is Deity. Divinity is an attribute of Deity. Deity is the essential, peculiar, lonely nature of God. That is the thought of the word used here. Here then we have the statement of the supreme fact concerning Christ, that the fullness, the pleroma of essential Godhead, dwelt in Him corporeally, that is in bodily manifestation.

In the context we have some phases of this fullness dealt with. The relation of Christ to creation is declared in the words, "The First-born of all creation; for in Him were all things created . . . all things have been created through Him; . . . and He is before all things, and in Him all things consist." Christ is the Creator and Sustainer of the universal order.

The relation of Christ to Redemption is revealed in the declaration that He is not only

First-born of all creation, but "First-born from the dead." Resurrection presupposes death. Death is due to sin. Between the original creation and the resurrection there was the tragedy of sin and its issue of death. In resurrection He was Victor over these. The result is peace, reconciliation between all that had been separated as the result of sin.

Thus with clear vision the writer looked back as far as human eyes can look, through all the processes of the things in the midst of which he found himself; he traced the material order back until he reached the beginning, and there he found Christ, the First-born of creation.

Again he looked and beheld the tragedy of evil, of sin, the rivers of darkness and of death sweeping through the centuries; until he saw death's power broken, the resurrection, life won out of death, and there again found Christ, God coming into the midst of human sin and human wrong, the First-born from among the dead.

Then he looked on, and where his gaze ended I cannot see, but his vision was that of an ultimate reconciliation of things on earth and things in heaven; and the Reconciler is this same Christ, Who is behind creation, and Who caused it to be; Who came into human history and broke the power of death. He is the Reconciler, having made peace through the blood of His Cross. These all are the activities of Deity and not of humanity. Humanity did not create, did not break the power of death, cannot produce peace and reconciliation where there is war and strife.

Having thus described the activities of Christ, he declared that "in Him dwelleth all the pleroma of the Godhead bodily," all the fullness of Deity; creating, rising out of death in triumph, reconciling to the utmost bound of the heavens. That is Paul's Christ. That is the Christ of the Christian Church.

The second part of the central teaching is; "In Him ye are made full." In days when I am discouraged and very fearful by reason of my own frailty, and my own near-sightedness, I come back and read this statement, and then I break into song in celebration of this Christ of mine. I am made full in Him. There is nothing I need which is not to be found in Him.

Let us interpret the making full of the saint by the pleroma of the Saviour. Let us explain the filling of the human by the fullness of Deity.

We will do so by the illustrations which the apostle used. This Christ is the Origin of creation, the Creator. We are made full in Him. That means that we are restored to our true place in the creation. It means that in Christ man regains his sceptre and his crown. Out of that fact grows part of our missionary responsibility. "Go ye into all the cosmos"; not merely travel over the earth, that is not all; but go into the cosmos, into the creation, crying, groaning, sobbing, agonized creation; go into it and preach the evangel of that risen Christ, Who is Lord and Master, and the Redeemer of all creation. Every true Christian is restored to the place of dignity and rule in the creation of God. I know we do not realize it. I know we are too often busy hunting among rubbish heaps, attracted by the glitter of straws. But the fact remains that in this sense we are made full in Him. He is the Creator and Sustainer of the universe, of mountains and hills; of beasts, birds, and flowers; and we are made full in Him. We come into relation with all the kingdom of nature, in Christ, as we never can come into relationship with it, save under His dominion and power. The animals will have a better time if we live in

Him. Flowers will become more beautiful under our touch if He energize it. All the glory and beauty of the cultivation of flowers has resulted from missionary enterprise. Nature runs riot in her beauty in the wilderness, where the foot of man comes not, and the hand of man does not touch; all the delicate and fine results of cultivation have come after the evangel to the creation. We are made full in Him, so that we are restored to our proper place in the creation. I begin there because Paul began there; but that, glorious as it is, is the lowest thought of all.

Let us take a step further. We are made full in Him, in our restored relationship to God by the way of His resurrection. By His resurrection the very life of God is communicated to the spirit of man, so that he takes his right place as subject to God, bending before Him, not by the breaking of his will, but by the capture and constraint of the will, by the indwelling grace of the life of Christ. Thus we are made full in Him.

That leads us to the final fact, we are restored to fellowship with God in Him. Fellowship does not merely mean that we receive from God; it also means that which to me is more and more amazing, indeed the most amazing fact of all, that we can give to God in service. I think every day I live, the thing about the grace of God which amazes me most, is not that He loves me, not that He saves me, but that He calls me to be a fellow-worker with Himself. Christ has made it possible for me to be a worker together with God. I can help Him to bring in His Kingdom, to establish His righteousness, to hasten the day of His ultimate victory.

We are made full in Him; for it is in Christ that we are restored to our true place in creation; in Christ that we are restored to our true relation to God; in Christ that we are restored to that fellowship with God which means coöperation in all His purposes.

These are the central teachings of this letter, stated in broadest, barest outlines; the doctrine of the fullness of Christ; and the doctrine of the fullness of the saint in Him.

The abiding appeal is threefold.

"Take heed lest there shall be any one that maketh spoil of you through his philosophy and vain deceit, after the tradition of men, after the rudiments of the world, and not after Christ" (ii. 8).

"Let no man therefore judge you in meat, or

THE MESSAGE OF COLOSSIANS 217

in drink, or in respect of a feast day" (ii. 16). "Let no man rob you of your prize by a voluntary humility and worshipping of the angels" (ii. 18).

"If ye died with Christ from the rudiments of the world, why, as though living in the world, do ye subject yourselves to ordinances? Handle not, nor taste, nor touch (all which things are to perish with the using), after the precepts and doctrines of men? Which things have indeed a show of wisdom in will-worship, and humility, and severity to the body; but are not of any value against the indulgence of the flesh. If then ye were raised together with Christ, seek the things that are above" (ii. 20—iii. 1).

It will at once be recognized that this threefold appeal is entirely dependent upon the great doctrines of the letter; that it is the necessary sequence and corollary of the provision made in Christ. The first note is a warning against false philosophy, the second is a warning against false mediation; and the third is a warning against false confidence.

The warning against a false philosophy; "Take heed lest there shall be any one that maketh spoil of you through his philosophy and vain deceit."

The warning against false mediation; "Let no man therefore judge you in meat, or in drink, or in respect of a feast day, or a new moon, or a Sabbath day," and "Let no man rob you of your prize by a voluntary humility and worshipping of the angels"; the mediation of ceremonialism, and the mediation of angel worship or symbolism in any form. The warning against false confidence; Why do you submit yourselves to ordinances and to severity to the body? These things are of no value against indulgence of things of the flesh. "Set your mind on the things that are above."

This false philosophy Paul summarized with a masterly hand as the tradition of men, the rudiments of the world; the tradition of men, speculation; the rudiments of the world, materialism. This philosophy is the result of human guessing; a philosophy which puts God out of His universe, and attempts to account for everything within the limitation of the material. Such false philosophy is to be corrected by recognition of the fact that Christ is the solution of the problem of the universe. There is no other solution. Beware of the philosophy which is vain deceit, which comes from the tradition of men; beware of it, because it is only speculation; because it is bounded by the cosmos, by the rudiments of the world, by elementary things, things having a beginning; you may call them atoms or electrons or anything you will, but if you attempt to account for the world by the world, then your philosophy is a philosophy of vain deceit. This is to be corrected by recognition of the fact that God through Christ is at the back of all æons and electrons. That is a philosophy characterized by dignity, by majesty. The vision of Christ as the First-born of creation, the Upholder of creation, gives a true view of the universe.

The next appeal is a warning against the false mediation of ceremonialism. Men will judge us in the matter of what we eat and drink, and as to whether we observe feasts, and new moons, and Sabbath days. They are shadows all; and we are to have done with them, because we have Christ, Who is the substance.

There is another false mediation, that of the worshipping of angels, a voluntary worshipping and humility which is of the essence of pride. With all this also we are to have done, by recognition of the fact that we need no intermediary, because we have access to the Lord Himself, direct, immediate communication with the Lord of all angels, the Master of all spirits. We are not to suffer ceremony or angel to come between us and Christ.

The final note of appeal is a warning against false confidences. The first is that of slavery to human opinion. If we have died with Christ from the rudiments of the world, we are not as though living, to subject ourselves to ordinances of men, which have no value against the indulgence of the flesh, and which are only matters of human opinion. Of such ordinances Paul gives an illustration in the words, "Handle not, nor taste, nor touch." I constantly hear Christian people saying that the Bible says, "Handle not, nor taste, nor touch." As a matter of fact the Bible teaches us that we are not to obey those who lay such restrictions upon us; and that, not in order that we may have licence to play with evil things, but because we are to take our commands from our living Lord, and not to allow anybody to interfere between us and Himself.

Another false confidence is that in ascetic practice. Severity to the body Paul dismisses as of no value against indulgence of the flesh. It is possible to wear a hair shirt and be sensual. It is possible to lacerate the body with whips and scourges and think indecently while we do it. We are risen with Christ; therefore we are to seek the upper things, to set our minds on the upper things; to have a true view of our Lord, to see Him Lord of creation, Master of death, Reconciler of the universe; and then by living union with Him, we shall need none of these things which never yet made men spiritual. All the fullness of the Godhead is in Christ, and we are made full in Him!

A final word as to the application of these things to the Church of God to-day. The matter of supreme importance to the Church, for her life and service, is that of her doctrine of Christ. I know that is hardly the view of current philosophy. We are being told that it does not matter what a man thinks, it matters what a man is. Yes; but let us not forget that as a man thinks, so is he. The supreme matter for the Christian Church is what she thinks of Christ. It is not enough that our conceptions should be Christocentric. The supreme question is, Who is the Christ at the centre? We may be Christocentric, and yet not be Christian in the New Testament sense of the word. If the Christ at the centre be the Christ, Who is the First-born of creation, the First-born from the dead, in Whom is all the pleroma of Deity; then our position is Christian according to the New Testament.

To hold fast the Head as He is revealed in this letter will make impossible all the failures which are here revealed. To hold fast this Christ will make it impossible to accept a philosophy of the universe which is the result of speculation, and which begins and ends in the material. We cannot be New Testament Christians without believing that every blade of grass flashes with the glory of God in Christ. We cannot be New Testament Christians without seeing tokens of His majesty and His infinite glory in the delicate beauty of the pencilling of the flowers, and in the rolling rhythmic order of the system of the stars. The New Testament Christian cannot consent to any solution of the riddle of the universe which shuts out God and Christ.

This doctrine of Christ will as certainly put an end to all false mediation and false confidence.

The New Testament Christian cannot be content with the mediation of ceremonialism in any form. The New Testament Christian will waste no time listening to the muttering of witches in the hope of discovering some secret of the spirit world, when it is possible to hold direct and immediate communication, in street and city, in the railway train, as well as in the sanctuary, with the Lord of angels, and the Master of all spiritual realms.

A Christless philosophy ends in animalism. Beware of it. A religion of added intermediation robs of the prize of religion. Beware of it. Asceticism is of no value against the flesh. Beware of it.

> " Christ ! I am Christ's ! and let the name suffice you,
> *Ay, for me too He greatly hath sufficed:*
> Christ is the end, for Christ was the beginning,
> Christ the beginning, for the end is Christ."

Whether we look up or down ; back or on ; to depth, height, length or breadth, we still see Christ, and all the pleroma of Deity resident within Him is our fullness ; so that in Him, for to-day, for to-morrow, and forever, we are filled to the full.

NEW TESTAMENT
BOOK TWO

CONTENTS

THE MESSAGE OF—

I. THESSALONIANS 9

II. THESSALONIANS . . . 27

I. TIMOTHY 47

II. TIMOTHY 63

TITUS 77

PHILEMON 91

HEBREWS 107

CONTENTS

THE MESSAGE OF—

JAMES 123

I. PETER 143

II. PETER 161

LETTERS OF JOHN 177

JUDE 195

REVELATION 211

THE MESSAGE OF I. THESSALONIANS

A THE ESSENTIAL MESSAGE	B THE APPLICATION

I. The Central Teaching
The Relation of the Second Advent to Christian Experience.
i. The final Argument producing Faith. i. 9, 10.
  To God from Idols.
  To Order from Disorder.
  The Completion of the Mission of the Son.
ii. The abiding Confidence inspiring Labour. ii. 19.
  To serve a Living and True God.
  By Faith in Suffering.
  The Final Rewards.
  Those won—at His Coming.
iii. The ultimate Victory creating Patience. iii. 13.
  Personal. The Certainty of Perfection.
  Relative. With God and the World.
 	
II. The Abiding Appeal
The Response of Christian Obedience to the Second Advent.
i. In Life. Sanctification. iv.
  { Personal Purity.
  { Love of the Brethren.
  { Honesty in the World.
ii. In View of Death.
  { The Comfort of the Bereaved.
  { The Joy of the Living.
iii. In View of Judgment.
  { Sons of Day.
  { Appointed to Salvation.
	I. To the Church
	i. The Light that failed.
	  Therefore.
	  { Unbelief. Idols.
	  { Indolence. Strife.
	  { Impatience. Sin.
	ii. The Light obscured.
	  { Knowing without Doing.
	  { Waiting without Work.
	  { Singing without Suffering.
	iii. The Light shining.
	  { The Passion for the Kingdom.
	  { The Service of Love.
	  { The Optimism of Hope.
	
	II. To the Individual
	Spirit.
	Soul.
	Body.
	  Waiting.
	  Serving.

THE MESSAGE OF I. THESSALONIANS

THIS letter thrills with conflicting emotions. On the one hand there are evidences of the apostle's unbounded joy and satisfaction in the work accomplished at Thessalonica. On the other hand there are equally clear evidences of his concern for the Thessalonian Christians in view of the circumstances of peril in which they lived.

The letter differs from any we have already considered; not because it was written at an earlier period in the ministry of the apostle; but because the need calling for it was different. I draw attention to this, because it has been said that this was one of the first of Paul's letters, and that when he wrote the later ones he had entirely departed from some of the positions he held when he wrote this one.

All Paul's letters were written with some very definite, immediate, and local purpose. Paul did not sit down intending to write a system of theology, or to write letters for the Catholic Church; but he nevertheless did both these things in the purpose and economy of the inspiring Spirit of God, though quite unconsciously to himself at the time. He wrote to the people whom he named, and on some subject of immediate importance to them.

In all the letters we have considered so far, some great doctrine of the faith, or duty of the Church has been discussed. Here there is no definite teaching of that kind. This is not a letter stating a great doctrine of the faith. This is not a letter insisting upon some special duty of the Church. In two verses only do we find anything in the nature of definite teaching which is new; "The Lord Himself shall descend from heaven, with a shout, with the voice of the archangel, and with the trump of God: and the dead in Christ shall rise first: then we that are alive, that are left, shall together with them be caught up in the clouds, to meet the Lord in the air: and so shall we ever be with the Lord" (iv. 16, 17).

In that brief paragraph we have the only passage which is of the nature of positive statement. And let us be careful even in regard to this. It is not an announcement of the fact of the second Advent. It does declare the fact, but that is not the purpose of the statement of the apostle. Neither is it a defence of the truth of the second Advent. It becomes a defence, for it is an apostolic and inspired declaration; but that is not its purpose. It is rather a simple statement of the order of events at the Advent, made for the comfort of bereaved Christians. It must be taken in connection with that which has preceded it, beginning at the thirteenth verse; "We would not have you ignorant, brethren, concerning them that fall asleep."

Having written this the apostle gave the order of events, showing that at the second Advent of Jesus those that have fallen on sleep will take precedence of those that remain. That is the purpose of the declaration. Thus, the only positive statement of truth in this letter is, after all, an incidental part of the argument.

It is nevertheless patent, alike to the casual and most critical student of this letter that the fact of the second Advent of Jesus was paramount in the mind of the writer from beginning to end. Its glory gleams on every page and shines through every argument, and was the supreme matter in all that he had to say to these Thessalonian Christians.

Let us attempt to discover the reason of this. Paul's work in Thessalonica had been characterized by the most remarkable spiritual awakening, and that in spite of peculiarly vindictive opposition and persecution, the history of which is found in the Acts of the Apostles. He came to Thessalonica and for three Sabbaths he spoke in the synagogue; then he turned to the Gentiles, and there was a marvellous awakening, followed by most vicious opposition, so that Paul was compelled to escape from Thessalonica, to Berea, to Athens, and finally to Corinth. At Corinth he was joined by Timothy, whom he had left behind, and from whom he learned of the state of his Thessalonian converts. Only a few months elapsed between his first coming to Thessalonica and the writing of this letter.

These Thessalonian Christians were firm in their loyalty to the gospel which had been declared unto them; but they were enduring suffering, persecution, and affliction for the sake of the Kingdom of God. To these people Paul wrote; and the letter therefore was one intended

MESSAGE OF I. THESSALONIANS 13

to comfort those who were suffering for their loyalty to that King Jesus, for preaching Whom, the apostle had been sent away. What more natural then than that His Advent of vindication and victory should be uppermost in his thought? He could best comfort them by reminding them that the unseen King to Whom they were loyal would again be manifested, and would vindicate their loyalty in the grace and glory of His second Advent.

The essential message of this letter, therefore, is that of the relation of the second Advent to Christian experience. The letter does not deal doctrinally with the Advent; it takes the fact for granted, and applies it.

It does take the fact for granted. No man can read this letter without seeing that when Paul wrote it he believed that as surely as Jesus had been seen in this world, He would be seen again; that as certainly as He had once appeared, He would appear again; that as certainly as there had been a coming to suffering, there would be a coming to sovereignty. To go back to the brief paragraph already quoted; the simplest honest reading of it can leave no doubt that the apostle referred to an actual coming of the same

Jesus Who had already come. That is the force of the introductory phrase, "the Lord Himself." Why the introduction of that word "Himself" unless it be to emphasize the fact of the personal Advent of Jesus? No comment is needed. Of course, it might be pertinent for us to discuss the question whether Paul was right or wrong. My business, however, is simply to emphasize what Paul said and meant. There are those who say that he was mistaken. In that view there is necessarily involved the question of the inspiration and authority of these letters. Our attitude is that of belief in their inspiration and authority. The teaching of Paul was in harmony with that of the Lord; "Whosoever shall be ashamed of Me and of My words, of him shall the Son of man be ashamed, when He cometh in His own glory, and the glory of the Father, and of the holy angels." "The Lord Himself shall descend from heaven, with a shout, with the voice of the archangel, and with the trump of God; and the dead in Christ shall rise first; then we that are alive, that are left, shall together with them be caught up in the clouds, to meet the Lord in the air; and so shall we ever be with the Lord." Thus Paul reaffirmed Christ's definite declaration.

MESSAGE OF I. THESSALONIANS

The central teaching of this letter then is that of the relation of the second Advent to Christian experience. This fact of the coming of Jesus is the final argument, producing faith. This fact of the second Advent of Jesus is the abiding confidence, inspiring labour. This fact of the coming of Jesus is the ultimate victory, creating patience. In the introduction to this letter the apostle declared that he remembered without ceasing their work of faith, their labour of love, and their patience of hope. These are the facts of Christian experience. The work of faith is that act of faith by which men become Christians. Said Jesus, "This is the *work* of God, that ye *believe* on Him Whom He hath sent." That work of faith is followed necessarily and inevitably by the labour of love. That labour of love is maintained through all circumstances by the patience of hope. These are the three attitudes of the Christian life.

Let us carefully notice how the first three chapters end. The first ends with the words "to wait for His Son from heaven, Whom He raised from the dead, even Jesus, which delivereth us from the wrath to come." The second ends, "What is our hope, or joy, or crown of glorying? Are not even ye, before our Lord Jesus at His coming? For ye are our glory and our joy." The third ends, "To the end He may stablish your hearts unblameable in holiness before our God and Father, at the coming of our Lord Jesus with all His saints."

These are all references to the Advent. The first indicates that which I have named as the first fact, the relation of the Advent to Christian experience in its beginning. The final argument producing faith is that of the coming of Jesus. They turned from idols to God to serve God and *to wait for His Son*. The last argument producing faith was the declaration that the One Who had come was coming again. They were to wait for Him. Think of the actual circumstances of these Thessalonians; they were living in the midst of idols that could be seen; their Lord was unseen. They were men who had been brought up in the midst of idolatry, worshipping things seen and handled, which appealed to the senses; and they turned to an unseen God. What was the last argument persuading them to do this? The fact that He would yet again be manifested; and that at His Advent there would be the vindication of faith in sight. When they turned to God from idols, they turned towards a restored order, from the disorder in the midst of which they were living; towards the establishment of the Kingdom, from the anarchy in the midst of which they had been living, from the anarchy of idolatry to the Government of God. When they did that, they did it, determining to wait for the Son. Faith acted not only upon the declaration that He has come, but that He is coming again. Faith is a venture which trusts in the first coming, and waits for the second. Thus the second Advent is the final argument producing faith.

Then, as in the power of faith they turned to their labour of love, the second Advent became their abiding confidence, inspiring that labour. They turned "to serve a living and true God." When they turned to the unseen God, having heard the declaration that the Son should be revealed again, determining to wait for the Son, they turned to serve this living and true God. The reward of service will be received when the Son returns. In order to comfort these Thessalonian Christians in the midst of their suffering, Paul spoke of his own experience; "What is our hope, or joy, or crown of glorying? Are not even ye, before our Lord Jesus at His coming?"

The reward of Christian service is, in its finality and completion, postponed until the second Advent. There is a sense in which rewards come in the act of service. In the Corinthian letter the apostle deals with that phase of the truth, "Be ye steadfast, unmovable, always abounding in the work of the Lord, forasmuch as ye know that your labour is not in vain in the Lord." The reward of service is in the service, in the immediate success of service; but the great reward, the ultimate gladness, will be when those whom we have led to Christ by patience and by perserverance and persistence, in the midst of toil and travail, are presented faultless at His coming.

As I watch this apostle on his journeys, the intrepid missionary, pressing ever on to the regions beyond, suffering perils by land and sea, from enemies and false brethren; glowing in his heart forevermore, as the inspiration of his labour of love, is that glad hour when those who are won for Christ will be presented faultless in the glory of the second Advent.

Finally, the Christian experience is made up not only of the work of faith and the labour of love, but also of the patience of hope. The ultimate victory, creating the patience, is to be won at the second Advent. "To the end He may stablish your hearts . . . before our God and Father, at the coming of our Lord Jesus with all His saints." That conviction of the heart produces patience. Patience in this matter of personal salvation, with ourselves; not with ourselves as severed from Him, or as apart from Him; not with ourselves as disloyal to Christ. But even when loyal to Christ we are disappointed. If we are satisfied with ourselves it is an evil thing for us spiritually. How dissatisfied with ourselves we become whenever we think of ourselves; but at His coming He will stablish us, unblameable in holiness. Not for a moment is this to be an excuse for carelessness in Christian life, but on the contrary it is to be a perpetual inspiration, driving us towards approximation to that final perfection, lest, as John says, we be ashamed from Him at His coming. We shall be patient with ourselves if we are loyal, in proportion as our hearts are resting in the glory of the Advent. We know that then we shall be perfected.

Then also this conviction will give us patience with God. We have all experienced hours in which, because of our frailty, we have been inclined to be impatient with God; impatient with God about the world. If we have ever come very near the world's agony, there have been moments when it has seemed as though God were doing nothing. But when we see this fact of the second Advent, and know that by a crisis in the future, as definite as the crisis in the past, God will consummate the thing that to-day is being prepared for by processes, then the heart is patient with God, and with all conditions. Here suffer a word of personal testimony. If you take away from me the doctrine of the second Advent of Christ, which is to be a crisis in human history as definite as the first, I am the most pessimistic of men. If you tell me that the work of the missionary is to convert the world by preaching, I am hopeless indeed! But when I realize that the work of missions is to evangelize the world by the preaching of the Gospel for a witness; and that beyond the Advent there will be a new age in which human history will be perfected; then I wait with patience for the crisis which is to come, and serve, as God helps me, in order to hasten that coming, the coming of our Lord Himself.

Thus the central teaching of the letter is of the

second Advent in relation to the whole fact of Christian experience. It is the last argument producing faith. How can I turn to God? He Who came is coming! Then I will trust and wait. The fact of that Advent is the abiding confidence which inspires labour. Then shall I know the real result of my toil, and that makes me quite careless about present statistics and figures. Then the sheaves of the harvest will be garnered; the statistics of God will be published. Then the heart will know its final joy, when in the presence of Christ we see men, women, and little children, whom we have tried to help and win for Him. The fact of that coming produces the patience which is the very strength of life, for then we shall be perfected and the ways of God vindicated.

The abiding appeal of this letter is that we should respond to this great truth of the second coming of our Lord. How are we to respond?

First in our own life, by sanctification. The life of sanctification is the true response to the doctrine of the second Advent. The life of sanctification is that of personal purity; love of the brethren; and honesty in the world. That is response to the doctrine.

If we believe that He may in any day disturb us in our work, or in any night wake us from our sleep by His own voice, how pure we shall desire our personal life to be, that we may be ready; how we shall love the brethren, lest He should come and find us quarrelling; how honestly we shall live before the world.

What is the response to this fact in the presence of death? First there is comfort for the bereaved. "If we believe that Jesus died and rose again, even so them that are fallen asleep in Jesus will God bring with Him." Then, what rapture and gladness, what uniting of severed friendships when partings are no more. Oh, the comfort of it. "Comfort one another with these words." This is the transfiguration of death, the abolition of death.

If there come what men call death to the child of God, then the child of God will lay down his head and sleep, knowing that when the Lord shall come, he will be awakened before those who are left; that he will be changed first, that in their transfiguration there may be perfect reunion. Yet we wait not for death, but for Him.

In view of the judgment that lies beyond

MESSAGE OF I. THESSALONIANS 23

death what is the response to this truth? The Advent is not a question of times and seasons; would God the Church believed that! It is the study of this Advent in connection with calendars and almanacs that has brought the whole subject into disrepute. There is a Day of God of which the ancient prophets spoke, which will be a Day of Judgment; but we are not appointed to judgment but to salvation and to deliverance from the disasters of that day.

It is my own personal and strong conviction that this truth of the second Advent is the light that has failed in the history of the Christian Church. I am sometimes inclined to think that I am a very lonely man as an expositor to-day in the view I take of the second Advent. I believe that the results of the loss of this doctrine to the Church are: unbelief, and return to idols; indolence, which issues in strife; and impatience, which issues in sin; the opposites of the great things which Paul describes, as the work of faith, the labour of love, and the patience of hope. The measure in which this great doctrine becomes vital and real is the measure of faith, the measure of labour, the measure of patience.

If this is the light that failed, it is also a light

which was given again, and then strangely obscured during the nineteenth century. God raised up certain men of vision, and restored this great truth; but the most amazing wonder and calamity is that they have so largely obscured the light by making it the one and only fact for which they have cared anything; waiting without working; singing about the Advent, without suffering in order to hasten its coming; treating the Advent as though it were a method by which God would gather them away to everlasting rest, while He let the rest of the world drift to darkness and death. That is a lie. It is a more terrible heresy than to forget the Advent. Belief in the second Advent of Jesus should be the inspiration of all things that are of service and sacrifice.

Paul ended his letter by the prayer, "The God of peace Himself sanctify you wholly; and may your spirit and soul and body be preserved entire, without blame at the coming of our Lord Jesus Christ. Faithful is He that calleth you, Who will also do it." The sanctification of the spirit, soul, and body, consists in that waiting for Jesus which is the waiting of unceasing service; not in gazing at the stars, not in attempting to decipher hieroglyphics, not in fatuous endeavours to fix a date.

With that music of the second Advent in our souls, with the assurance in our hearts that He Who came will come; we will wait and watch, while we love and labour. Thus waiting, the time will soon pass, and we shall see Him and be like Him.

THE MESSAGE OF II. THESSALONIANS

A THE ESSENTIAL MESSAGE	B THE APPLICATION

I. The Central Teaching. The Truth about the Day of the Lord
i. A Distinction concerning the Parousia.
  "Our Gathering together unto Him."
                   See 1 Thess. iv. 16, 17.
  "The Day of the Lord."
                   See 2 Thess. ii.
ii. The Day of the Lord.
  a. The present Facts.
    { "The Mystery of Lawlessness. . . ."
      "That . . . One . . . He . . . restraineth."
  b. The Crisis.
    { "He (that restraineth) taken away."
      Man of Sin. Son of Perdition. Lawless One. Apocalypse. Parousia.
  c. The Ultimate.
    { Epiphany of Parousia.
      Destruction of lawless One.
 	
II. The Abiding Appeal
i. A Call to Courage.
  The Heart comforted, established.
  In Word. In Work.
ii. A Call to Conduct.
  Work and thus wait.
  Wait and thus work.
	I. To the Church
	i. Interpretation of the Times.
	  Lawlessness.
	  Restraint.
	ii. The coming Crisis.
	  The Unveilings.
	    { The Man of Sin.
	      The Lord Jesus.
	iii. The Church the Instrument of Restraint.
	    { Salt.
	      Light.
	
	II. To the Individual
	i. The Responsibility for Restraint.
	ii. The Principle.
	  Against Lawlessness.
	iii. The Secret of Courage.
	  The Day of the Lord.

THE MESSAGE OF II. THESSALONIANS

THE second letter to the Thessalonians was a sequel to the first; but the purpose was different. The purpose of the first letter was comfort, while that of the second was correction.

To understand this letter it is important that we should recognize the circumstances of these Thessalonian Christians at the time when Paul wrote. Of these, we have no historical picture. The Book of the Acts tells the story of the founding of the church, and of the departure of the apostle; but gives no account of the subsequent history of the church. From these letters we may learn the condition of affairs in Thessalonica so far as these Christians were concerned.

We must bear in mind the conditions referred to in our last study. They are distinctly described in the beginning of this letter;

" We ourselves glory in you in the churches of God for your patience and faith in all your persecutions and in the afflictions which ye endure;

which is a manifest token of the righteous judgment of God; to the end that ye may be counted worthy of the Kingdom of God, for which ye also suffer" (i. 4, 5).

These people were enduring persecutions and afflictions, and the apostle recognized the reason of the persecution and affliction; they suffered for the Kingdom of God. These experiences of trial had called forth the first letter, and they had not changed when this second was written.

In this, however, new conditions are clearly revealed. These arose in all probability from a misreading of the first letter, accentuated perhaps by the arrival in Thessalonica of spurious letters, purporting to be from Paul himself, but in reality sent by some one else; and also from the teaching of certain people in Thessalonica.

The new conditions are seen in the first two verses of the second chapter;

"Now we beseech you, brethren, touching the coming of our Lord Jesus Christ, and our gathering together unto Him; to the end that ye be not quickly shaken from your mind, nor yet be troubled, either by spirit, or by word, or by epistle as from us, as that the day of the Lord is now present."

They were in danger of being *shaken from their mind*. That phrase is an attempt at literalness in translation, which it is not easy to improve upon, and yet it hardly conveys the idea of the text. Dr. Findlay's translation is very graphic because more literal; he renders it " shaken out of your wits." These Thessalonian Christians were alarmed, perturbed; and the apostolic word was a protest against that attitude of mind; because such mental disturbance produced another condition which is described in verse eleven of chapter three;

" We hear of some that walk among you disorderly, that work not at all, but are busybodies."

In these two references we have a description of the new conditions. In the midst of their trials they were suffering from mental disturbance, which resulted in disorderly conduct. Their mental disturbance was caused by the fact that they were expecting the immediate manifestation of Jesus in judgment to set up the Kingdom of God. The result was disorderly conduct. A great many abandoned their toil, gave up work in order to wait; yet they had to live, and consequently they were eating at other people's charges; and they became busybodies. In Paul's actual statement there is a play upon words, as though he should say, you are busy about everything except your own business.

Thus it is seen that the conditions obtaining when he wrote his first letter were still continued; they were in affliction and persecution for the sake of the Kingdom of God. But now there was this added trouble, they were mentally disturbed, by his first letter partly, and by letters received " as from us "; they were expecting that the day of the Lord was close at hand, that He would immediately manifest Himself in judgment to set up the Kingdom; and the result of it was that very many of them had given up their daily callings, and had become busybodies. Paul had written his first letter dealing with the fact of the second Advent in order to comfort them. Now he heard from Thessalonica, that many of them were giving up work, and waiting for the coming of the Day of the Lord and the establishment of the Kingdom. This second letter was written in order to correct that false view.

It may be said therefore that Paul wrote this letter for two purposes. First, to correct a false view of the Advent; and secondly, to correct alse conduct arising out of such a false view. In

MESSAGE OF II. THESSALONIANS 31

these two purposes of the apostle we discover the essential message of this letter, its living, lasting, and immediate teaching; and in that part in which he corrected the false conduct, we discover the abiding appeal.

The central teaching of this letter is that of its setting forth of the Christian position concerning *the day of the Lord*. Students of Holy Scripture will at once recognize that phrase. So far as we are able by internal evidence to date the writings of the Old Testament we believe that the prophecy of Joel must be placed at a very early period, and therefore that he was the first to make use of it. From that time the phrase constantly recurs in the writings of the prophets. When we come to the New Testament the idea and the phrase are still present. In this letter the apostle explained to these Thessalonian Christians the relation of the Day of the Lord to the New Testament covenant, and the New Testament economy.

The importance of this teaching cannot be overestimated. The old phrase of the Hebrew prophets and the New Testament writers obtains until now. We are constantly using it in our common speech. Yet while the phrase is Scriptural and valuable, we very often use it in entire ignorance of its meaning according to Scripture. Consequently difficult and mystical as this subject may seem to be, we have no right to pass it idly over. It is most important that we should know what Holy Scripture says to us concerning "the Day of the Lord" and its relation to the Christian covenant.

There are two things we need specially to notice in considering this teaching; first the careful distinction which the apostle made; and secondly, his definite teaching concerning the Day of the Lord.

First then as to the distinction. He had written to them telling them that "the Lord Himself shall descend from heaven, with a shout, with the voice of the archangel, and with the trump of God." He had written in such a way as to fasten their attention upon that Advent as the hope of Christian souls. He now wrote to them to tell them that "the day of the Lord" was not near, that it could not come until certain things had happened. Now the question is, did Paul in his second letter contradict the teaching of the first? Some expositors say, yes; that when Paul wrote his first letter he said one thing, and that when

MESSAGE OF II. THESSALONIANS 33

he wrote his second letter he modified his statement in the direction of actual change of teaching.

Now let us carefully observe the distinction which he made, a distinction which has given rise to the view that the second letter contradicted the first. The whole burden of the first letter is this; He is coming again; wait for Him. The whole burden of the second letter is this, He cannot come yet; continue your work. Here is the apparent contradiction. As a matter of fact there is no contradiction.

The first chapter of the letter is largely introductory. When we come to the second chapter we find this distinction made;

"We beseech you, brethren, touching the coming of our Lord Jesus Christ, and *our gathering together unto Him;* to the end that ye be not quickly shaken from your mind, nor yet be troubled, either by spirit, or by word, or by epistle as from us, as that *the day of the Lord* is now present; let no man beguile you in any wise: for it will not be, except the falling away come first, and the man of sin be revealed."

The distinction there between "our gathering together unto Him," and "the day of the Lord" is patent. The whole purpose of the paragraph is to show the difference between the two.

In the first place let us carefully notice the Greek word Parousia. That word simply means presence; it does mean the actual, positive, personal Presence. We shall see that the same word is used about the antichrist; the man of sin is to have a parousia. It is a word always used with reference to the second Advent, and suggests that it is to be personal as was the first, as definite, as positive, as visible. No man can make his appeal to the authority of Scripture without believing that He Who came is coming. We may differ as to the details; but the fact that Jesus is to come again, as surely as He came, the New Testament most certainly teaches. Parousia is the word used to describe that Coming. That Coming, that Presence, was the theme of his first letter to these people. At the close of every great section therein that word occurs. It is as though he now said: I wrote to you about the Presence; I want to say something else about it, I desire to make a distinction.

That distinction is not between the Parousia and the "Day of the Lord"; but between "our gathering together unto Him" and "the Day of the Lord." The trouble in the Thessalonian church resulted from confusion between two aspects of the Parousia, or Presence of Jesus; those namely of "our gathering together unto Him" and "the day of the Lord."

They had received his first letter, in which he had said;

"The Lord Himself shall descend from heaven, with a shout, with the voice of an archangel, and with the trump of God: and the dead in Christ shall rise first: then we that are alive, that are left, shall together with them be caught up in the clouds, to meet the Lord in the air: and so shall we ever be with the Lord."

That is a description of "our gathering together unto Him" at His Parousia or Coming.

He now wrote to tell them they were not to be troubled and disturbed as though "the Day of the Lord" were at hand.

Thus he revealed the fact that there is a distinction to be made when considering the Parousia or Coming of the Lord, between "our gathering together unto Him," and "the day of the Lord." The apostle desired to teach these Christians that their relation to the Parousia was that of people waiting to be gathered unto Him; and that "the day of the Lord" was not that in which they were personally interested, so far as their habits of life were concerned.

Nevertheless it is an interesting subject; and one full of importance. Therefore he proceeded with care to deal with the subject.

He first declared that before "the day of the Lord" comes, there will be apostasy and a revelation of the man of sin; and then clearly described the man of sin, and the method of his manifestation;

"He that opposeth and exalteth himself against all that is called God or that is worshipped; so that he sitteth in the temple of God, setting himself forth as God. Remember ye not that, when I was yet with you, I told you these things? And now ye know that which restraineth, to the end that he may be revealed in his season. For the mystery of lawlessness doth already work; only there is one that restraineth now, until he be taken out of the way. And then shall be revealed the lawless one, whom the Lord Jesus shall slay with the breath of His mouth, and bring to nought by the manifestation of His coming; even he, whose coming is according to the workings of Satan with all power and signs and lying wonders."

In that paragraph there are three matters we need specially to notice; first, the description of existing conditions; secondly, the declaration that there will be a crisis; and thirdly, the teaching concerning the ultimate day of the Lord.

First as to the present facts. The apostle mentions two; first, the fact that the "mystery of lawlessness doth already work"; and secondly, the fact that there is "One that restraineth."

I am perfectly well aware of how many interpretations there have been of this passage. Everything depends upon the view held of the person here referred to. There are three descriptions; "lawless one," "son of perdition," "man of sin." The history of the interpretation of this passage is the history of the Christian Church for almost nineteen hundred years. Early Christians believed that the power that hindered the manifestation of the antichrist was the Roman Empire. Then there came a time when Christians believed that the power that prevented was the State. Views as to the man of sin have changed in the same way. There are those even to-day who say that the spirit of antichrist is Romanism, and that the ultimate man of sin will be the Pope of Rome. And some believe that the State, organized under the government of God, is the restraining force. My own view is that they are all right, and that they are all wrong. They are all right in that they all discover the working of the mystery of lawlessness; but they are wrong in that they have not apprehended the fullness of the apostolic teaching. "The mystery of lawlessness" is one of the most remarkable of Bible phrases as a definition of sin; I cannot say of evil, because evil is not only the actual moral wrong, but all that results from it, of pain and suffering. Lawlessness is the root trouble with human life individually, socially, nationally, and racially. The apostle spoke of it "as the mystery of lawlessness," and he used that word mystery as he did in all his letters. A mystery according to the Greek philosopher was something that could only be known to an inner circle of initiated, and hardly known to them. A mystery, according to Paul, was something that no man could discover, but which God reveals. The "mystery of lawlessness" is that hidden, subtle, underlying force, ruining, blighting, spoiling humanity and creation. That lawlessness has been revealed. Jesus Christ came not only to reveal God and man, but the Devil also, by dragging him out of darkness into light that man might see him. The mystery underneath; the root of all humanity's maladies and diseases; the hidden spring of poison from which the polluting rivers flow; is lawlessness. This, the apostle declared, is already at work.

But he declared also that there is a restraining power opposing it, so that it cannot come to full manifestation; "there is one that restraineth" and I believe that he referred to the Church of God, as created by and indwelt by the Holy Spirit of God. As all these great truths are found in germ and potentiality in the teaching of Jesus, let us go back to the Manifesto of the King. He said to His disciples: "Ye are the salt of the earth . . . ye are the light of the world." What is the effect of salt? It is aseptic. What is the effect of light? It is illuminative. Lawlessness is corruption; it is darkness. The Church is salt, to prevent the spread of corruption; it is light flashing upon the darkness, so that lawlessness is hindered from full victory, and the men of lawlessness cannot accomplish all their dastardly works. That is true of the

Church of God and the Spirit of God in the world at this present moment. Lawlessness is working; it is an attitude of heart, of mind, of will. If the Church of God, the whole company of new-born souls, were lifted out of the world, and taken right away, what would be the result? Lawlessness would have its full manifestation. The thing that saves London from unutterable corruption, and from the deepest darkness is the presence in it of the Holy Spirit of God through Christian men and women. That then is the present condition of affairs. The mystery of lawlessness working, but the Holy Spirit through the Church restraining.

The second matter to be observed is the apostle's declaration that there will presently come a crisis. It will come when He that restraineth is taken away, that is when the Spirit is withdrawn. When will the Spirit be withdrawn? When the Church of God is withdrawn, and never until then. "I will pray the Father, and He shall give you another Comforter, that He may be with you forever." When will the Church be withdrawn? At "our gathering together unto Him" at His coming. When He that restraineth is withdrawn, the man of sin, the son of perdition, the lawless one, will have his apocalypse, his parousia. The apostle teaches with great distinctness that at last lawlessness will have its final manifestation in some one person, a despot far worse than any the world has ever yet seen; and yet one characterized, not by the old-fashioned brutality of the beast, but by the oppression and cruelty of culture and refinement. If you would know the character of that one, the man of sin, we have the revelation in Paul's description; "He that opposeth and exalteth himself against all that is called God or that is worshipped." He will be entirely godless, but of so remarkable a character as to persuade men that he is himself divine.

The final matter is that of the ultimate fact which will bring the Day of the Lord. At last, all evil focussed in a person and manifested; there will be an epiphany of the parousia of the Lord—that is a very remarkable phrase; not His parousia merely; that includes the whole fact of the Advent. There will be first of all that aspect of the coming which will result in the gathering together of His own to Himself; when that happens, that which restrains being taken away, lawlessness will come to its head, and will have its manifestation in a person. Then the parousia, the presence of Christ in which His own have been gathered to Him, will become an epiphany; a flaming, shining glory; destroying the man of sin, and setting up that Kingdom on the earth which is the Kingdom of the iron rod; the rule of perfect, inflexible justice; the reign of the One Who does not judge by the seeing of the eyes or the hearing of the ears, but with righteous judgment.

How often as we look at human life, or see its portrayal in literature, we feel that this is what the world supremely needs. Then for the first time the world will come to the realization of the breadth, beauty, and beneficence of the will of God. I have no hope in kings, or parliaments, or policy, for the ultimate establishment of the Kingdom. Only by the presence of the Christ, returning with the saints He has gathered to Himself, shall be set up and established His Kingdom in the world. The manifestation of the presence will be for the destruction of the lawless one, and the establishment of the Kingdom.

The abiding appeal of this letter is first a call to courage. Paul said: Do not let your mind be

MESSAGE OF II. THESSALONIANS 43

disturbed, do not be shaken out of your wits. Let your heart be comforted and established. Courage is always an affair of the heart. Comforted is from the same root as the word which is used for the Holy Spirit; a word of great strength, which suggests a sense of peace and quietness. Let your heart be comforted and established.

It is also a call to conduct. Get on with your work! Wait and work! The man who gives up the fulfillment of his daily vocation to wait for Christ is doing exactly what some of these Thessalonian Christians had been doing. The work to which the apostle referred is the practical, commonplace work of every-day life; that actual work by which a man supplies the necessities of his physical life.

So let us wait, with calm and steady hearts, knowing that there will be a gathering together to Him; and afterwards, an epiphany of the presence, when lawlessness having come to manifestation in a person, will be smitten to its death, and the Kingdom of God will be established.

The application of this letter to the Christian Church is in its interpretation of our own times;

these are days of lawlessness, and, thank God, of restraint also. The gravest peril that we have to confront is not that of socialism, nor that of feudalism; it is rather that of a growing spirit of rebellion against all government; lawlessness. It is abroad everywhere. The gravest menace to our national life is that of the man who leaves out God, mocks at authority, and vaunts his own independence. Wherever you find him, the mark of the beast is on him. It is well that the Church should realize this.

But let the Church remember that there is One that restraineth; the mighty grip of God is on all the forces which seem to be making for lawlessness, restraining them until He be ready that they shall manifest themselves. The crisis is coming, it will be for the world, first the unveiling of the man of sin; and then the unveiling and apocalypse of the Lord Jesus. Our hearts are to be firm and steady in absolute assurance that in that last unveiling it is not the Lord Jesus Christ, but the man of sin, who will be destroyed. Only let us also remember that in the interim the Church is the instrument of restraint. She is salt, and she is light, by the indwelling and power of the Holy Spirit.

What is the application to the individual? The measure in which I share the life of the Christ is the measure in which I am exercising restraint. Let each Christian ask then: How far am I by influence of speech and work restraining lawlessness? And then let us remember that the measure in which we restrain lawlessness in the world is the measure in which there is no lawlessness in our own hearts.

THE MESSAGE OF I. TIMOTHY

A THE ESSENTIAL MESSAGE	B THE APPLICATION
I. The Central Teaching i. The true Function of the Church. 　The Proclamation of the Truth in the World. 　　*a.* The Instrument. Church. Pillar. Ground. 　　　　　　　　　　　　　　iii. 15, 16. 　　*b.* The Truth.　　The Mystery of Godliness. 　　　　　　　　　　　　　　iii. 15, 16. ii. The true Function of the Minister. 　The Exposition of Truth in the Church. 　　*a.* By Teaching and Exhortation. 　　*b.* By Example.	**I. To the Church** 　　The Things that hinder. i. False Doctrine. ii. Failure in Prayer. iii. False Government.
II. The Abiding Appeal i. To the Church. 　The Instrument fitted for the Fulfillment of Function. 　　*a.* Her Gospel unchanged. 　　*b.* Her Worship unceasing. 　　*c.* Her Ministry unfailing. ii. To the Minister. 　The Instrument fitted for the Fulfillment of Function. 　　*a.* Loyalty to Truth. 　　*b.* Consistent in Behaviour. 　　*c.* Personal Life.	**II. To the Minister** 　　The Things that hinder. i. Failure in Doctrine. ii. Failure in Duty. iii. Failure in Diligence.

THE MESSAGE OF I. TIMOTHY

THIS letter is the first of three; which, while separated from each other in that they were written at different times and to two persons, are yet correlated in that they deal with one subject, that of the relation between the minister and the Church. They were all written to men occupying positions of responsibility in regard to churches of Jesus Christ; Timothy in Ephesus, and Titus in Crete.

The doctrine of the Church, and the fundamental doctrine concerning the ministry, we find in other of Paul's writings which we have already considered; and the things therein taught must be borne in mind as we come to these letters which, while so largely personal, are yet full of relative values. We find in our study of the New Testament that sometimes the Church is spoken of, sometimes the churches, sometimes a church. That is to say, the word is used in reference to the whole Church, the complete Church. It is also used of local churches.

Whereas it is perfectly true that there is one Church of God; it is equally true that there was the church at Ephesus, the church at Corinth, and so on. In that sense therefore we use the word "churches"; not that these churches are divided each from the other; but that the whole Church is divided by locality, by circumstances, by geographical distances, into churches. In the New Testament it is evident that every local church was a microcosm of the catholic Church, and all the great fundamental doctrines concerning the catholic Church are equally applicable to the local church. Timothy was in oversight of the church at Ephesus; Titus was fulfilling a special work in connection with the church in Crete; and these letters were written to these men, holding positions of spiritual responsibility for very definite and specific purposes, and their theme is that of the inter-relation of the minister of the Word, and the Church.[1]

---

[1] A glance at our analysis of contents will show an inter-relation between these letters which is remarkable and interesting.

In 1 Timothy, there are two divisions A and B. In 2 Timothy, the theme of B in 1 Timothy is elaborated in three divisions, A, B, C, which cover the same ground as III., II., I. of B in 1 Timothy.

In Titus the theme of A in 1 Timothy is elaborated; the application is different, but the general conceptions are the same. See "The Analyzed Bible," Vol. iii., p. 248, and on.

The first part of 1 Timothy deals with the charge of the minister, that over which he has care, the church. The second part is the apostolic charge to the minister concerning his consequent responsibility. In these three letters then the great theme is that of the church and the minister. The first letter to Timothy is general and fundamental; the letter to Titus deals particularly with the method by which the minister is to set the church in order; and in the second letter of Timothy the particular subject is that of the minister's personal responsibility.

Having thus recognized the inter-relationships of these letters we may now turn our attention to the first.

The central teaching of this first letter to Timothy is that of its revelation of the true function of the church; and the true function of the minister.

The true function of the church is the proclamation of Truth in the world. The true function of the minister is that of the exposition of Truth in the Church. The one function for which the Church exists is that of the proclamation of Truth in the world. The one function for which the ministry is created is that of the exposition of Truth within the Church. That is the exact thought underlying Paul's teaching in the Ephesian letter concerning the catholic Church. In that letter, when we turn from the discussion of the Church's predestination, edification, and vocation, to the application of the truth in detail, we find Paul writing "I therefore, the prisoner in the Lord, beseech you to walk worthily of the calling wherewith ye were called"; and in close connection declaring that when Jesus ascended and received gifts, "He gave some to be apostles; and some, prophets; and some, evangelists; and some, pastors and teachers; for the perfecting of the saints, unto the work of ministering"; that is to say that the saints are to fulfill the ministry, and men qualified by gifts are to perfect the saints for the fulfillment of that ministry. The ministry of the Church is that of the proclamation of the truth of God in the world. The ministry created by gifts bestowed is that of perfecting the saints. The saints are to be perfected by the truth. The one function of the ministry then is the exposition in the Church of the truth which the Church is to proclaim to the world.

That is the central teaching of this letter in application to the local church.

The true function of the Church then is that of the declaration of the Truth to the world.

"That thou mayest know how men ought to behave themselves in the house of God, which is the church of the living God, the pillar and ground of the truth. And without controversy great is the mystery of godliness; He Who was manifested in the flesh, justified in the spirit, seen of angels, preached among the nations, believed on in the world, received up in glory."

There we reach the central light of the epistle concerning the true function of the Church. The Church is an instrument; it is "the pillar and ground of the truth"; it is that upon which the truth is to be displayed; it is that upon which the truth is to be so raised up that men may see it. This is in perfect agreement with the teaching of our Lord.

"Ye are the light of the world. A city set on a hill cannot be hid. Neither do men light a lamp, and put it under the bushel, but on the stand; and it shineth unto all that are in the house. Even so let your light shine before men, that they may see your good works, and glorify your Father which is in heaven."

The value of the Church in the world is that of the Truth which the Church reveals, proclaims; that Truth is light, which flashes upon the darkness, rebuking it, dissipating it, making it easy for men who are stumbling to find their way.

The apostle immediately, comprehensively, and most marvellously described the Truth in the words "without controversy great is the mystery of godliness."

The word which most simply conveys the meaning of the Greek work here translated "godliness" is the old word *piety*. It has largely dropped out of use in recent years, and for some reasons we are not sorry, for it was very much abused. Yet that is the real thought of godliness, and if we use it, as did our fathers, to describe religion in life, relationship to God in the actualities of every-day life, we have the true thought of godliness.

Where is this piety? Where is this life of relationship to God to be seen? The answer to such inquiries is to be found in the fact that the apostle immediately passed from the abstract ideal of godliness to a concrete and positive Person in Whom the idea was perfectly revealed;

"He Who was manifested in the flesh." For poetic beauty of expression Humphrey's translation of this passage in the Cambridge Bible is very fine ;

> " Who in flesh was manifested,
> Pure in spirit was attested ;
> By angel's vision witnessed,
> Among the nations heralded ;
> By faith accepted here,
> Received in glory there ! "

According to that setting of the passage, the three couplets suggest the central facts in the life and work of Jesus ; the first the life-story ; the second the angels desiring to look into the mystery, and the nations hearing the ministry ; the third the victory among men by faith, and the ascension.

Though it is poetic and beautiful, I do not think that it reveals the deepest values of the passage.

Rotherham thus translates ; —

> " Who was made manifest in flesh,
> Was declared righteous in spirit,
> Was made visible unto messengers ;
> Was proclaimed among nations,
> Was believed on in (the) world,
> Was taken up in glory."

So far as I have any right to express an opinion, I do not hesitate to say that I consider that to be a most accurate, and beautiful translation. It covers far more than the life-story of Jesus when He was in the world, including the whole mystery of godliness manifested, beginning with the life-story, and ending with the second Advent.

The first line deals with the whole fact of the human life; "Who in flesh was manifested." The second line, "Was declared righteous in spirit," refers to the resurrection from the dead, for it was by the resurrection from the dead that He was "declared to be the Son of God with power, according to the spirit of holiness." The third line, "Was made visible unto messengers," needs to be carefully noticed. The Greek word is sometimes translated "angels," and sometimes "messengers"; and here I believe Rotherham is quite right in translating it *messengers*. The messengers were not angels in our general sense, but those who saw Him after resurrection, and who became the first apostles of the new movement. The immediate result of that manifestation to the messengers is declared in the fourth line "Was proclaimed among nations"; and the

THE MESSAGE OF I. TIMOTHY 55

spiritual result in the fifth " Was believed on in (the) world." These two facts of proclamation and belief are going forward now. The last line, "Was taken up in glory," refers to the Ascension of our Lord, and ultimately to that hour when, completed in His saints, His whole body perfected at the second Advent, Christ and His Church as an eternal unit pass into the heavens.

The great mystery of godliness then, according to this earliest hymn of the Church, is that of the manifestation of godliness in the flesh of the Son of Man; the declaration of His righteousness by resurrection; that risen One made visible to messengers, who proclaim the resurrection which is the foundation truth of Christianity; the proclamation issuing in the belief which brings men into living union with the manifested One; and ultimately, the complete manifestation in the Church in her union with Christ.

Thus the true function of the Church of God in the world is that of the proclamation of godliness; the Christ, and all those associated with Him, manifesting to the world the true life of piety, of religion, of godliness.

The true function of the minister then is that of the exposition of Truth in the Church. This is to be done by teaching, by exhortation, and by example.

The word is full of solemnity, one that always searches the heart of those who are called to the ministry of the Word. It is not by orthodoxy of intellectual comprehension merely that this work can be done. It is only as Truth is incarnate in the life of the teacher that the teacher has the power to prepare others to reveal the Truth. The responsibility of the Church in regard to the ministry is that it shall incarnate the Truth taught, in order that it may fulfill its function in the world as the pillar and ground of the Truth, that from which the glory and light of the Truth flashes upon the darkness of the world.

The abiding appeal to the Church is that the instrument must be fitted for the fulfillment of the function. The supreme matter of importance in the life of the Church is that she shall be an instrument able to proclaim the Truth. First her gospel must be an unchanged gospel. There must be no turning aside to false knowledge and heresies, such as Gnosticism and others that were then creeping in; no turning aside from the one doctrine of godliness manifested in flesh; the great faith once delivered to the saints in the

Person of Christ, and multiplied in exposition through all these who share His life. The Church must be true to her gospel.

Secondly her worship must be unceasing; hence that whole section which deals so wonderfully with the subject of prayer.

Finally she must be responsive to the authority of a faithful ministry.

In order to be an instrument fulfilling her true function the Church needs a gospel unchanged, worship unceasing, and an unfailing ministry.

The responsibility of the minister may be described in the same way. The instrument must be fitted for the fulfillment of function. That fitness on the part of the minister consists of unswerving loyalty to truth; consistent behaviour, that is behaviour towards others in harmony with the truth proclaimed; and realization of godliness in personal life; that is personal life harmonious with the truth, mastered by the truth, responsive to the truth.

There is an immediate application of this message to the Church of God, and I choose to make it, having thus seen the positive teaching, by a negative statement. Let the Church beware of the things that hinder. They are false doctrines; failure in prayer: false government. False doctrine is any doctrine that denies the essential truths focussed in the apostolic statement. When the Church relaxes her hold upon any vital part of the essential truth of the New Testament, she is weakening her testimony. Failure of prayer is so patent a secret of failure that it only needs to be stated. False government is government by men who lack the godly character. Both bishops and deacons must be men of true Christian character. We have been too eager to seek men for other reasons than for the highest; and to put them in charge of the affairs of the Christian Church. Those in oversight should be men full of faith and the Holy Ghost, men whose lives are transformed by the great doctrines for which the Church stands. Oversight must be in fulfillment of the truth, by incarnation of the truth; or what hope is there that the Church will rise to the fulfillment of her function in the world?

The application to the minister is that he is warned against failure in doctrine; failure in duty; and failure in diligence. No man can be in the ministry of Jesus Christ and fulfill the ideals of this letter to Timothy without putting into the business of his ministry, the business of his study, the business of his exposition, the business of his life, all the forces of his being.

Our sources of strength are sufficient. Truth itself, if known and responded to, will make us free from all the things that hinder us in the fulfillment of our service. Let those who teach the Word of God, whether in the larger assembly, or in the smaller circle, remember that teaching is only valuable and dynamic in the measure in which it is given, not by intellectual processes merely, but by volitional obedience and the changed life that results. How often we need to remind ourselves of the word of Emerson, "I cannot hear what you say for listening to what you are." Let us solemnly remember it in the presence of God. However orthodox the thing we say, however godly the method of our presentation of the truth, unless the life harmonizes, it is not only true that the things said will have no effect, it is true that the things said become a blasphemy and an impertinence.

The Church of God in the world to-day has as her function the proclamation of the truth of godliness. Those who teach the Word of God have as their responsibility that they give such exposition of the truth in teaching and life that the Church shall be equipped for her great work. May He Who has honoured us with the sacred responsibility fit us for the fulfillment of the duty

THE MESSAGE OF II. TIMOTHY

A THE ESSENTIAL MESSAGE	B THE APPLICATION

I. The Central Teaching
    The true Minister of Jesus Christ.
i. His perfect Equipment.
    Gifts and Grace.
ii. His prevailing Methods.
    Construction.
    Character.
iii. His supreme Work. Know the Writings.
    Preach the Word.
 	
II. The Abiding Appeal
    "Fulfill thy Ministry." iv. 5.
i. As to Equipment.
    a. Gift.
        "Stir up the Gift."
    b. Grace.
        "Be Strengthened in the Grace."
ii. As to Methods.
    a. Construction. "Give diligence . . ."
    b. Character. "Flee . . . follow."
iii. As to Work.
    a. The Writings. "Abide."
    b. The Preaching. "Instant."
	I. To the Church
	i. The Preaching of the Word as the Corrective to abounding Perils.
	ii. The Importance of the Ministry.
	iii. Recognition.
	    Of Gift and Grace in choosing.
	    Of Time and Teaching in work.
	
	II. To the Minister
	i. The Safety of the Deposit.
	ii. The Trusteeship of the Deposit.
	iii. The Fidelity to the Deposit.
	    Because of
	    Christ's Appearing.
	    Formalism.
	    Paul's Departure.

THE MESSAGE OF II. TIMOTHY

IN our consideration of this letter, in order to discover its main teaching, the central teaching of the first letter is assumed. That letter teaches us that the true function of the Christian Church is the proclamation of the Truth in the world, and that the true function of the Christian minister is that of the exposition of the Truth in the Church.

Between the writing of the first letter and this one, some period had elapsed. Paul, who was in prison when he wrote the great epistles, had been liberated when he wrote the first letter to Timothy; but was again in prison before he wrote this second one; and there is practically no question that this is the last writing that ever came from his pen.

The reason of the writing of this second letter to Timothy was that of the perils threatening the church, which were likely to prevent the church fulfilling its function as the pillar and ground of the truth. These perils he described in the words:

"Know this, that in the last days grievous times shall come. For men shall be lovers of self, lovers of money, boastful, haughty, railers, disobedient to parents, unthankful, unholy, without natural affection, implacable, slanderers, without self-control, fierce, no lovers of good, traitors, headstrong, puffed up, lovers of pleasure rather than lovers of God; holding a form of godliness, but having denied the power thereof."

That is a picture of what the apostle saw happening in the Church; it was being invaded by godlessness and worldliness. The Church is the pillar and ground of the Truth, and if the Church fails, then the Truth ceases to be proclaimed to the world; and that was the reason of the writing of this letter. The great missionary heart of Paul was troubled about the Church, because where the Church fails to give its testimony, the city abides in darkness. In view of these perils he wrote to Timothy, upon whom there necessarily rested grave responsibility.

The purpose of the letter then was that of preparing Timothy for the fulfillment of his responsibility for the Church, in order to the maintenance of its testimony; and therefore it is preeminently a letter to those who are in the ministry of the Word.

The central teaching of this letter is that of its revelation of the true minister of Jesus Christ. The content is the message. The order is so systematic, the movement is so regular, the method is so logical, that any young man preparing for the ministry, or any man in the ministry, may read it as a letter to himself from this great apostle, and from God Himself by the Spirit through the apostle.

The letter gives us a perfect picture of the true minister of Jesus Christ, and that in three respects; those namely of his perfect equipment; of his prevailing methods; and of his supreme work.

The perfect equipment of the Christian minister is revealed in two words, *gifts* and *grace*. In the old days when a candidate presented himself for the work of the ministry, the questions asked were: Has this young man gifts, and has he grace? I am not sure that we always ask those questions to-day. Yet these are the supreme qualifications; and no man can be a true minister of the Word in the Church, and no church can call a man to be a minister, and no college can make a man a minister if he lack these.

A man can become a minister of the Word only when a gift is bestowed upon him by the Head of the Church through the Holy Spirit. That is the supreme qualification. Roman Catholics speak of a vocation ; it is a great word. The vocation, according to the New Testament, is received with the bestowment of the gift. The gift bestowed is the first qualification for the Christian ministry.

But grace also is necessary, with all that word means, of fellowship with Christ and with God, and the consequent approximation to the character of Christ and of God ; the appropriation of the very resources of Christ and of God, and these so reacting upon the character as to make it the character of light and life and love.

The gifts are described in the Ephesian letter:

"When He ascended on high, He led captivity captive, and gave gifts unto men. . . . He gave some to be apostles ; and some, prophets ; and some, evangelists ; and some, pastors and teachers."

The gift of the apostle is that of the first messenger, the pioneer, the missionary. The gift of the prophet is that of the ability to discover what the Word of God has to say, not so much to the individual as to the nation, the age. The gift of the evangelist enables a man to tell the story of Jesus with such wooing winsomeness that men are drawn towards Him, and are won for the Kingdom and the Church. The gift of the pastor and teacher enables a man to watch the flock and to feed them. A gift is in itself a Divine deposit, flaming in fire, burning in heat, driving in energy; that is the first thing.

Beyond this there must be grace, that infinite resource of God at our disposal through Christ, which creates the tone of our preaching and the temper of our living, bringing all into harmony with the character of God.

The prevailing methods of the true Christian minister are those of construction and character. He is to aim at the development in holiness of those to whom he ministers; and this by the guarding of his own character, so that it may express concretely the truth he preaches. These are the true methods. As to constructive work, he builds upon foundations, and watching the building, patiently corrects it where it is faulty, testing it ever by the Word.

"Every Scripture inspired of God is also profitable for teaching, for reproof, for correction, for instruction." The whole idea of that passage is that of character building. The first word refers to authoritative teaching, upon which a man can depend, upon which he can build. Reproof does not mean rebuke, it means proof over again. The Greek word is figurative and suggests the letting down of a plumb-line by the side of a building to test its straightness. Correction means pulling the thing that is out of line into the straight. Instruction means construction, that is carrying the building higher. That is the work of the Christian minister. All the gifts of the ministry of the Word tend to the building of character according to the will of God.

The supreme work of the Christian minister is twofold; first to know the writings; and then to preach and teach the Word. No man can exercise the Christian ministry, whatever be the nature of his gift, who does not abide in the Scriptures. His business is to preach the Word, not to destroy it, not to defend it, but to preach it.

The abiding appeal of this letter to the Christian minister is contained in the charge of the apostle, "Fulfill thy ministry." This is necessary as to equipment, methods, and work.

THE MESSAGE OF II. TIMOTHY 69

As to equipment, the first responsibility concerns the gift; and is declared in the words, "Stir up the gift of God which is in thee." To stir up is to set on fire, to fan to a flame. The gift received for the ministry is a thing of fire; we are to fan it to a flame; and not allow it to burn to an ember. Are we not all in danger of allowing the fire to die down? There is nothing the Christian minister has to guard against more earnestly than the danger that he should come to the hour when the Word of God ceases to move him. It is a subtle danger. We are always handling the Word, reading it, studying it; and unless we are careful, it will cease to surprise us, cease to amaze us; and the gift, whether of apostle, prophet, evangelist, or pastor, will become dull and dead.

The second responsibility as to equipment concerns the grace, and is revealed in the words: "Be strengthened in the grace that is in Christ Jesus." We must not neglect the means of grace, in the true full sense of the word. Let no minister imagine that he of all men can afford to neglect prayer and devotional study of his Bible, and that fellowship with God which, being neglected, the fire always burns dimly, the pulse beats slowly, and the Christian life is poorer than it ought to be. "Be strengthened in the grace." "Fulfill thy ministry."

As to methods, our responsibility for construction is declared in the simple and yet incisive charge, "Give diligence"; while our responsibility as to our own character, if we are to construct character in others, is declared in the words; "Flee youthful lusts, and follow after righteousness, faith, love, peace . . . foolish and ignorant questionings refuse." "Fulfill thy ministry."

As to work, we fulfill our responsibility as to the Scriptures when we abide in them; and as to the Church, by being instant in season and out of season.

All this is but the gathering out of sentences, the whole teaching of the letter being in mind. These are the revelations of the secrets of success in the Christian ministry.

This letter emphasizes the fact that the teaching of the Word is the corrective of all the perils that threaten the Church; just as the preaching of the Word, and the Word incarnate in the lives of the saints who constitute the Church, is the corrective of all the perils that threaten the city and the nation. In proportion as we really know this Word of God, all the things which sap the life of the Church and make her devoid of power are corrected. The Church must flourish by the preaching of the Word. Nothing will take its place. Whether it be a church, or an organization taking the name and responsibility of Christian work in the world, if it neglect the Word, it robs itself of power, and sooner or later the whole must crumble to pieces. The churches that have placed the preaching of the Word at the centre of their life, and have aimed at its embodiment in the lives of their members, are the churches which have truly served their day and generation.

Consequently the Church must recognize the importance of the ministry of the Word. I think a grave peril threatening us to-day is that the churches take so little interest in the men who go to our colleges. I think the hour must come when the colleges will have to say, We will accept no man for training unless he not only brings his minister's recommendation, but one also from a church which knows that he possesses a gift for the work of preaching. We take men too often before we are sure that they have the gift. We give such men training, and then are surprised that no church wants them. Let the Church take over this responsibility and understand how important and sacred a thing this ministry of the Word is. The Church should be able to say: We recognize this man has gift and grace, and because he has gift and grace he is called to the ministry; therefore we will see to it that he has time for preparation and training, in order that his gift may be realized and his ministry fulfilled.

The first note of application to the minister is one of comfort if he be indeed a minister of Jesus Christ. If he have the gift and grace, then this letter brings him comfort, and it is comfort coming from the testimony of a man whose ministry of the Word was closing. This man, anxious about Timothy, and anxious that the Church should fulfill its function, anxious therefore that this young minister should be able to fulfill his function in order that the Church might fulfill her function in the world, said: "I know Him Whom I have believed, and I am persuaded that He is able to guard my deposit." That phrase, "my deposit," may mean something deposited with Him, or something deposited

THE MESSAGE OF II. TIMOTHY 73

with me. The popular interpretation has been that He is able to take care of something we have given over to Him. I think the apostle meant that the Lord is able to take care of a deposit which He commits to us, the deposit of Truth. If I have gift and grace, I need waste no time guarding the truth or defending it. I am sorry for the man who thinks his business is to go about defending the Truth. The Lord is able to take care of that. The safety of the deposit is the fundamental word of comfort to the man who wants to preach the Word of God.

The responsibility of the minister is that of the trusteeship of the Word of God. I hold the Word of God as a trustee; it is mine for others. If I am called into this ministry and am given a gift, the gift means power to convey; that is the peculiar quality that makes a man a minister. Consequently the Truth is a deposit which He is able to guard and of which I become the trustee. I am in debt to other men for all I know of the Truth, and I cannot get out of debt so long as there remains one single sphere of my influence, in which that has not been heard which has been entrusted to me.

The final application of this letter to the minister is that it calls him to fidelity to the trusteeship of the deposit, fidelity to the exercise of the gift in order that the Truth may be known to other men ; fidelity because of Christ's appearing presently ; because of the formalism that is growing within the Church ; and because gaps in the ranks are always occurring.

The appeal is a constant appeal. The apostles, prophets, evangelists, pastors and teachers fulfill their ministry and pass on ; but the Word abides, and the responsibility of those who follow in their train abides. When next we hear of some labourer fallen in the forefront, some teacher of the Word, let us say : So help us God, a little more faithfulness, a little more of passion, a little more of suffering, a little more of outpoured life, and the victory will be won.

THE MESSAGE OF TITUS

A THE ESSENTIAL MESSAGE	B THE APPLICATION

I. The Central Teaching. The true Church of Jesus Christ
i. The Motive of its Order.
   a. General. "The Truth which is according to Godliness." i. 1. (*Cf.* 1 Tim. iii. 16.)
   b. Negative. "To convict the Gainsayers." i. 9. { Liars. Evil Beasts. Slow Bellies.
   c. Positive. "Instructing ... live." ii. 12. { Soberly. Righteously. Godly.
ii. The Method of its Order.
   a. General. Oversight. Bishops. i. 7.
   b. Passive. Clear Vision.
      { Of Truth.
       Of prevailing Conditions.
       Of true Method.
   c. Active. Authority. ii. 15.
      { "Speak." Enunciation of Truth.
       "Exhort." Application to Need.
       "Reprove." Insistence upon Obedience.
iii. The Might of its Order. The Facts and Forces of the Epiphanies. ii. 11–14.
   { "Grace hath appeared."
    "The ... appearing of the Glory."
II. The Abiding Appeal. The Church true to Jesus Christ
i. The inclusive Church Responsibility. "To adorn the Doctrine." ii. 10. (See "Trimmed," Matt. xxv. 7.)
ii. The individual Christian Responsibility. "Careful to maintain good works." iii. 8.
iii. The consequent Responsibility of those in Oversight. "To affirm confidently." iii. 8.
	I. To the Church
	i. The Power of the Church in the World is that of her Revelation of Truth.
	ii. All her Overseers must be Men themselves under the Dominion of Truth.
	
	II. To the Overseers
	i. The Power of the Overseer is that of the Truth to be revealed.
	ii. The Measure of the Success of Oversight is the Measure in which the Church exercises the Power of Truth.

THE MESSAGE OF TITUS

IN considering this letter we need again to remind ourselves of the inter-relation between the two letters to Timothy and this one to Titus.

In the first letter to Timothy we saw that the true function of the Church is that it should be the pillar and ground of the truth. In order that this function may be fulfilled, it is necessary that every local church should be properly organized.

As in the second letter to Timothy we saw the perfect equipment of the minister, his prevailing method, and his special work; in this letter we see the true Church of Jesus Christ so far as her ecclesiastical order is concerned. It is a very remarkable thing that this letter has to do with a church of Jesus Christ in a most difficult place. Paul described the Cretans by quotation from one of their own poets as "liars, evil beasts, slow bellies." In this letter also the most startling and amazing thing as to the possibility of Christian life is said concerning those who are in this most difficult position, and of those who are in the most trying circumstances, the bond-slaves. The apostle declared that they were to "adorn the doctrine of God."

Thus in order to show the true spiritual power of the Church, and the possibility of the lowest exercising it, the most difficult soil was selected, the most difficult circumstances were employed; and of those in the midst of trying and impossible conditions of life the finest possibilities were postulated. Thus the Spirit of God teaches us that the Church of God can be the pillar and ground of the truth in the most dark, desolate, and difficult places of the earth; and that men and women whose circumstances are most trying and difficult, can fulfill the highest function of Christianity, that of "adorning the doctrine of God our Saviour in all things."

The central teaching of this letter is that of its revelation of the true Church of Jesus Christ; and its abiding appeal that the Church be true to Jesus Christ. The Church of Jesus Christ is revealed in its true order; as to motive, method, and might. We could appropriately write as a

THE MESSAGE OF TITUS

motto over this letter the words, "Let everything be done decently and in order."

The motive of church order is revealed in a phrase at the very beginning of the letter; "The truth which is according to godliness." That word "godliness" we found in the first letter to Timothy, "great is the mystery of *godliness.*" That is the truth of which the Church is to be the pillar and ground. More than half our disputes within the one catholic Church are disputes about order; whereas if we were more occupied with the reason for order, there would be very much less division about it. The passion of the apostle when he sent Titus to Crete and wrote to him there, was a passion for the truth which is according to godliness, that godliness of which the mystery is great.

The motive of the order is further explained, first negatively as the apostle shows that the result of the setting in order of the church will be that of convicting the gainsayers. In that connection we have the threefold description of the Cretans already referred to, "Liars, evil beasts, slow bellies." These are the things of animalism; and the business of the church, by its revelation of truth, is to correct and convict the gainsayers, those who by their animalism speak against godliness.

Secondly, there is a positive value. That we find stated in the second chapter in the midst of the great passage on grace, in which the apostle declared that "the grace of God hath appeared, bringing salvation to all men, instructing us, to the intent that, denying ungodliness and worldly lusts, we should live soberly and righteously and godly in this present world." The Cretans were liars; Christians were to live soberly. The Cretans were evil beasts, sensual, animal, and fierce in their passions as against one another; Christians were to live righteously, that is, in right relationships with the world around them. The Cretans were slow bellies; Christians were to live godly.

That is the motive for setting the church in order. The saints who constitute it are to deny ungodliness and worldly lusts in their own lives, and so become God's negatory forces, in the midst of the cities in which they live and move and have their being. To set our church in order so that we may worship as we desire to worship, is to act from a low motive. That the church may be the pillar and ground of the Truth; upon which and from which shall flash

THE MESSAGE OF TITUS

the light of truth; in order that the forces of death and darkness and devilry may be rebuked; ought to be the motive behind all church organization.

The method of church order is that of oversight. Elders were to be appointed, and the apostle explains the office by the use of the word "bishop." A bishop is one in oversight, one who watches, one who sees clearly. I am not now discussing as to whether the bishop is to be a pastor of one flock, or whether there are to be two or three bishops for one flock or whether one bishop is to have a diocese. I do not believe that there is any final word in the New Testament as to ecclesiastical government. The matter of supreme importance is that we understand that the office of a bishop is that of oversight. Ruskin draws attention to this fact, and in his caustic way he asks whether the bishop is aware that down yonder alley Bill has been knocking Nancy's teeth out, and if not, he declares that he is not a bishop, though his mitre be as high as a steeple. The function of the office may be described as first, active; and then, passive. The one placed in oversight by the Holy Spirit through the gift bestowed and through grace abounding, must have a clear vision of the truth of God of which the Church is to be the pillar and ground; he must also have a clear vision of the prevailing conditions in the midst of which the Church is to flash and shine; he must finally have a clear vision of the true method in oversight.

The bishop is to speak, exhort, reprove; and these words are not idly chosen. He is to speak, that is, to enunciate truth. That is his first business, but it is not his last business. He is to exhort, that is, he is to apply the truth to local conditions. That is his second business, but it is not his last business. He is to reprove, that is, he is to insist upon obedience to the truth. That is the threefold activity of the man in oversight. He is placed in oversight by the Holy Spirit of God, or he has no claim to oversight. The method of the order of the Church is that of oversight by men appointed by the Spirit of God.

The might of the Church's order is revealed in that great passage already quoted, the recitation of which is always a revelation and interpretation. How does the passage open? "The grace of God hath appeared." How does it end?

"The appearing of the glory." The facts and forces of the two epiphanies constitute the true strength of church government, and church order, and church service. "The grace of God hath appeared . . . looking for the appearing of the glory." I have sometimes said that if I were to build a new church I should like to call it the church of the two Epiphanies; the epiphany of grace; and the epiphany of glory. When was the first? When He came. When will be the second? When He comes. The first was the Advent of grace; the second will be the Advent of glory. When we see the first Advent we see "Glory as of the only begotten from the Father." That was the Advent of grace. When we see the second Advent, we shall see the final unveiling of grace. The one catholic Church of God; the assembly of believers by whatever human name it is called; lives between the light of the first Advent and the light of the second; the first Advent, which was the setting of the Sun in blood, and the second, which shall be the rising of the Sun in glory. Between these we live, and the forces of the first and the forces of the second, the dynamic that came from the Cross, the inspiration which comes from the Crowning, constitute the might of church order, both for the overseer and for the flock in order that the Church may be the pillar and ground of the Truth.

The abiding appeal of this letter is that the Church shall be true to Jesus Christ Who is the Truth. The inclusive church responsibility is to adorn the doctrine. The individual Christian responsibility is to be careful to maintain good works. The consequent responsibility of those in oversight is to affirm confidently these things.

The inclusive responsibility of the Christian Church is to adorn the doctrine. Paul says this of the bond-slave, a servant in the most difficult situation and condition of life, and certainly if such can adorn the doctrine all others can. The word translated "adorn" is *kosmeo*, and is derived from the Greek word *kosmos*, a word suggesting order and beauty. When our Lord spoke of the virgins wise and foolish, and declared that at midnight the cry went out, Behold the bridegroom cometh; He said that they *trimmed* their lamps. "Trimmed" is the same word as here is translated "adorn." To trim the lamp was to snuff the wick. That is the way to adorn the doctrine. A wick is snuffed that the flame may burn the brighter; and in proportion as that poor carbon of our life knows the principle of the Cross, which is the snuffing of the wick, we adorn the doctrine. It does seem so impossible to adorn the doctrine; but it is not so. I once heard Dr. Watkinson illustrate this. He said: Here is a piece of music. I take it up and look at it. I notice that the marks upon the page are darker and thicker here, and more straggling there; I am told it is a wonderful piece of music, but I cannot comprehend it. Presently some one comes and takes the piece of music, and plays it upon an instrument; and so the player *adorns* the music. The player does not compose it, is quite unequal to composing it, but he plays it, interprets it, *adorns it*, to his fellow man who has no knowledge of it. That is the great business of the Christian Church, to adorn the doctrine. We cannot create the doctrine; the doctrine is created; but this great mystery of godliness the Church is to adorn by living it. That is the supreme responsibility of the Church.

The individual Christian responsibility is to carefully maintain good works. That phrase does not refer to charitable philanthropy. It does not mean doing meritorious things in order to win salvation. It means doing all good, true, noble, beautiful things, out of the forces of salvation. Alone I cannot perfectly adorn the doctrine; but I can watch and be careful to maintain good works, and in that measure I contribute to the adorning of the doctrine. That is the individual responsibility.

The consequent responsibility of those in oversight; bishops, elders, those gifted and having grace, is that they affirm confidently. We do not help men and women to adorn the doctrine when we debate our doubts in their presence. We may have doubts; I suppose every man has them. I have them, doubts and difficulties, questionings, problems, but I never preach them. Let us wait until the light has become clearer if there be a subject on which we are in doubt, before we speak about it. We are to affirm confidently the essential, fundamental things of the Christian faith epitomized in that passage concerning the mystery of godliness.

Our general application may be briefly made. First this letter reveals to me the fact that the power of the Church in the world is that of her revelation of the truth of God. I dare not begin an exposition of that, yet ponder it well. The Church is not influential because she is able to manipulate the affairs of the State. The Church is powerful in the measure in which she is revealing the truth of God in her own life. That is the central truth of this letter. Concerning the Church this also is revealed, that all overseers must be men themselves under the dominion of the truth; and the principle of selecting a leader, a bishop, must be that of his mastery by the truth; and I am not now referring merely to those who preach; but to all those who hold office in the Christian Church. Trustees, managers, deacons, stewards, who have been appointed because of their wealth or social influence, are a hindrance and not a help. It is on the basis of spiritual life, resulting from mastery by the truth, that all must be placed in office in the Christian Church if she is to fulfill her function.

The application of the letter to overseers therefore is; first that the power of the overseer is that of the truth and not that of his office. No man has any real power because he holds office. The only power of the overseer is that of the truth he proclaims, and confidently affirms, until it captures and masters those who hear it. The measure of success in oversight, therefore, is the measure in which the Church exercises the power of the truth. The test of success is not the crowd; but the souls transformed under the power of the Word who adorn the doctrine, and thus fulfill the holy function of being the pillar and ground of the truth.

THE MESSAGE OF PHILEMON

A THE ESSENTIAL MESSAGE	B THE APPLICATION

I. The Central Teaching. Pictures of Christianity in its Outworking
i. Of Individuals.
    a. Paul. { 1. Triumph over Circumstances in the Fellowship of Christ. 1 and 9.
              2. Triumph over personal Authority in the Power of Love. 8, 9.
              3. Triumph over Inclination in a Passion for Righteousness. 13, 14.
    b. Onesimus. The Change. 11.
    c. Philemon. The Principles. 5–7. { Love. Faith.
ii. Of Social Relations.
    a. Paul and Philemon. "Love seeketh not its own." 14.
    b. Paul and Onesimus. "Love beareth all things." 17–19.
    c. Onesimus and Philemon. "Love suffereth long, and is kind."
        1. The Slave to return. 12.
        2. The Master to receive him. 16, 17, 21.
    d. The Church. "Love never faileth." { Interested. 1, 2. Coöperative.
	I. To the Individual
	i. Life in Christ changes every Relationship.
	
	ii. Our Relationships to others test our Relationship to Christ.

II. The Abiding Appeal. The Power of Christ in its Inworking
    a. Ephesians. "Be filled with the Spirit." v. 18.
    b. Philippians. "Have this mind." ii. 5.
    c. Colossians. "Let the Word of Christ. . . ." iii. 16.
	II. To the Church
	Social Evils are to be changed by transformed Lives.

THE MESSAGE OF PHILEMON

IN this letter as in the second and third letters of John, we have pictures and portraits which serve as illustrations.

The letters of the first imprisonment of Paul, in the order of their placing in our Bible, were those to the Ephesians, the Philippians, the Colossians, and Philemon. The value of the last consists in the fact that it is an illustration of the outworking into every-day life of the great doctrines dealt with in the other three. It is a page of pictures of Christianity in its outworking. They are all boldly drawn, in bare outline, yet full of beauty. We have first, pictures of individuals; Paul, Philemon, Onesimus. Secondly, pictures of social relationships; Paul and Philemon; Paul and Onesimus; Paul, Philemon, and Onesimus; and finally we have a picture of the Church. Thus in this one page of the New Testament we have at least seven pictures presented to the mind. Let us first look at these pictures in bare outline.

The first is that of Paul. Of course we have no biography, no autobiography; no detail about those minor matters of human life which we so perpetually emphasize when we tell the story of the lives of men; but the essential facts of his character are revealed in this letter all unconsciously by the writer.

First this letter reveals Paul as a man of triumph over circumstances in fellowship with Christ. He is seen secondly as a man triumphing over the right to exercise personal authority in the power of his love. He is also seen as a man triumphing over personal inclination in a great passion for righteousness. If there were no other revelation of Paul in the whole of the New Testament, this in itself reveals the transformation wrought in him, and manifested through him, as the result of his life in Christ, and consequent fellowship with Christ.

Paul was a prisoner in Rome, and by his imprisonment all his missionary journeyings were at an end; the burning passion of his heart to be out upon the highway of missionary endeavour, pressing ever on to the regions beyond, might have been quenched as he found himself held by the irksome chain of his imprisonment. That, however, is not the way in which Paul refers to his imprisonment. He describes himself as "Paul a prisoner of Christ Jesus." That is perfect triumph over circumstances in the power of fellowship with Christ. That is the first fact of the outworking of Christianity in individual experience. Fellowship with Christ gives the individual perfect triumph over circumstances. Paul was a prisoner not of Rome, not of the Roman emperor, but of Jesus Christ. He saw through all the secondary, incidental things, to the primary and fundamental fact, that, to the man abandoned to the will of his Lord, nothing can happen outside the good and perfect and acceptable will of God. How many of us really know what it is, in circumstances of limitation, when all our highest aspirations seem checked and thwarted, when our passion to work for God is not allowed to find vent and exercise, to sit down and write of ourselves as the prisoners of Christ Jesus? That is the privilege of all the saints, but it is only possible to those who are living in true fellowship with Jesus Christ.

The next note is that of triumph in the power of love over the right to exercise authority. Not that the authority of Paul was lessened; not that his appeal would fail to produce the effect he desired; but here was a man who had the right to enjoin that which was befitting, but who said, I will not enjoin, command thee; I prefer to beseech thee for love's sake. That is the perfect victory of love in the life of a man; when he is able not to command, though his authority for so doing may be vested in Christ, but chooses rather to deal with others as God does, by beseeching in love. That is the Divine method; "As though God were intreating by us; we beseech you on behalf of Christ, be ye reconciled to God."

Then finally there was triumph over personal inclination in a passion for righteousness. Notice the two *I woulds* of Paul in verses thirteen and fourteen. "Whom *I would* fain have kept with me" is the "*I would*" of personal inclination. Onesimus was the child of his bonds, he would have ministered to him and made things easier for him, so that the apostle said, I would like to keep him with me. But the second "*I would*" is the revelation of his sacrifice of personal inclination, because he knew the other course to be right. It was a triumph over inclination in the passion for the right.

THE MESSAGE OF PHILEMON 95

When I think of Paul I am usually impressed by the magnificence of his intellect sanctified by the indwelling Spirit; and by his tremendous devotion to his Lord; but here I see the profoundest things of his character. Christianity outworking through his experience was manifested as triumphing over circumstances in the fellowship of Christ, so that he could say I am the prisoner of Christ, while to all human seeming he was the prisoner of Rome; triumphing over the right to exercise personal authority on highest levels, in the power of love, so that rather than enjoin, he besought; triumphing over inclination to keep Onesimus to be useful to himself, in the passion which was in his heart for the doing of the right thing in all circumstances.

The next picture is more briefly drawn. It is of "Onesimus, who was aforetime unprofitable to thee, but now is profitable to thee and to me." There was a sanctified humour in Paul's play upon words here. It was Martin Luther who said, "We are all the Lord's Onesimi, we are all the Lord's profitable servants. How have we been made profitable to the Lord? We were unprofitable." This man, said Paul in effect, when he was with you, Philemon, bore a name to which he was not true; he is now Onesimus in reality, profitable to thee and to me.

The picture of Onesimus is that of the radical change which Christ works in the life of any man of whom He gains possession; the unprofitable becomes profitable. It is a perpetual picture of what Christ does with men. The waste, unprofitable material He makes valuable, profitable.

The last of these single pictures is that of Philemon; "Hearing of thy love, and of the faith which thou hast towards the Lord Jesus, and towards all the saints . . . for I had much joy and comfort in thy love, because the hearts of the saints have been refreshed through thee, brother."

Philemon was a man governed by two principles, faith and love. These were associated in his practical life. As to faith Paul said, "The faith which thou hast towards the Lord Jesus, and towards all the saints." Faith towards the Lord Jesus, and faith towards the saints. The preposition employed in each case is the same; and what is meant in one case is meant in the other. The fundamental principle in the life of the Christian man is faith towards the Lord Jesus, and towards the saints; and that faith towards the Lord Jesus and towards the saints is expressed in love; love works through faith.

The experimental order is revealed if we take the portraits in the other order. Beginning with that of Philemon, we see the principles of faith and love; glancing next at Onesimus, we see a man changed from unprofitable to profitable; finally, looking at Paul, we see the triumph of Christianity in its outworking in a threefold application.

Turning to the picture of social relationship we come first to that of Paul and Philemon. I should be inclined to write underneath the picture of these two men as I see them here, "Love seeketh not its own." The apostle wrote to his friend, "Without thy mind I would do nothing; that thy goodness should not be as of necessity, but of free will." That is very simple and very human; yet the very simplicity and humanness of it constitute its sublimity and beauty. In effect Paul said: I should like to have kept Onesimus, but I would not without thy mind. If I had kept Onesimus you would not have complained; but you would have been helpless, and your goodness would have been of necessity. I want your goodness to be manifested towards this man, of your own free will. I am seeking the development of your Christian character at its highest, noblest, and best. I would have kept him; but I am seeking not only his blessing, and his restoration to favour; but your blessing, and the development of all that is highest and best in you. If you did a good thing of necessity, it would not be on the highest level; but if a good thing be done of your own free will, it is on the highest level. Thus in this beautiful, tender, gracious regard of Paul for Philemon is revealed the love which seeketh not its own.

The next picture is that of Paul and Onesimus. Beneath that I would write the words: "Love beareth all things." The Greek word translated *beareth* suggests a roof upon which the rain falling, the person standing underneath is protected. Love is a covering roof; sheltering the friend beneath. "If he hath wronged thee at all, or oweth thee aught, put that to mine account," wrote Paul. Onesimus the unprofitable runaway slave was the child of Paul's very heart, the child of his bonds; and Paul's love was the roof over Onesimus which protected him. Love beareth all things. That is the relationship which Christ creates between men.

The third picture of relationship is of that between Onesimus and Philemon. Here let us write the words "Love suffereth long, and is kind." What will Christianity do in this case? Onesimus was the runaway slave of Philemon. What will Christianity do with him? Send him back. The slave must return. What will Christianity do in the case of Philemon? It will prepare him to receive him as a brother; "No longer as a servant, but more than a servant, a brother beloved"; and as a partner, "if then thou countest me a partner, receive him as myself." Then followed that touch, which did not say the last thing, but pointed the way to it as the apostle wrote, "Having confidence in thine obedience I write unto thee, knowing that thou wilt do *even beyond what I say.*" That something beyond was almost certainly the giving of his freedom to the slave. Christianity sent Onesimus back to fulfill the obligations of the law. Christianity taught Philemon to receive the slave kindly, and cancel the obligations of the law in the power of indwelling love.

Finally we have a picture of the church in the house of Philemon. Its title may fittingly be "Love never faileth." Paul wrote to the church, because in the highest ideal of Christianity you cannot write to the individual without the church being interested and being brought into coöperation. The true fellowship in Christ Jesus is such that if one member suffers all suffer, and if one member rejoices all rejoice; when one member fulfills obligation and goes back to duty, all the members coöperate with him in his return; if one member fulfills the law of love and receives the runaway, all the members enter into the joy of heart that comes to the one. We have here then a picture of an ideal church in which the runaway slave is to be received on his return as a brother and a partner by all who share the common life, and walk in the common light, in the power of the common love.

If this be the central teaching of these pictures of Christianity in the outworking, what is their abiding appeal? I am constrained to say that it is not to be found stated in words in the epistle. The pictures themselves create the appeal. They appeal to all who look upon them and who share the life which produces these results, to yield themselves to that life entirely, absolutely.

In order to find the appeal of this letter stated in actual words I go back to the other epistles written in imprisonment. It has often been pointed out that some of the greatest things we have ever had for our spiritual instruction were written in prison. Paul never rendered greater service to the Church of God than in those days when he was shut up in prison. No others are more wonderful, more full of light and glory, more evidently the revelation of the Spirit of God to His servant, than the letters of the imprisonment. The apostle was thinking the Ephesian, Colossian, and Philippian letters, and while such thoughts filled his mind he wrote this letter to Philemon about a runaway slave. There was a time when some thought that this page should be left out of the New Testament because the subject was not worthy the dignity of an apostle; but thank God that in His overruling in the arrangement and selection and preservation of the writings which are essentially of the Spirit, Philemon is not left out. In this epistle we see the commonplaces of every-day life set in the atmosphere and power of the sublimest things of the eternities. Philemon is but a page of pictures resulting from Ephesians, Philippians, and Colossians.

I go then to these great epistles and take from them the central words of each in order to find the words of appeal. In Ephesians, that great unveiling of the glorious Church, "Be filled with the Spirit." In Philippians, that great unveiling of Christian character, "Have this mind in you, which was also in Christ Jesus." In Colossians, that great unveiling of the glory of Christ as at the disposal of the Church, "Let the word of Christ dwell in you richly." That is the threefold abiding appeal of the letter to Philemon.

How is it possible for me to live the life of faith and love? How is it possible for me, who have been most unprofitable, to be indeed a man profitable? How is it possible for me ever to know such triumph over circumstances as Paul manifested; such triumph over personal authority in the power of love; such triumph over personal inclination in the passion for righteousness?—How can I fulfill this life?

All the necessary resources are in Christ. Then the power of Christ must have full sway, and right of way in and through me; and my responsibilities are stated in the words of these

THE MESSAGE OF PHILEMON 103

great epistles, "Be filled with the Spirit," "Have this mind in you, which was also in Christ Jesus," "Let the word of Christ dwell in you richly."

What then are the applications of this brief letter? First as to the individual. This letter teaches me that life in Christ changes every relationship. All the relationships that might be suggested do not appear upon this page; but those which do appear have a bearing on all the rest. My son, my daughter, my father, my husband, my wife, my neighbour; all bear new relationship to me the moment I am a man in Christ. I bear a new relationship to them, and consequently they bear a new relationship to me. I have a new relationship to my servant if I am a man in Christ. I have a new relationship to my master if I am a man in Christ.

I learn also that our relationships to others test our relationship to Christ. Not by what I sing about my Lord, not by what I affirm of relationship to Christ, but by my relationship to other men, is my relationship to my Lord made manifest. Philemon angrily refusing to receive Onesimus would have contradicted all the profession he made of love for Jesus Christ. Onesimus refusing to return to Philemon would have rendered null and void all his profession of faith in Jesus Christ. Had Paul yielded to personal inclination he would by that act have proved a measure of disloyalty to Christ. It is the relationships I bear to other men which constitute the real test of my relationship to Christ.

If I am living in true fellowship with Him, letting His mind be in me by being filled with His Spirit, and having His word richly dwelling in me, my relationship to others will be changed; and my relationship to Christ will be revealed.

There is one word of application to the Church at large. From this letter one of the profoundest matters is learned; that social evils are to be ended by the transformation men, and in no other way. There is no protest here against slavery. There was a day when Christian teachers used this very letter in defence of slavery. We know full well that any such use was absolutely unwarranted. Onesimus was sent back to Philemon, but Philemon was charged to receive him in a new way. The supreme work of Christianity is to transform men, so that out of their transformed lives shall come the transformation of all social conditions, and the victories of righteousness and of love.

THE MESSAGE OF HEBREWS

A THE ESSENTIAL MESSAGE	B THE APPLICATION

I. The Central Teaching
i. The Perfection of the Revelation through the Son.
   a. Superseding all others.
      Angelic. Human. Ritualistic.
   b. Meeting all Needs.
      Prophetic. Priestly. Kingly.
   c. Ensuring all Victories.
      Individual. Social. Universal.
ii. The Principle of Life by Faith.
   a. Faith defined.
      Volitional Surrender (In spite of Appearances).
   b. Faith active.
      Doing. Suffering. Waiting.
   c. Faith triumphant.
      In the Deed. Over the Suffering. Ultimately with God.
iii. The Peril of Death through Apostasy.
   a. Apostasy defined.
      Disobedience (Because of Appearances).
   b. Apostasy active.
      Doing. Suffering. Waiting.
   c. Apostasy hopeless.
      In the Deed. Under the Suffering. Ultimately without [God.
 	
II. The Abiding Appeal
i. Warnings.
   a. As to Speech of Son. ii. 1*a*. "Lest."
      1. Haply we drift. ii. 1.
      2. Haply . . . falling . . . God. iii. 12.
      3. Hardened. iii. 13.
      4. Haply . . . rest . . . short. iv. 1.
   b. As to Goal of God.
      1. "Falleth short of Grace." xii. 15. Life.
      2. "Root of Bitterness." xii. 15. Love.
      3. "Profane Person." xii. 16. Light.
ii. Encouragements.
   "Let us."
   a. As to Son.
      1. Prophet. "Fear." iv. 1.
               "Give diligence." iv. 11.
      2. Priest. "Hold fast." iv. 14.
            "Draw near." iv. 16.
      3. King. "Press on." vi. 1.
   b. As to Saintship.
      "Draw near." x. 22. "Hold fast." 23.
      "Consider one another." 24.
   c. As to Service.
      Towards the Goal. "Lay aside." "Run." xii. 1.
                          "Have Grace." xii. 28.
      Suffering. "Go forth." xiii. 13.
                "Offer praise." xiii. 15.
	I. To the Church
	i. The Message assumes the Biblical Conception of God.
	   a. Universal Sovereignty.
	   b. Knowable and revealing.
	   To deny this Conception is to destroy these Conclusions.
	ii. The Message depends upon the Christology of the Writer (See i. 2, 3).
	   To deny this Christology is to destroy these Appeals.
	
	II. To the Individual
	i. The Power of Faith.
	ii. The Peril of Apostasy.

THE MESSAGE OF HEBREWS

FOR inclusive value, suggestive teaching, beauty of statement, perfection of system, perhaps there is no writing of the New Testament more wonderful than this letter to the Hebrews.

Its central teaching is threefold; first, the perfection of the revelation through the Son; secondly, the principle of life by faith; thirdly, the peril of death through apostasy.

As to the first, the perfection of the revelation through the Son, there are three values of the revelation set forth; that it supersedes all others; that it meets all needs; and that it ensures all victories.

This letter does not reveal Christ to us in His personal glory as some others do; but it does show that through the Son, God has given us His most perfect revelation of Himself. God is the first word of the letter; it is the theme of the letter. It is God revealed; God at work; and God triumphing. As we take our way through this letter, we are following the pathway of God through human history to consummation. It begins where the first verse of Genesis begins; and ere it closes, we find ourselves upon the mount, amid all the hosts of glory, as we find them in the Apocalypse.

It teaches us first of all that the revelation through the Son supersedes all others; angelic, human, and ritualistic. It supersedes the angelic; for the Son is superior to angels. It supersedes the human, as represented by Moses and Joshua; for the Son is greater than the servants. It supersedes the ritualistic method, the method of the priest and the altar, the method of the temple and sacrifice, and all the things through which God did by picture and symbol speak to men of Himself; because when the Son came, there was fulfillment of all of which these were but the shadows. When the Son came to speak from God, angels were no longer required, human teachers and interpreters were set on one side, all ritualism was rendered unnecessary.

The revelation through the Son was sufficient to meet all human need. The first need of man is a prophet who shall utter the word of God as the standard for his life. He needs also a priest, whose mediation shall reconcile him to God. He needs finally a king who shall govern according to the will of God.

When the Son came He came as Prophet, Priest, and King, meeting all these needs; and this is clearly set forth in the argument of the writer. God speaks through the Son; and angels, and Moses, and Joshua are silent. So the prophetic need is met. Then He establishes a new covenant; and His priesthood is higher than that of Aaron, higher than the Levitical order, being of the order of Melchizedek. Thus the priestly need is met. Finally, He, as King, establishes the Kingdom of God in this world. So the kingly need is met.

Once again, the revelation through the Son ensures all victories. The individual is perfected through the Son. The old economy is abolished because it made nothing perfect. Social victory is realized through the Son; "Ye are come unto mount Zion, and unto the City of the living God, the heavenly Jerusalem." Finally, universal victory is made certain, for the ultimate glory is that triumph of God wherein He Who suffered shall find His perfect satisfaction.

All that, so far as we are concerned, may be said to be objective. Faith is revealed as the principle by which these things become subjective, part of our own experience. If there is one book of the Bible which more carefully than any other defines faith, it is this letter. It contains one passage in which faith is defined in so many words, but that is not the only definition of faith which it affords. Faith, according to the whole teaching of the writer, is volitional surrender, and obedience in spite of appearances. Faith is not merely intellectual conviction. Faith is the action of the will which follows intellectual conviction and harmonizes with intellectual conviction. That is the only faith that saves. Faith as a creed, apprehended by the intellect, never saves. If we carefully follow the argument of the writer, when he is dealing with the subject of the people who could not enter in because of unbelief, we discover that unbelief is described as disobedience. The men who triumphed by faith were men who did things because they believed, when all appearances made it seem as though their doing was the doing of unutterable folly. Think of the unutterable folly of any man turning his back on Ur of the Chaldees and going, no one knew whither, not even himself, because he believed God, and looked for a city. That is faith; volitional surrender and obedience in spite of appearances. That is how the letter to the Hebrews in its wider teaching defines faith.

Faith is not only defined, it is revealed at work. Faith is not merely a sentiment, an attitude of mind; it is energy that drives and accomplishes. These men did something. Faith also suffers, and the story of suffering is graphically told. And finally, faith waits, the most difficult thing that faith ever has to do; "These all died in faith, not having received the promises. . . . God having provided some better thing concerning us, that apart from us they should not be made perfect.' And they are waiting still! The life of faith does not end when we die. The life of faith runs on into the paradise of God. There is no uncertainty in the waiting, no unhappiness, no misery; but they are waiting because the victory is not yet won, the work is not done, and God's Kingdom has not yet come. For us the most heavenly activity, and the most difficult activity of faith, is to wait. So long as I can work, even though I may suffer, it is not so difficult; but when I can no longer work, or suffer, and simply have to wait, that is the most trying activity of faith.

Finally, this letter gives us a picture of faith triumphant. It is triumphant in the deed. Go through the eleventh chapter again, and see how constantly those men did things, and how in the doing there was triumph. The things that they did are the things that have made the world what it is to-day, in so far as it harmonizes with the will of God. Faith suffers, but in the suffering it is triumphant. It makes sorrow the occasion for song. Finally faith is triumphant in its waiting, for it is in itself the assurance of things hoped for, the certainty of the ultimate accomplishment of the will of God.

The final note of the teaching of this letter reveals the peril of death through apostasy. Apostasy is defined here. It is the exact opposite of faith, and consists of disobedience because of appearances. Let the history interpret the teaching. The men of old said, The land is full of Anakim, and walled cities; these were appearances; because of them they disobeyed; that is apostasy; and so they failed to enter into rest.

Therein is revealed the whole truth about apostasy. Men are not apostate because the doctrine they hold is wrong. They are apostate when they hold the true doctrine, and refuse to obey it. Disobedience is the unbelief that hardens the spirit, and ends in death. Apostasy is active also, it will do things. Apostasy will suffer; and will wait. Let no man imagine that by apostasy he will escape from effort, or suffering, or waiting. The strain of effort, the actuality of suffering, the tragedy of waiting all continue; but mark the difference. As faith is always triumphant in deed, and over suffering, and ultimately with God; apostasy is always hopeless in the deed, in the suffering, and ultimately without God. The end of apostasy is restlessness, just as surely as the end of faith is perfect rest.

In the light of this central teaching, let us hear the abiding appeal of the letter. The first note of that appeal is one of warning, and the application is introduced in every case by the use of the word "*Lest.*" There are two groups of such warnings. The first deals with perils threatening us in view of the finality of the speech of the Son; and the second with perils confronting us in view of the ultimate victory of God.

The first group is found in the section of the letter specially dealing with the speech of the Son. God has spoken to us by the Son; we ought therefore to give most earnest heed to the things we have heard.

Take the four warnings;

"*Lest* haply we drift."

"*Lest* haply there shall be in any of you an evil heart of unbelief, in falling away from the living God."

"*Lest* any of you be hardened by the deceitfulness of sin."

"*Lest* haply, a promise being left of entering into his rest, any one of you should seem to come short of it."

That is a sequence. Lest we drift; that is the first thing; it is the picture of a vessel dragging its anchor and drifting. What next? "An evil heart of unbelief, in falling away from the living God." If I drift from the things the Son has said, I fall away from the living God Whom the Son reveals. With what result? I am "hardened by the deceitfulness of sin." With what issue? "A promise being left," I "come short of it." To avoid the first is to be saved from all the rest. To fail in the first is inevitably to pass through all the experience described in the rest. No storm is sweeping the sea; we are still close to the shore; but drifting just a little way. If by God's grace we recognize the drift, and hasten back, we shall not fall from the living God, we shall not become hardened, we shall not lose our rest.

The second group is found in the twelfth chapter;

"Follow after peace with all men, and the sanctification without which no man shall see the Lord: looking carefully *lest* there be any man that falleth short of the grace of God; *lest* any root of bitterness springing up trouble you, and thereby the many be defiled; *lest* there be any fornicator, or profane person, as Esau, who for one mess of meat sold his own birthright."

These three warnings occur in that part of the letter which has to do peculiarly with the ultimate victory of God. In the eleventh chapter we pass through the hall of the heroes and heroines of faith in the past; the last note is that which declares that the whole of them are not yet made perfect. Then in chapter twelve, we are brought face to face with our own experience in its relation to the ultimate victory of God.

The first warnings had to do with the revelation of the Father through the Son, and the notes were those of personal relationship; Lest we drift, Lest we fall away from the living God, Lest we become hardened, Lest we lose our rest. But now there is something more important than our rest, our heaven. It is God's glory which is in view, the joy that was set before the Christ. We are responsible about that.

"Lest there be any man that falleth short of the grace of God." Falling short of the grace of God means being unable to run the race, or to coöperate with God in the work that makes His Kingdom come.

"Lest any root of bitterness, springing up . . . the many be defiled" and therefore cannot run the race.

Lest there be a profane person who will turn his back upon the high, supernal glory of God for some mess of earthly pottage, and so fail to coöperate towards the consummation.

These warnings do touch personal salvation, but that is not the ultimate meaning of them. If we fail, we fail to coöperate with God for the bringing in of His Kingdom and His glory. Falling short of grace is falling short of life; the root of bitterness is falling short of love; the profane person is falling short of light. If we fall short of life, of love, and of light, we cannot run this race and be fellow-workers with God. These three warnings then have ultimately to do, not with the matter of personal salvation, but with the matter of our fitness for coöperation with God in order to the winning of His victory in the world. Thus, warnings greet us at the beginning of the letter, and confront us at its close.

The appeal of this letter is also one full of encouragement, and the notes are introduced by the words: "Let us." They fall into three groups; words intended to encourage us in our relation to the Son through Whom the final speech has been uttered; words to encourage us as to our own saintship; and words to encourage us in our service.

Those referring to the Son touch upon His threefold work as Prophet, Priest, and King.

The first two are;

"Let us fear therefore.

"Let us therefore give diligence."

We are to fear lest the promise being made we

do not enter in. We are to be diligent "that no man fall after the same example of disobedience." Both these words of encouragement have to do with the prophetic work of Christ, the teaching of Christ. "The word of God is living, and active, and sharper than any two-edged sword, and piercing even to the dividing of soul and spirit." Let us fear lest we fail of the promise made in the Word, and let us be diligent in order that there be no disobedience to the Word.

The next two are;

"Having then a great high Priest, Who hath passed through the heavens, Jesus the Son of God, let us hold fast our confession."

"Let us therefore draw near with boldness unto the throne of grace, that we may receive mercy, and may find grace to help us in time of need."

These words have to do with the priestly work of the Son, and need no exposition.

The last word is;

"Wherefore let us cease to speak of the first principles of Christ, and press on unto perfection."

That is a picture of the ultimate victory of the King, Who will build the city, and establish the Kingdom; and towards that victory we are to press on.

Then we come to words of encouragement concerning our saintship;

"Let us draw near with a true heart in fullness of faith, having our hearts sprinkled from an evil conscience, and our body washed with pure water:

"Let us hold fast the confession of our hope that it waver not; for He is faithful that promised:

"Let us consider one another to provoke unto love and good works."

As in the first group of five words we have encouragement as to the Son as Prophet, Priest, and King; here we have words of encouragement as to the experience of saintship in the present life, and they again need no exposition.

Finally, we have words of encouragement in our service;

"Let us also, seeing we are compassed about with so great a cloud of witnesses, lay aside every weight, and the sin which doth so easily beset us;

"Let us run with patience the race that is set before us."

"Let us have grace."

In order to coöperate in the work which will

eventuate in the victory we are to lay aside all that hinders, run with patience, and have grace.

"Let us therefore go forth unto Him without the camp, bearing His reproach. . . . Let us offer up a sacrifice of praise to God continually."

In such service we are to have fellowship with Him in suffering; and fellowship in praise.

The teaching of this letter assumes the Biblical conception of God. Its first note is that of His universal sovereignty. The God of the Bible is not a Being within the universe, enslaved by it. He is Sovereign. The God of the Bible moreover is knowable and revealing. He spake in times past; He has spoken in His Son. If we deny these things we shall of course find no teaching in the letter to the Hebrews. There can be no meaning in it, apart from these fundamental conceptions of God.

Again, the teaching depends upon the Christology of the writer. We have it set before us in the early part of the letter. There is a sevenfold description of Christ, leaving no question as to the position He occupied in the mind of the writer. To deny the Christology of the writer is to deny his appeals. If our Christ is not the

Christ of this writer; He is not superior to angels, to Moses, to Joshua, to Aaron, to all that magnificent ritualism which the writer knew so well.

If this letter is to be of any value to us in the Christian Church, we must be true to its conceptions of God and its presentation of Christ.

To the individual, the word of application is that of its teaching as to the power of faith, and the peril of apostasy.

THE MESSAGE OF JAMES

A THE ESSENTIAL MESSAGE	B THE APPLICATION

I. The Central Teaching
i. Positive. Faith in God produces Life according to the Will of God.
  a. Personal Life.
    1. In Trial. Patience.
    2. In Enticement. Steadfastness.
    3. In Religion. Love.
  b. Relative Life.
    1. In Thought. No Respect of Persons.
    2. In Speech. The Silence of heavenly Wisdom.
    3. In Action. Peace.
ii. Negative. Life contrary to the Will of God denies Faith in God.
  a. Personal Life.
    1. In Trial. Storm-tossed.
    2. In Enticement. Drawn away.
    3. In Religion. Unbridled.
  b. Relative Life.
    1. In Thought. Respect of Persons.
    2. In Speech. Set on Fire of Hell.
    3. In Action. Strife.
 	
II. The Abiding Appeal
i. Prove your Faith.
  a. Venture on it.
  b. Vindicate it.
ii. Perfect your Patience.
  a. It comes by proving Faith.
  b. It issues in perfect Life.
	I. Individual
	i. The Life of Faith is a Life of Peril.
	  a. It challenges the Spirit of the Age.
	  b. It denies the Call of the Flesh.
	  c. It provokes the Enmity of the Devil.
	ii. The Life of Faith is the Life of Power.
	  a. It is superior to the Spirit of the Age.
	  b. It triumphs over the Claim of the Flesh.
	  c. It causes the Devil to flee.
	iii. Life lacking these Signs is not the Life of Faith.
	
	II. Church
	i. In the Assembly Faith kills Class Distinctions.
	ii. In the Assembly Faith makes Strife impossible.
	iii. In the Assembly Faith is the Principle of Communion.

THE MESSAGE OF JAMES

IN dealing with the content of this letter we indicated its theme by suggesting as a subtitle, Christ and His Ethic. Its burden is ethical, not doctrinal. Some of the fundamental truths of our most holy religion are hardly referred to from beginning to end. The writer was preëminently occupied with the practice of Christianity.

There are many parallelisms between the Manifesto of Jesus and this letter of James. Let us recall three passages in that Manifesto (Matthew v. 20; v. 48; vi. 1);

"I say unto you, that except your righteousness shall exceed the righteousness of the scribes and Pharisees, ye shall in no wise enter into the Kingdom of heaven."

"Ye therefore shall be perfect, as your heavenly Father is perfect."

"Take heed that ye do not your righteousness before men, to be seen of them: else ye have no reward with your Father which is in heaven."

I have taken these three because in some senses they are inclusive. In the first one, by way of introduction our Lord uttered the fundamental demand of His ethic; "Except your righteousness shall exceed the righteousness of the scribes and Pharisees, ye shall in no wise enter into the Kingdom of heaven." These words were spoken immediately before the actual enunciation of His laws.

In the second the King revealed the ultimate aim of His ethic; "Ye therefore shall be perfect, as your heavenly Father is perfect."

Immediately following we have the King's revelation of the abiding principle of His ethic; "Take heed that ye do not your righteousness before men, to be seen of them."

The fundamental demand was for righteousness exceeding the righteousness of the scribes and Pharisees, which was intellectually orthodox, but lacked the harmony of the corresponding life.

The ultimate aim was that of the perfecting of humanity in harmony with the character of God.

The abiding principle was that of doing everything as in the sight of God, and to be pleasing to Him, rather than in the sight of men, to be pleasing to them. In these three words then we have the master principle of the ethic of Jesus.

For the purpose of the present study and by way of introduction let us give a little closer attention to the word revealing the ultimate aim; "Ye therefore shall be perfect, as your heavenly Father is perfect." With that in mind we turn at once to the letter of James, and within the first few sentences we find these words, "Let patience have its perfect work, that ye may be perfect and entire, lacking in nothing." The interpretation of the perfection which James enjoined must be discovered by an understanding of the perfection which Jesus demanded.

Before uttering His laws, Jesus had said that righteousness must exceed the righteousness of the scribes and Pharisees. Righteousness is not to be a thing of words, but of works; not of creed, but of conduct; not orthodoxy of doctrine, but fulfillment of duty. Perfection is righteousness according to the will of God, rather than according to the opinion of men.

That perfection, the perfection of righteousness which seeks to be pleasing to God, and makes that the one unending, unceasing, unbending aim of the life, can only result from faith in God. So that the root of righteousness is faith, and the fruit of faith is righteousness. That takes us back to that central enunciation of the master principle of life in the prophecy of Habakkuk, "The just shall live by his faith." That word of Habakkuk reappears constantly in the teaching of Jesus. He consistently linked life to belief. One supreme illustration is found in a word recorded in the third chapter of John, "He that believeth on the Son hath eternal life." We must not be narrow in our interpretation of that great word. It has to do most certainly with the initial fact that a man believing on Jesus receives the gift of life; but it has a much wider application. Life is the outcome of faith. "The just shall live by his faith," both as to the beginning, and as to the continued victories and manifestations. The proof of a man's belief in Christ is the manifestation of the Christ-life in that man's life.

Paul argued for the same principle and always in relation to Christ Himself. In Galatians he declared that there is no righteousness by law, and quoted the word of Habakkuk. In Romans he put the declaration into close connection with faith in the gospel of the Son of God. In

THE MESSAGE OF JAMES 127

Hebrews, he—or some one else—put the same quotation in relation to the second Advent of our Lord.

That principle is recognized by James. It was stated to the prophet; the fulfillment of it was claimed by Christ in His own Person; it was argued by the great apologist of the gospel, Paul; it was illustrated by James. The theme of James was preëminently that of faith producing works. James did not argue against faith; he argued for faith.

Recognizing this fact we turn to consider the essential message of the letter, and find that its central teaching has a positive and a negative emphasis. The positive teaching may be summarized thus; Faith in God produces life according to the will of God; while the negative teaching is that life contrary to the will of God denies faith in God.

It may appear at first sight that the teaching of this letter is entirely negative, but the negative is only of value as we discover the positive behind it. It may be said that the negative is really the central teaching; if a man say he has faith, let him show it by his works; life contrary to the will of God denies faith in God; if a man shall say he has faith, and his life is not life that springs out of faith, then his affirmation of faith is false. But it is at once evident that such a negative statement implies a positive truth. Consequently we have in this letter quite as surely the positive teaching that faith in God produces life according to the will of God.

The abiding appeal of the letter is twofold; first, prove your faith; secondly, perfect your patience. The two injunctions are intimately associated.

There is an application of the letter; first to the individual, and secondly to the Church.

Familiarity with the movement of the letter, with its content and line of argument, will show how James first of all declared that faith in God produces life according to the will of God; and that in two respects. He gave those to whom he wrote two pictures, one of personal life, and one of relative life; and in each case he illustrated the fact that where there is faith in God, the life harmonizes with the will of God, insisting that it must do so, that there can be no escape.

His first picture is one of individual life in circumstances of trial. He shows that where a man lives by faith in such circumstances his attitude is that of patience. Faith produces patience in trial. His next picture is one of individual life in the midst of enticement to evil. In such circumstances the man living by faith remains steadfast, and is victorious over every temptation. His final picture is one of individual life in the matter of religion. When there is faith in God, " Pure religion and undefiled before our God and Father is this, to visit the fatherless and widows in their affliction, and to keep himself unspotted from the world "; that is to say, religion is love. The one and only principle which enables a man to live this life harmonizing with the will of God is faith in God.

When a man of faith is in the midst of circumstances of trial and difficulty, his attitude is that of calm patience. We know how true this is when we test the matter by personal experience. When the child of God in circumstances of trial is impatient, it is always because confidence in God wavers. Faith failing, patience passes away. Christian souls living by faith in God in the midst of circumstances of trial are not callous, not hardened. They are conscious of the sweeping of the storm ; but they are filled with quietness and patience. Faith in God is the only principle which can produce that patience in the soul of any man or woman in circumstances of trial.

In dealing with the subject of enticement to evil, James gives us a wonderful definition of the genesis of sin. No man is lured towards evil by God. A man is drawn away, enticed of his own lust. By faith in God there is steadfastness, and refusal to answer the enticement. There is no other secret of victory over temptation to sin than that of faith in God. No man is safe to-day by reason of the fact that for ten, twenty, thirty, forty years he has been a Christian. Men are not safe one moment longer than they live by simple faith in God. It is perfect faith in God which gives perfect victory over enticement towards sin.

So also in the matter of the life of religion in the truest, deepest sense of the word. There is no more wonderful definition of religion in the New Testament than this; and it is only faith in God which inspires a man to give expression to his religion in acts of love and sympathy. Destroy faith in God, and by that act you destroy love towards man.

THE MESSAGE OF JAMES 131

With regard to relative life, James shows what faith does for a man in these respects ; in thought, in speech, in action.

In thought, by faith in God a man ceases to be a respecter of persons. As he looks upon his fellow men, if he have faith in God, he sees these men as they are related to God, and thus loses sight of the things that the man who lacks faith in God sees. If a man has no faith in God he is material in his outlook upon his fellow men, and expresses it by differentiating between rich and poor. The man who lives by faith in God sees every man as related to God. I have sometimes said in speaking of our Lord that which is not literally true, but which is true in spirit; that Jesus looked upon scribes and Pharisees and never saw their phylacteries ; and looked at poor men and never saw their rags. That is not literally true, for He saw everything ; but it is spiritually true that His mind was not affected by the incidentals, but by the essentials. We divide as between men, and hold them in differing approbation on the basis of the incidentals. By faith in God every man is seen to be a man. The thought of every man as to his fellow man is determined by his faith in God, or his lack of such faith. Faith in God creates that attitude of mind towards our fellow men which may be described as having no respect of persons. "There is no respect of persons with God." The man who is living by faith shares the Divine attitude of mind towards men; he is without respect of persons.

As to speech, we must look for the positive carefully. James is emphatic about the negative, the evil of the tongue. The paragraph which immediately follows is one that speaks of the heavenly wisdom that will not lie. The speech of the man who lives by faith in God is characterized by the silence of heavenly wisdom. Faith in God makes more for silence than for speech about our fellow men.

As to action; faith in God brings peace as between man and man. Wars, strifes, enmities, these are never the outcome of faith in God. War in any kind never results from faith in God. When we come to the individual aspect, it is certain that strife as between man and man cannot be the outcome of faith in God.

The life of faith in God is a life that has no respect for persons; and is characterized by that carefulness in speech which is most often mani-

THE MESSAGE OF JAMES 133

fested in the silence of heavenly wisdom, and by those activities which produce peace between man and man. That constitutes the positive teaching of this letter.

We turn now to the negative. Life contrary to the will of God denies faith in God.

Personal life in trial is storm-tossed, like the waves of the sea; and such experience is proof of lack of faith in God. I say it very carefully because I know how it searches the heart, and yet I know it is true. When in hours of trial and suffering we murmur and complain, it is because we are failing in faith.

In the matter of enticement towards evil, a man is drawn away of his own lust, and enticed. If he yield, it is because he fails in faith towards God. It is a searching, practical word. We cannot attend to the message of this letter without feeling how very practical it is. Whenever we sin it is because our faith fails. Discussions as to whether it is necessary for the believer to sin or not are surely unnecessary. Whenever we listen to the clamant cry of lust, and answer it independently of the Divine will, it is because we fight in our own strength; but it is finally because we fail to trust in God. No man need be overcome by enticement towards evil, if he live by faith in God.

In regard to religion, one illustration is sufficient, that of the unbridled tongue. That is the expression of an attitude of mind which is the opposite of love. Whenever the tongue is unbridled, untamed, unmanaged, there is evidence of lack of faith in God.

The negative teaching concerning relative life is equally clear. Where there is no faith in God there is respect of persons. If we show a man into a back seat in the church because he wears shabby clothes, we are saying by that action that we have lost faith in God. We have no business to know whether he has on goodly apparel or not. It is quite as possible to have respect of persons in the opposite direction, as in the one which we most often condemn. It is as possible to hold in contempt the man who is well dressed as to hold in contempt the man in rags. Faith in God does not see the incidentals. It is always conscious of the essentials.

In speech, lack of faith means the tongue set on fire of hell. Is there a more startling and awful word than that in the whole of Scripture? A tongue set on fire of hell is the result of lack of faith in God. Where there is faith in God there is the silence of heavenly wisdom. Where it is lacking the tongue is set on fire of hell. It is almost impossible to read this word without feeling that James had in mind the symbol of the tongue of fire. Speech is always inspired in hell or in heaven. It is always the expression of heavenly wisdom or an utterance inspired of hell. When the tongue is used to say things that are contrary to love and truth, it is because there is failure of faith in God. The master principle of true speech is that of faith in God.

As to action; wars, strifes, fightings, are all the outcome of fleshly lusts, all the result of the fact that the life is not governed by the principle of faith in God. The forces that overcome and spoil individual life, and relative life, are all the result of the absence of the master principle of faith in God.

The abiding appeal of this letter is first, Prove your faith. "Count it all joy, my brethren, when ye fall into manifold temptations; knowing that the proof of your faith worketh patience. And let patience have its perfect work, that ye may be perfect and entire, lacking in nothing." In this connection, prove your faith means venture on it, put it to the test. So to prove faith is to vindicate it. Vindicate your faith by venturing on it. When you venture on it, it immediately produces a definite result, and that result proves, or demonstrates, your faith.

A man says, I have faith. Let him prove it. How shall he prove it? By argument? No, by venturing on it, by doing the things that are in harmony with faith in God. If a man says that he has faith, and does not venture on it, then no results are produced. If he do not thus prove it, he cannot prove it at all. If he do not put this principle of faith into active proof, he cannot demonstrate the fact that he has faith; he rather demonstrates the fact that he lacks faith. As we pass through this letter and read the things that are denounced as evil things, and then look at our own lives, and find these things existing, we know that the measure in which these things are present is the measure of our lack of faith. On the other hand the measure in which life perfectly harmonizing with the will of God is manifest in conduct, is the measure in which we are proving that we have faith. We prove the faith we have, and so we prove that we have faith. A man says, I have faith. I have no right to deny it;

but I have the right to say: Prove your faith, put it to the test; live by faith homed in God, aiming at the perfection upon which the heart of God is set, and expect that by your faith in Him He will coöperate with you in that activity. He always does. In every victory won by faith there is the evidence of faith.

The second note of the appeal is, Perfect your patience. Patience comes by proving faith; and patience issues in perfect life. "Let patience have its perfect work, that ye may be perfect and entire." Notice the process. Faith is first. I believe the thing that God says. I will prove my faith by venturing on it, and doing the thing I could not do without it. In that deed I prove my faith to another man. In that victory won, patience fills my soul, I come to quietness and strength. When that patience, which is the outcome of faith, has completed its process, I shall be "perfect and entire, lacking in nothing."

Thus it is clear that James was not arguing against faith; he was arguing for it. He revealed the fact that faith is the one and only principle that is equal to that perfection of life, upon which the heart of the Lord is set.

The application of this letter to the individual is twofold. It teaches me first that the life of faith is a life of peril ; and secondly, that the life of faith is a life of power.

The life of faith is a life of peril. We cannot live the life of faith in God without being immediately in great peril.

The life of faith challenges the spirit of the age. The spirit of the age is not in favour of faith ; it never has been, it is not to-day. The spirit of the age is the spirit of life by sight, by wit, by wisdom, and by human cleverness. To live the life of faith is immediately to challenge the spirit of the age.

The life of faith denies the call of the flesh. The moment we begin the life of faith in God, we begin where Christ said we must, "If any man would come after Me, let him deny himself."

The life of faith provokes the enmity of the devil, because the life of faith is the only life that challenges the empire of sin. When a man begins to live by faith he inevitably therefore provokes the enmity of the devil. That is why the young Christian so often asks, How is it that since I gave myself to Christ I have been tempted as I have never been tempted before?

THE MESSAGE OF JAMES 139

Immediately a man is regenerated he becomes the object of the attack of all spiritual antagonisms. The life of faith is not a soft, dilettante life in which we sing hymns all the time. It is a life of conflict, demanding heroism and courage and definiteness. It is a life of peril.

> "They climbed the steep ascent to heaven,
> Through peril, toil and pain,"

is always true of the saints.

But the life of faith is a life of power. If it challenge the spirit of the age, it is superior to the spirit of the age.

If the life of faith denies the call of the flesh, it triumphs over the claim of the flesh.

If the life of faith provokes the enmity of the devil, it causes the devil to flee. "Resist the devil, and he will flee from you." There is no other way in which you can compel him to flee.

Wherever a man is living by faith he is living the life of power. I suppose one would have to argue that in the case of many a man. Some one is saying, This is all theory. No, it is more; it is experience. For that simple faith in God that obeys and ventures I am not an advocate merely. As a witness I declare that I have, and can, and do, overcome where else I were overcome. The life of faith is a life of peril; but it is also a life of power.

The last word is an application of this teaching to the Church.

In the assembly of the saints faith kills class distinctions. A community of men and women living by faith in God is at the end of the distinctions which are of the world, the flesh, and the devil. Let every church then test its faith not by recitation of its creed, but by that inner atmosphere of true communism and fellowship. The life of faith destroys all class distinctions.

In the assembly of the saints faith makes strife impossible. In that aspect of the assembly which is local, or in that which is catholic, where there is strife there is lack of faith in God.

In the assembly of the saints faith is the principle of communion. If we would correct the things of difference and hatred that are amongst us, we need to say to our Lord and Master what one said to Him of old, "Lord, I believe; help Thou mine unbelief."

THE MESSAGE OF I. PETER

A THE ESSENTIAL MESSAGE	B THE APPLICATION
I. The Central Teaching. The Sufficiency of Grace i. The Fountain and the River. i, 2. 　　{ Grace, interpreted by i. 1. 　　{ Multiplied, interpreted by the Letter. ii. The Secret of Confidence. 　　{ Foretold by Prophets. i. 10. 　　{ Supplied by the Advents. i. 13. iii. The Secret of Conduct. 　　{ Servants. ii. 19, 20.　{ Enduring wrong. 　　{ 　　　　　　　　　　{ Enduring patiently. 　　{ Husbands and Wives. iii. 7. Joint Heirs. iv. The Secret of Character. 　　{ The Resource for Communion. iv. 10. 　　{ The Crown of Humility. v. 5. v. The Secret of Courage. The Guarantee of God. v. 10. vi. Emmanuel's Land. This is the true Grace of Glory. v. 12. **II. The Abiding Appeal. "Stand ye fast therein"** i. The inclusive Thought. 　　In the Country watered by the River. Cf. i. 2, v. 12. ii. The Application. 　　When Faith is tried. 　　When Circumstances are difficult. 　　When Suffering for Conscience' Sake. 　　When assaulted by the Adversary.	**I. To the Individual** "For you . . . is the Precious- ness." ii. 7. **II. To the Church** "Ye are . . . the Excellencies of Him." ii. 9.

THE MESSAGE OF I. PETER

THE final paragraph of the first letter of Peter is one of salutation, but in the midst of it occurs this statement: "I have written unto you, briefly, exhorting, and testifying, that this is the true grace of God; stand ye fast therein." This closing affirmation of the writer, inserted parenthetically, startles, demands attention, and compels a consideration of the message in the light of what it says.

In these words the apostle first described his method: "I have written unto you, briefly, *exhorting* and *testifying*." The word translated "exhorting" suggests all the qualities of the ministry of the Holy Spirit, coming from the same root and having the same values as the word Paraclete. In the word translated "testifying," we find the same values as in the word of Jesus describing the work of His disciples, *witnessing;* and the root from which the word comes is the same as that from which our word martyr is derived. The methods of the apostle then were those of *exhortation*, that is such teaching as was for instruction and encouragement; and *testimony*, that is, witness out of personal experience.

Then he declared his theme, "That this is the true grace of God." That is to say, the real subject of all his exhortation and testimony was the grace of God.

Finally, he made his last appeal in the words "Stand ye fast therein"; that is in the grace of God, which had been the theme of his exhortation and testimony.

The central teaching of the letter then is that of the sufficiency of grace; while its abiding appeal is that we stand fast therein.

Now it must be admitted that this is a startling statement, for at first it does not seem that the grace of God has been the definite, specific theme of the letter. Let us therefore first read a selection of passages;

"According to the foreknowledge of God the Father, in sanctification of the Spirit, unto obedience and sprinkling of the blood of Jesus Christ; *Grace* to you and peace be multiplied" (i. 2).

"Concerning which salvation the prophets sought and searched diligently, who prophesied of the *grace* that should come unto you" (i. 10).

"Wherefore girding up the loins of your mind, be sober and set your hope perfectly on the *grace* that is to be brought unto you at the revelation of Jesus Christ" (i. 13).

Thus in the first chapter this great word *grace* occurs three times.

"For this is *acceptable*, if for conscience towards God a man endureth griefs, suffering wrongfully. For what glory is it, if, when ye sin, and are buffeted for it, ye shall take it patiently? but if, when ye do well, and suffer for it, ye shall take it patiently, this is *acceptable* with God" (ii. 19, 20).

In these verses we must substitute "*grace*" for "acceptable"; and thus we find it twice in the second chapter,

"Ye husbands, in like manner, dwell with your wives according to knowledge, giving honour unto the woman, as unto the weaker vessel, as being also joint-heirs of the *grace* of life" (iii. 7).

"According as each hath received a gift, ministering it among yourselves as good stewards of the manifold *grace* of God" (iv. 10).

Thus we find the word once both in chapter three and chapter four.

"Likewise, ye younger, be subject unto the elder. Yea, all of you gird yourselves with humility, to serve one another: for God resisteth the proud, but giveth *grace* to the humble" (v. 5).

"And the God of all *grace*, Who called you unto His eternal glory in Christ, after that ye have suffered a little while, shall Himself perfect, stablish, strengthen you" (v. 10).

"This is the true *grace* of God: stand ye fast therein" (v. 12).

Thus we find it three times in chapter five.

That very simple exercise at least reveals the fact that the word is found in every chapter of the letter.

In considering the content of this letter, we found that the thought is ever that of the establishment of Christian people, and the word grace is in every division. The first great statement of the letter is the expression of desire, "Grace to you and peace be multiplied"; the final declaration of the apostle is, "I have written unto you briefly, exhorting, and testifying that this is the true grace of God: stand ye fast therein"; and in every division the word appears not by some studied arrangement, but incidentally, naturally; it is the central word of the argument, and the appeal finds in it its value and force.

It is also remarkable that in every case the word grace occurs, not in the earlier part of the division dealing with doctrine, but in the application.

There is first the introduction, in which the writer introduced himself as the apostle, and described his readers as elect; but it was when he came to the explanation of the word elect, and breathed the desire of his heart that these people might come to practical experience of what it is to be elect, that he said "Grace to you and peace be multiplied."

The second occurrence is in the latter part of the first division; not in that section describing the life of faith, the statement of doctrine; but in that section in which doctrine is related to duty.

So also in the second division, the word is found; not in the first part dealing with the doctrine of holiness, but in the section dealing with the practice of holiness.

In the third division, the word occurs, not in the part dealing with the theory of victory, but in that showing the process of victory.

So also in the last case; not when the apostle was describing the life of conflict or the fellowship of conflict, but when he wanted men to understand the secret of strength for that conflict did he use the word.

All that may seem technical. It does, however, help us to realize that throughout the letter the fact of the grace of God was present to the mind of the writer; and it serves to explain his concluding word, "This is the true grace of God."

As we saw in studying the content, the main purpose of the letter is that of the establishment of such as were passing through suffering and difficulty and testing. The writer established his brethren by showing that all that was needed for strength was provided in the grace of God. Indeed, I should be inclined to say that, if we want a perfectly accurate sub-title for the message of this letter, we may quote from Paul, "My grace is sufficient for thee." That, as I understand it, is the living message of this letter.

In the essential message then the central teaching is that of the sufficiency of grace. That we may divide into six parts suggested by the passages to which we have referred.

First, The Fountain and the River. i. 2.

Secondly, The Secret of Confidence. i. 10, 13.

Thirdly, The Secret of Conduct. ii. 19, 20; iii. 7.

Fourthly, The Secret of Character. iv. 10; v. 5.

Fifthly, The Secret of Courage. v. 10.

Sixthly, Emmanuel's Land. v. 12.

The waters of the river, to quote the figurative language of Ezekiel, come by the way of the altar; that is the river of the living grace, the river of which Ezekiel declared, everything lives whithersoever it comes.

> "Grace is flowing like a river,
>   Millions there have been supplied,
>   Still it flows as full as ever
>   From the Saviour's wounded side."

Go farther back than that, and we find that the river proceeds from the very heart of God. "Grace unto you and peace be multiplied." "This is the true grace of God."

The central teaching of this letter is that of the sufficiency of grace. It opens not by a doctrinal statement or by argument; but with a great expression of the apostolic desire for those to whom he wrote, "Grace unto you and peace be multiplied."

Then it proceeds to show how forevermore grace is the secret of maintained confidence, the secret of triumphant conduct, the secret of holy character, the secret of victorious courage. It is grace the whole way through, until at last the apostle wrote, "I have written unto you, briefly, exhorting, and testifying that this is the true grace of God. All that experience, the true Christian experience of triumph, is the experience of the Christian in Emmanuel's land. Do not forget that this is Emmanuel's land. Do not postpone Emmanuel's land to heaven; we are already in Emmanuel's land by grace;

> "I've reached the land of corn and wine,
> And all its riches freely mine;
> Here shines undimm'd one blissful day,
> For all my night has passed away."

Only the man who lives in the land fertilized by the rivers of grace can sing that hymn, and understand its meaning.

In the opening passage the word "grace" must be interpreted by that which immediately precedes it. "To the elect . . . according to the foreknowledge of God the Father, in sanctification of the Spirit, unto obedience and sprinkling of the blood of Jesus Christ." In those words we see the great fundamental verities of our faith homed in the being of that one triune God who is Himself Father, Son, and Spirit. We must interpret "grace " by these phrases, and by these doctrines of the faith. "Grace unto you and peace be multiplied."

Recognizing the source whence this river springs, we see how it is the secret of confidence. Take the whole passage in the first chapter and let me summarize it thus. There are two things to notice in the operation of grace. First; it was foretold by the prophets, "Concerning which salvation the prophets sought and searched diligently." Secondly; it is supplied through the Advents of Jesus, "Set your hope perfectly on the grace that is to be brought unto you at the revelation of Jesus Christ." What were the prophets looking for? They were searching what time or what manner of time the Spirit testified when it testified the suffering of Christ and the glory which should follow; these are matters into which the very angels desire to look. The prophets foretold that grace. For the interpretation of that fact we need the four, and the twelve. Their theme was ever that of grace which was to come. It came by the suffering of Jesus, and assures the glories that follow His suffering, those glories which will have their full outshining at His revelation. The two Advents are in view. Thus Peter shows that our secret of confidence is the certainty of that grace to which all the prophets bore testimony, and which became operative in human history and life through the work of Christ.

It is also the secret of conduct. This is illustrated in the simplest relation. In all the apostolic writings, the most radiant, beautiful things of the Christian life are spoken of as being exhibited where the world would be least likely to look for them. The grace, that is the glories and beauties flowing out as the result of this life communicated by Christ, is most radiantly revealed in the most trying and difficult circumstances. Servants, if you endure wrong patiently, this is grace. Conduct can have its most beautiful manifestation of the power of this grace in circumstances the most trying and most difficult. Conduct can be manifested most perfectly and beautifully, as Paul suggests, by that most sacred union between husband and wife, the most perfect revelation of the union between Jehovah and all trusting souls; for we are "joint-heirs of the grace of life"; and in the power of that grace we are to meet all the difficulties of every-day life, that our prayers be not cut off, or hindered. Servants whose masters are ungodly and unjust have a great opportunity to reveal the grace of God. That is the point you miss if we read "acceptable with God," when the word is the same, and we should read "This is grace with God." If to-day in some house of business, for Christ's sake men and women have suffered wrongfully, and patiently; God has there plucked the fairest flowers that have blossomed in London. This is grace with God. The commonplaces of home-life may be sanctified, glorified, and made to flame with the beauties of the grace of God. This is the true grace of God.

Yet again, grace is the secret of character.

Peter urged those to whom he wrote to use "hospitality one to another without murmuring, according as each hath received a gift ministering it among yourselves, as good stewards of the manifold grace of God." What a strange and wonderful merging of the commonplace and the sublime according to the measurements of men. Hospitality, and the ministry of the Word in the assembly of the saints! The grace of God is the secret of such character. Or again, " All of you gird yourselves with humility, to serve one another : for God resisteth the proud, but giveth grace to the humble." Grace is not only the source of hospitality and communion, it is the ground of humility. These are the things of high character. The Christian character is revealed in beauty in these commonplaces of life. What is at once the inspiration of character that is filled with hospitality and with love ; and the ultimate crown of beauty upon that character ? The humility that girds itself for service. The Greek word there will bear translation by a phrase; Gird yourself as with a slave's apron of humility. Peter was surely thinking of the day when Jesus took a towel and girded Himself and washed the disciples' feet. He was remembering that the towel, the sign and badge of slavery, was made by Jesus the insignia of nobility in His Kingdom. The secret of such character is the grace of God.

Then we come to the question of conflict. " Your adversary the devil, as a roaring lion, walketh about, seeking whom he may devour. . . . The God of all grace, Who called you unto His eternal glory in Chist, after that ye have suffered a little while, shall Himself perfect, stablish, strengthen you." Grace in the conflict is the guarantee of the glory which will be perfect, and of final victory over the forces of evil that are against us.

The inclusive thought of the abiding appeal is that we are to live in the country watered by the river of grace, and that the apostle expressed in the charge "Stand ye fast therein."

Go over the four thoughts again. When faith is tried, remember that in grace there is perfect resource which being appropriated will make us strong in the Lord, and in the power of His might.

When faith is trembling, let us come into new understanding of the sufficiency of this grace of God, and faith will triumph.

When circumstances are difficult—and do not let us be afraid of the simplest illustrations—in the place of service which is not appreciated when it ought to be, in all the constant difficulties of the home, if we would manifest that conduct which is in harmony with the will of God, the resources are in grace. When we fail, it is because we neglect the grace of God.

When suffering for conscience' sake, being persecuted because we bear the Christian name, how shall we bear it, how shall we still manifest the Christian character? Only in the power of this grace.

When assaulted by the adversary who goeth about like a roaring lion seeking; how are we to overcome? Only by remembering that our God is the God of all grace; and that through suffering and the assault of the adversary, He will perfect that which concerneth us.

The abiding appeal I can venture to make in no other way than by using the great words, " For you therefore which believe is the preciousness." Link that very carefully with the teaching which goes before it; living stones coming to the living Stone, and the living Stone, " elect, precious." Then follows the declaration, " For you therefore which believe is the preciousness." When we come to Him He communicates to us those virtues which constitute His preciousness, and we become precious also. Preciousness is the result of having the elemental forces compacted together into consistent strength. Peter was an elemental man, lacking preciousness until Christ gave him His own nature, His own life; then he became precious. What is a precious stone? It is the embodiment of passion mastered by principle. That is the thought in the figurative language of one of the old prophets, "the stones of fire"; the diamond is a stone of fire; it is precious, solidified, mastered by principle. This is the great truth about grace. Grace communicates to us the preciousness of Christ; all that which in Him was precious to the heart of God, that which made Him the one supreme and lonely glory in the diadem of Deity, is made over to us.

If we take the individual stones that thus receive His preciousness, and build them into the whole assembly, what then? Then the description follows, "Ye are an elect race, a royal priesthood, a holy nation, a people for God's own possession, that ye may show forth the excellencies of Him Who called you out of darkness into His marvellous light." The preciousness of Christ being communicated to individuals, the whole company of such individuals will reveal the excellencies of God.

Grace is the secret of all establishment in

the Christian life. It is the river that flowing through the desert makes it blossom as the rose until it becomes Emmanuel's land.

> " All the rivers of Thy grace I claim.
> Over every promise write my name.
>
> .   .   .   .   .
>
> Grace there is my every debt to pay,
> Blood to wash my every sin away,
> Power to keep me spotless day by day."

"This is the true grace of God: stand ye fast therein."

THE MESSAGE OF II. PETER

A THE ESSENTIAL MESSAGE	B THE APPLICATION

I. The Central Teaching. Responsibilities of Grace
i. Resources creating Responsibility.
   a. The Power. i. 3.
      { 1. Things for Life according to His Glory.
      { 2. Things for Godliness according to His Virtue.
   b. The Coming. i. 4 and 11.
      { 1. The final Escape from Corruption.
      { 2. Entrance into the eternal Kingdom.
ii. Responsibilities created by Resource.
   a. Appropriation of the Resources.
      { 1. Remembrance.
      { 2. Response.
   b. Avoidance of the Perils.
      { 1. Test the Prophets.
      { 2. Holy Living and Godliness.
 	
II. The Abiding Appeal. Give Diligence
i. In Coöperation with the Power.   i. 5.
   a. Faith appropriating Power.
   b. Diligence developing Character.
ii. In View of the Coming.   iii. 14.
   a. Faith looking for the Coming.
   b. Diligence guarding Character.
	I. To the Individual
	i. Relation to the Power.
	   Remembrance in order to Diligence.
	ii. Relation to the Coming.
	   Anticipation in order to Realization.
	
	II. To the Church
	i. Her only Perils.
	   a. Denying the Master ii. 1.
	   b. Denying the Coming iii. 4.
	ii. The Inter-Relation of these.
	   To deny Him is to deny His Coming.
	iii. The Issue of these.
	   Near-sightedness.
	   Lust.
	   Destruction.

THE MESSAGE OF II. PETER

THE main purpose of this second letter, like that of the first, is the establishment of believers in their faith and in their life. Both were undoubtedly written in fulfillment of the charge of the Lord Jesus to Peter; "When once thou hast turned again, stablish thy brethren."

The first letter was written to "the elect who are sojourners of the Dispersion in Pontus, Galatia, Cappadocia, Asia, and Bithynia"; and the opening words of the third chapter of the second epistle lead us to believe that it was written to the same people. In each case the method is the same, although the apostle was dealing with different difficulties. In the former, he dealt with perils threatening the spiritual life of the Church from without. In this, he dealt with perils threatening the spiritual life of the individual believer from within.

There is a sense in which this second letter touches a deeper note than the first. Perhaps it would be more accurate to say that it has a more searching effect; its note is deeper, in the sense that it deals with us personally, individually, whereas the first presented to us in a more general way the great and sublime truth of the sufficiency of that grace wherein we stand. Grace is sufficient; that was the theme of the first letter. That is still the message; but now it is insisted on that grace is only sufficient as its laws are obeyed. No man has any right to say God's grace is sufficient to keep him if he is breaking the laws of grace, and so putting himself in peril. God's grace is not sufficient to keep a man from falling who is not obedient to the law of that grace, and to the revealed will of God. The first letter began "Grace to you and peace be multiplied," and ended "Stand ye fast therein." The second letter begins, "Grace to you and peace be multiplied," and ends "Grow in the grace." The same beginning in each case reminds us of the fountainhead and the flowing river. The final word of the first is, "Stand ye fast therein," that is, live in Emmanuel's land, watered and fertilized by this great flowing river of grace. The last word of the second letter is "Grow in the grace," that is, being in the land, appropriate its resources and grow. It is not enough to abide, to stand fast; there must also be growth. In the first epistle the burden is that of the sufficiency of grace, and the consequent first responsibility of standing fast. In the second letter the burden is that of the responsibility which the fact of being in grace creates.

This must be clear. The great burden of the first letter is the sufficiency of grace; grace in every time of need; ending with the one note indicating responsibility, "Stand ye fast therein." The burden of the second letter takes for granted the burden of the first, that grace is sufficient, and sets forth the responsibility that rests upon those who are in grace, revealing two grave perils forever threatening the life of those in grace. While its burden is that of responsibility, and while it ends with the note which insists upon responsibility, "Ye therefore . . . grow in the grace"; the thought of this last word is also that of sufficiency, as it really means, being in the grace, grow; you are in the grace, God has put you in His grace, you are in the land watered by the river of His grace, therefore grow.

Let us then consider the essential message of this second letter as to its central teaching; and as to its abiding appeal.

The central teaching has to do with the responsibilities of grace; first, the resource creating the responsibilities, and secondly the responsibilities created by that resource.

After the introduction in the first two verses, the apostle wrote: "Seeing that His divine power hath granted unto us all things that pertain unto life and godliness, through the knowledge of Him that called us by His own glory and virtue." An interpretation of this letter must be sought in the light of the mount of transfiguration. If that be borne in mind, this declaration immediately becomes full of meaning. The central thought is that of Divine power. This power grants us "all the things that pertain to life and godliness, through the knowledge of Him that called us by His own glory and virtue." Put the things of grace which are there referred to, "glory and virtue," against the things for which power is provided, "life and godliness," and it is at once seen that they are mutually explanatory. The Divine power being at our disposal, we have everything that is necessary for life, according to His glory; and for godliness, according to His virtue.

His glory these men had seen on the holy mount. What they saw was not the outshining of the Deity of our Lord, but the coming to final perfection of His humanity. Deity has never had that kind of outshining. Deity has no manifestation to the eyes of sense. When God hid Himself in flesh, then men saw God; the glory of Deity was revealed not in any splendour, but in the humanity of our Lord. That humanity came to its perfection on the holy mount. The story of the life of Jesus may be told thus; innocent in babyhood and childhood; holy in youth and manhood; coming to ultimate glory on the mount of transfiguration. There humanity was revealed at its highest and best.

It was glory, but it was also virtue; that is, it was not merely what life was in itself, inherently, in its perfection, but it was the fact that that life was filled with every excellency which made God declare, "This is My beloved Son, in Whom I am well pleased."

The word virtue here has not the meaning which it usually has when we make use of it. We recall the great passage in the first letter,

"Ye are . . . that ye may show forth the *excellencies*," "the praises," as the Authorized Version has it. The word excellencies or praises is exactly the same word as virtue. Virtue refers there to that in Him which was excellent, that in Him which satisfied the heart of God.

His Divine power has given us all that we need, in order that life may come to the pattern of that glory; and that godliness may be the realization of that virtue. These are the resources of His power.

Then there are the resources of His coming. These are also referred to in the first chapter; "Whereby He hath granted unto us His precious and exceeding great promises; that through these ye may become partakers of the Divine nature, having escaped from the corruption that is in the world by lust." "For thus shall be richly supplied unto you the entrance into the eternal Kingdom of our Lord and Saviour Jesus Christ." "The eternal Kingdom" is an arresting phrase, and this is the only occasion in the New Testament in which it is used. In this letter the subject of the Second Advent is not dealt with as it is in some of the other writings of the New Testament. The main thought of the

THE MESSAGE OF II. PETER 167

apostle is not that the Second Advent will mean the setting up of the Kingdom of God in this world, but that it will result in the perfecting of the saints. We should always draw a distinction between the Coming of the Lord and the Day of the Lord, that day of judgment ushering in the reign of righteousness. The apostle is here dealing with the value of the Coming to the saint. In that Coming we shall finally, perfectly escape from the corruption that is in the world by lust. In that Coming we shall enter into the age-abiding Kingdom of our Lord and Saviour Jesus Christ.

Here again is the resource provided for us in grace. If I stand in grace, I have power sufficient to conform my life to the perfect pattern of His life, so that it shall be well pleasing to God. If I stand in grace I stand in the light of the Parousia, the Presence, the Coming; which for the world will lead to His process of judgment establishing righteousness; but which for me, standing in grace, will be the hour when I finally escape from corruption. There is a sense in which every believer has already escaped in the economy and purpose of God; but in the hour of that Coming, that Advent at which scoffers are still scoffing, we shall finally escape from corruption. This corruptible must put on incorruption. Then shall be brought to pass the word that is written. That is the final outcome of our Christian life; and we lose a very great deal if we forget or neglect, as a part of the resources of grace, the presence or coming of our Lord.

What then are the responsibilities which these resources create? They can be expressed in two words; appropriation of the resources; and avoidance of the perils.

Two words will indicate the method of appropriation; first remembrance, and secondly, response. In proportion as we forget the beginning we are in danger of wandering from the pathway that leads to the end. It is an ill day in my Christian life when I do not remember my Lord's death, and that Cross from which I receive the benefit of my life. There is a great value in the Lord's command, "This do in remembrance of Me." When gathering about the table, one of our first responsibilities is that there we remember the beginning of our Christian life by His atonement; and we must keep our life day by day set in relation to these things, the first things.

But we are to remember not only the first things, but also the ultimate things. When I forget the ultimate, forget the Coming, then my life becomes careless. I am perfectly sure that Dr. Denny is right when he says in his volume on Thessalonians that the very bloom of the beauty of the Christian communion in the early days was that of their ever expecting the return of the Lord; and I believe he is perfectly right when he says that the measure in which the Church has lost that expectation is the measure in which the bloom of that beauty has been brushed from her character. By remembrance of these things, I appropriate them.

But infinitely more is needed. If I remember them only as an intellectual exercise, there is no value in that. I must respond to them. Remembering the Cross and what it means with regard to sin, I am to put sin away and yield myself to its inspiration for service. Remembering the Advent, His return, then "what manner of persons ought ye to be in all holy living and godliness, looking for and earnestly desiring the coming of the day of God?" So, resources are to be appropriated by remembrance and response.

That necessarily involves the second thought, avoidance of the perils. The solemnity and searching power of the second chapter are great. There is no pity in the heart of this man for false prophets; for very love of truth, there cannot be. He warns against the false prophets; and in the next chapter he charges them that they "remember the words which were spoken before by the holy prophets." How are we to avoid the perils? By remembering the truth, the messages of the prophets, of the Lord Himself, of the apostles. We are to test prophecy by the established prophecies of essential truth. We are to avoid the peril of evil living that grows out of listening to false prophets, by all holy living and godliness resulting from obedience to the holy prophets.

The abiding appeal of the letter is that we give diligence. This we do first by coöperation with the Power. "Adding on your part all diligence, in your faith supply virtue; and in your virtue knowledge; and in your knowledge temperance; and in your temperance patience; and in your patience godliness; and in your godliness love of the brethren; and in your love of the brethren love." First faith appropriates power; then diligence develops the character which is potentially taken hold of by faith. Faith is the first thing. Faith appropriates the Divine power. The Divine power has put all things at my disposal, and faith appropriates that power. That is not enough. I am to give diligence to supply. That process is described through the flowering of faith, until the fruit is reached, which is love. The figure is that of the opening flower. The root principle is faith taking hold of the resources of power; then we see the flower open; until we get at last to the fruit, love. If we want to know what love is, we leave Peter and go to Paul, "The fruit of the Spirit is love, joy, peace, long-suffering, kindness, goodness, faithfulness, meekness, temperance." In order to that development from faith to love, cultivation is needed; self-cultivation, and diligence withal. It is perfectly true we grow; and it is perfectly true that not by effort can we grow, not by taking thought can we add one cubit to our stature even spiritually; but it is equally true that we are to be diligent in adding, not adding to, as though we got from somewhere else a new quality; but bringing out the thing that is already there; reaching down into the Divine power until all the petals of the perfect flower are unfolded, and until the fruit itself is formed, which is love.

The appeal of the letter goes farther. We are to give diligence, not only to coöperate with power, but also in view of the Coming. "Seeing that ye look for these things, give diligence that ye may be found in peace, without spot and blameless in His sight." Just as we saw faith appropriating power, now we see faith looking for the Coming. It is faith and nothing else that looks for the Coming. The scoffers are always present, saying: "Where is the promise of His coming?" As things have been, so they will remain. Faith looks up, and expects the fulfillment of the sure word of prophecy. Faith is certain that what God has spoken He will do. Faith does not attempt to explain away the prophecies of the Old Testament as though they had happened, when most evidently they have not happened. Faith looks and expects, and affirms that though there be no flush of dawn to the eyes of sense, He is coming, and the day is coming in which the elements shall melt away with fervent heat.

I speak out of my own experience. Unless I

looked for that coming I would be of all men the most miserable, and the most hopeless. In this matter God is working as He always has worked, through processes leading to crises. Faith is looking for the coming, and it must give diligence that in the crisis we may be found in peace, without spot, and blameless in His sight.

That is the abiding appeal. Give diligence with regard to the power, to coöperate with it for the development of character. Give diligence with regard to the Coming, to look for it and to guard character so that at any moment— to quote from John for the illumination of Peter —we may not be ashamed from Him at His Coming.

The application of the letter to the individual is first that it reveals the law of relation to that Divine power which is at his disposal in Christ; remembrance in order to diligence, remembrance the inspiration of diligence. To forget is to become negligent; to remember is to be forever more diligent.

It also reveals the law of relation to the coming; anticipation in order to realization. If I really anticipate His coming, if I really live so that I may be ready when He comes—how the thought touches all life—if I really believe He may disturb me at my work, or worship, or play, then I shall work and worship and play so as not to be ashamed when He comes. If we have lost that, how much we have lost.

The application of this letter to the Church is first that it reveals her only perils. The first is that of denial of the Master. "There arose false prophets also among the people, as among you also there be false teachers, who shall privily bring in destructive heresies, denying even the Master that bought them, bringing upon themselves swift destruction." Denying the Master; His glory and His virtue, those essentials concerning Him which were revealed to Peter and the Church for all time upon the holy mount. Denying all that He is in Himself, denying that which was the central subject of the converse of the holy mount, the *exodos*, not death, but the fact that through death He would break a highway into life. The second peril is that of denying His coming; "In the last days mockers shall come with mockery, walking after their own lusts, and saying, Where is the promise of His coming? for, from the day that the fathers fell asleep, all things continue as they were from the beginning of the creation." When the Church joins in the mockery of the mocker, and denies the prophetic utterance of the Scriptures, and the definite declarations of the Lord and His apostles, then she is in peril, for to lose the sense of His coming is to lose the most powerful force and inspiration for holy living.

The inter-relation of these perils is manifest. To deny Him in any sense is to deny His coming. To deny Him by making Him merely a moral exemplar is to doubt the saving value of His death, and to deny His resurrection; and to deny the resurrection is to deny His Second Advent.

The issue of such denial is near-sightedness, seeing only the things that are near. This issues in lust. And lust brings forth death.

The note of the letter is one of great solemnity, I had almost said severity; but it is the severity of a great love and a great desire for the strengthening of believers. Let us ever hear its great words to us; In remembrance, give diligence. Grace is sufficient; but we must discover and obey its laws, or it is valueless.

THE MESSAGE OF THE LETTERS OF JOHN

A THE ESSENTIAL MESSAGE	B THE APPLICATION

I. The Central Teaching. The Life of Fellowship explained
 	
i. As to Resources.
   a. Objective. The Pattern provided.
      1. Of Light. The Sinless One. ii. 6.
      2. Of Love. "He loved us." iv. 10.
   b. Subjective. The Power provided.
      1. For Light. "Begotten we see." ii. 20, 27.
      2. For Love. Begotten we love. iv. 7.
ii. As to Realization.
   a. Its Value to us. The Fulfillment of Life.
      1. The perfected Being.
      2. The Friendship of God.
   b. Its Value to God. The Fulfillment of Purpose.
      1. Media of Manifestation.
      2. Instruments of Accomplishment.
	I. To the Individual
	
	Life must be tested by Light and Love.

II. The Abiding Appeal. The Responsibilities of Fellowship declared
 	
i. As to Light.
   a. Its Testing must be sought.
   b. Its Revelation must be obeyed.
ii. As to Love.
   a. Its Impulse must be yielded to.
   b. Its Holiness must be maintained.
	II. To the Church
	The Law of its Fellowship is that of Life expressed in Love tested by Light.
	"Believe not every spirit."
	"Look to yourselves."
	"Welcome such."

THE MESSAGE OF THE LETTERS OF JOHN

THE three letters of John are intimately related to each other. In the first we have teaching, and in the second and third, illustrations; but the message is one.

There is, moreover, a close relation between these letters and the Gospel according to John. Two statements, one in the Gospel, and one in the letters, in which the apostle declared the purpose of his writing in each case, reveal that relation.

The purpose for which the Gospel was written was that those reading it should believe that Jesus is the Christ, the Son of God, and that as a result of their belief, they might themselves enter into life. This the writer clearly declared in the words,

"These are written that ye may believe that Jesus is the Christ, the Son of God; and that believing ye may have life in His name" (John xx. 31).

The purpose for which the letters were written was that those reading them, having already believed on the name of the Son of God, might have the means whereby to find assurance of their possession of eternal life. This with equal clearness John declared in the words,

"These things have I written unto you, that ye may know that ye have eternal life, even unto you that believe on the name of the Son of God" (1 John v. 13).

In the Gospel, then, we have the unveiling of eternal life in its manifestation in the Son of God; and the revelation of the fact that this life is, through Him, placed at the disposal of men through the mystery of His death, and the victory of His resurrection. When we read the Gospel story, we know what eternal life really is, for it is clearly manifested in the Son of God; and further, we learn that we may share in that life by believing in His name. Thus the theme of the Gospel is that of eternal life; as it is revealed in the Son of God; and as the Son of God is able to communicate it to believing souls.

In the letters, the theme is still that of eternal life, only in these we see its manifestation in the children of God, that is, in those who through faith in the Son of God have received that life. So that the theme of the letters is that of eternal life, as it is revealed in the children of God, as they are under the mastery of the Son of God.

The theme of the Gospel and the letters is thus seen to be the same. It is that of age-abiding life, that is, life according to the will and purpose of God. In the Gospel we see one lonely figure, that of the Son of God, revealing and communicating eternal life. In the epistles we see the children of God, those whom the Son brings into this life, that is all such as believe on His name.

In the prologue of the Gospel, John wrote of the Son of God,

"In the beginning was the Word, and the Word was with God, and the Word was God. . . . And the Word became flesh, and dwelt among us . . . full of grace and truth" (John i. 1 and 14).

In the parenthesis of the fourteenth verse, John, in evident exultation of spirit, wrote,

"And we beheld His glory, glory as of the only begotten from the Father full of grace and truth," and in that brief and almost abrupt phrase, "full of grace and truth," he gave the distinguishing facts of the " glory."

When we turn to his letters, we find the same facts of grace and truth dominating his thought: the first of them illustrating the power of grace in the life of all those who believe in the Son of God, and the second and third insisting upon the importance of truth, by showing the necessity for loyalty thereto on the part of those who share the privileges of grace.

These letters, then, afford a teaching and a test. They teach us what eternal life is in the experience of the child of God; and they enable us therefore to test our life, and to know whether it is eternal life.

In dealing with the essential message we find that its central teaching is an explanation of the life of fellowship; while its abiding appeal is that of a declaration of the responsibilities of fellowship.

As we commence our reading of the first letter, the word *fellowship* is found, and it is the key-note of the three epistles, the master-thought of the writer being that eternal life is life in fellowship with God; we enter upon eternal life when we are brought into fellowship with God;

we continue in eternal life as we abide in fellowship with God.

The explanation of the life of fellowship falls into two parts, the first dealing with resources, and the second with realization.

The resources of the life of fellowship are objectively presented in the pattern provided in the Son of God; and subjectively received in the power provided when we are begotten children of God.

The pattern of eternal life is given in Christ, and the writer dealt with it in its twofold aspect of light and of love.

When dealing with the subject of light, the apostle wrote,

"He that saith he abideth in Him ought himself to walk even as that One walked" (1 John ii. 6).

It is evident from that literal translation that as John wrote, he had before his vision the Lord and Master Whom he knew so intimately. If we desire an accurate interpretation of the phrase, "that One," we must go back to the Gospel to find it, for there we see the One upon Whom John was looking in spirit, and by faith, when he wrote the words. In that Gospel the Son of

God is revealed, walking in light, and, therefore, as the sinless One, never consenting to darkness, never hiding from God, or attempting so to do; the One of Whom it was preëminently true that in His spirit there was no guile, no deceit. He is the pattern, therefore, of eternal life, as perfect conformity to light. In the measure in which we walk as He walked, we walk in light.

It must be remembered that this writing was for the children of God, that the Lord Jesus Christ is not presented as a pattern to men until they have yielded themselves to Him; for the perfection of His life is such that to present it as an ideal to be realized would be but to mock the impotence of unregenerate men. It is perfectly true that we may present Him as the great Ideal to men who have not yet received His gift of life; but in doing so we only succeed in discovering to them their inability to imitate the pattern, and so to reveal to them the necessity for the new birth. Having become His by the gift of life, we are called upon to live the life of fellowship with God, and our first resource is that of the pattern which He thus presents.

In dealing with the subject of love, the apostle wrote,

"Herein is love, not that we loved God, but that He loved us, and sent His Son to be the Propitiation for our sins" (1 John iv. 10).

In all the life of the Son of God thus sent by the Father there was a revelation of the attitude and activity of perfect love. No word ever passed His lips but that was love inspired. He wrought no deed but in answer to the demand of love. Thus in Him we see eternal life in the sinlessness of light, and the selflessness of love.

If, however, as we have already indicated, our resources in Christ are only objective, then we are left helpless indeed. The more carefully I contemplate the revelation of eternal life in Christ, the more impossible do I feel it to be to imitate the pattern given. Those who speak of imitating Jesus Christ, and seem to hope to realize the ideal in their own strength, have surely never seen Him in that marvellous wonder of perfect sinlessness and absolute love which John has presented to us in his Gospel. The pattern is not enough, and therefore in dealing with our resources, he shows that Christ is not merely objectively presented to us as from without, that we may gaze upon Him; but that by the communication of His own life to us He becomes a subjective, an actual power, working within our lives.

This is true both with regard to light and to love. The light only comes when comes the life, and the love only comes when comes the life. When a man is begotten of God, he sees, he becomes sensitive in the matter of sin, he knows exactly what he ought to do. Moreover, when a man is begotten of God, the first impulse of his new life is love, which drives him out upon the pathway of sacrificial service on behalf of other men.

The relation of life to light in the case of the children of God is revealed in two statements;

" Ye have an anointing from the Holy One, and ye know all things."

" And as for you, the anointing which ye received of Him abideth in you, and ye need not that any one teach you; but as His anointing teacheth you concerning all things, and is true, and is no lie, and even as it taught you, ye abide in Him " (1 John ii. 20 and 27).

While there are many values in these statements, for the purpose of our present meditation we may summarize their teaching in this respect by saying that the child of God is never left in doubt by God as to the thing which is sinful, and the thing which is right. That statement may be challenged, but let it be carefully pondered in the light of Christian experience. There are times when we may be tempted to argue with ourselves that we are not sure; but in the deepest fact of our life in Christ we always know. As we have received His life, that life is always light, and though there may be moments when on some threshold between light and darkness we waver and wonder, that very uncertainty does but demonstrate the necessity for fleeing the danger, and pressing back into the clear light. The man begotten of God sees, and if we are conscious of the loss of a keen sense of sin, we may know that our life is at a low ebb.

The relation of life to love in the case of the children of God is revealed in the words;

"Every one that loveth is begotten of God, and knoweth God" (1 John iv. 7).

The man begotten of God loves. That is the very essence of Christianity. The first movement in the soul of a man born of God is a movement inspired by love and impelling to service. Let that be illustrated in the simplest possible way. Here is a man born again in some service, or, it may be, in the loneliness of his own home. Then immediately, and without any exception, he thinks of some one else whom he loves, and desires that such an one may share his joy ; and is consequently impelled to go and tell that one the secret of his new-found life. There is no exception to this. The life of God is love, and the moment we share it, we love. We may quench love, be afraid to let it lead us to full expression, but all such action reacts upon life itself. The truth of infinite value is that the most loveless become love mastered as they are born of God.

These writings reveal not the resources of life alone, but also the values of its realization. These are twofold, the value to us, and the value to God.

The value of the life of fellowship to us is that of the realization of our own life, the perfection of our being, in friendship with God.

Some time ago I received a letter, in which the writer said, "How am I to find the secret that will admit me to the realization of all of which I am conscious ? Life seems to me as though it ought to be made up of love and laughter, but I am afraid that this is an improper definition of life." In answer to that letter I said that such is life indeed, according to the will of God, and that life only becomes love and laughter as it is eternal life, or life in fellowship with God. It is self-evident that when I use the word laughter I am not referring to such laughter as the preacher described in the book of Ecclesiastes, when he wrote,

"For as the crackling of thorns under a pot, so is the laughter of the fool: this also is vanity" (vii. 6).

I refer rather to that exultant hilarity which results from full consciousness of life. When a man is born of God, he is made to realize what God meant when He first made man. That is eternal life.

That way of stating the fact may surprise a great many truly Christian people who seem to have an idea that eternal life changes a man into some other order of being. Let us ever carefully remember that what we are essentially, in our first creation, we are by the will and power of God. He creates each human being a member of the great commonwealth of humanity, necessary for the perfecting of the whole. We never come to a realization of these powers, or make our contribution to the larger whole, until we are living eternal life, that is, life in fellowship with God. The words of Jesus are most significant in this respect, in which He declares, "Whosoever loseth his life shall find *it*," that is, the very life he loses. He that loses his life for Christ's sake does not find a different life. He finds rather the key to his own life, which unlocks its secrets; and the power which enables him to realize its potentialities. The value of eternal life to us then is the perfecting of our personalities in friendship with God, according to the will of God. Eternal life is true life, life as God intended it should be.

Realization of eternal life by the children of God is valuable to God Himself, in that He finds in every human being who lives in fellowship with Himself a medium through which He can manifest Himself, and an instrument through which He is able to accomplish His purposes. When a man begins to live the life eternal, God gains in him an opportunity to show Himself in the shop or the office where he works, in the circle of men and women among whom he moves.

The abiding appeal of these letters consists in

their declaration of the responsibilities of the life of fellowship. These responsibilities are those of light and love.

With regard to light, the first responsibility is that its testing must be sought. It is not enough that I should say that light must be obeyed. Our first duty is to seek the light. We often say that we have no light on a given subject. Let it be remembered that if that is so, the fault is with us. We can have light if we will. That fact is most clearly taught by Paul in one of his letters, in which he said, "Awake, thou that sleepest, and arise from the dead, and Christ shall shine upon thee." This does not merely mean once, at the beginning, but along the whole pathway of life. It is possible for us not to seek the light, not to want to have the light, not to desire its shining; and our first responsibility therefore is that we do seek the light. If indeed we bear His name and profess to live the life of fellowship, we have no right to undertake any business without seeking light, no right to enter upon any pleasure without desiring to know His will. There must be the testing of the life by light on the part of all those who are living in fellowship with God.

Then when the light shines, it must be obeyed wherever it leads, and at whatever cost.

Our responsibilities as to love are that its impulse must be yielded to, and its holiness must be maintained.

It is a matter for the most solemn consideration that we may destroy our capacity for love by not yielding to its impulse. There is a time in the earlier experiences of all Christian life when the soul is conscious of a great passion for lost men and women. It is possible to lose this. It is possible to continue the service, and yet to have lost the love. We lose the love impulse when we refuse to obey its suggestions. Love asks for some sacrificial service, and we listen to some calm, calculating, satanic voice, and caring for ourselves, we stifle love. If the life of God in the soul of a man is in its first movement an impulse of love, our first responsibility is that of obedience thereto. Love will lead us to the doing of such things that the world will be unable to understand. Judas will still inquire, "Why this waste?" If we listen to that criticism, and cease to respond to love, love will die. If we turn a deaf ear to such suggestions of Satan, and yielding ourselves to love, serve in answer to its impulse, love will deepen and intensify.

We are not only to yield to love; we are to guard its holiness. It is possible to be led astray from the activity of true love by yielding to a false charity. At the very centre of love is light. That is not true love which sacrifices principle. God has never acted in love at the expense of light. If I could be persuaded for one moment that God can be so loving as to pass lightly over sin, then I should feel that the government of the universe was insecure. The fact is otherwise. He loves with such intensity that He never can excuse sin. In all our love, therefore, we must see to it that the light is shining, and that holiness is maintained.

These letters have an immediate application to the individual and to the Church. That to the individual may thus be briefly stated. Life must be tested by light and by love. That is a word full of solemnity. We talk of our fellowship with God. How are we to prove to ourselves that we are really living in fellowship with Him? The test of the life is that of light and love. If the light is not shining clearly, or if shining, we are disobedient to it; if the love that once burned and inspired is no longer operative, then may God deliver us from mere satisfaction with the formulæ of orthodoxy, or correct intellectual apprehensions of the doctrines of grace.

As to the Church, the law of its fellowship is life, and as in the case of the individual, life must be tested by light and by love. We have no right to be so broad in our Church fellowship as to receive men who deny Christ as He is presented in the Gospel, and as He has accomplished His victories in the souls of men in the centuries of the Christian era. We may respect the convictions of these men, but there can be no fellowship with them in Church life, which does not weaken the testimony of the Church. It would be infinitely better that the fellowship of any Church should be smaller than that its numbers should be enlarged by the inclusion of those who fail to walk in light, or to respond to love.

It is a remarkable fact and not to be lightly passed over, that in these writings of John, who has become known preëminently as the apostle of love, we find the sternest words as to the necessity for loyalty to truth; and the Church of

God needs to remember that fellowship with God necessitates separation from all who fail to fulfill the responsibilities of fellowship in light, or in love.

THE MESSAGE OF JUDE

A THE ESSENTIAL MESSAGE	B THE APPLICATION

I. The Central Teaching. The Peril of Apostasy
i. Apostasy defined.
   a. Its Character. (Verse 4.)
   b. Its Characteristics. (Verses 12, 16, 19.)
ii. Illustrations of its Nature and Issue.
   a. Israel.   Unbelief.   Destruction.
   b. Angels.   Rebellion.   Kept in Bonds.
   c. Sodom and   Fornication.   Age-abiding Fire.
      Gomorrah.
   d. Cain.   Self-righteousness.
   e. Balaam.   Greed.
   f. Korah.   Presumption.
      NOTE.—All these contrary to Faith.
 	
II. The Abiding Appeal
i. The inclusive Command. (Verse 3.)
   a. Passionate and determined Effort.
   b. The Abandon and Cautiousness of the Athlete.
                              (Verses 20–23.)
ii. The Exposition.
   a. Keep yourselves.   Building.
                        Praying.
                        Looking.
   b. "Some." . . .
iii. The Inspiration. The Doxology.
	I. To the Church
	    The Faith for which
	    we are to contend.
	i. The System of Truth.
	ii. That Truth centred in a Person.
	iii. That Truth operating in Grace.
	
	II. To the Individual
	    The Contending which defends the Truth.
	i. Constant Loyalty.
	ii. Ceaseless Caution.
	iii. Courageous Confidence.

THE MESSAGE OF JUDE

THIS letter is one of the briefest of the New Testament writings; but it is by no means unimportant. It is characterized by great and grave solemnity, making appeal to "them that are called, beloved in God the Father, and kept for Christ Jesus." It is catholic, and has perpetual application to the people of God.

Its purpose is evident. We have to spend no time in seeking to discover its message; it is in itself a definite message. Its solemnity is increased by the fact that the writer declares that whereas he had purposed writing on an entirely different subject, he turned aside from that original purpose, in view of the urgency of the need, as he saw it, for solemn warning.

Glancing at the early verses of the letter, let us notice first the reason for the writing; secondly, his own declared purpose in writing; and then, before turning to the statement of the message, let us notice the method he adopted in the writing.

The reason is declared in verse four; there were certain "ungodly men, turning the grace of our God into lasciviousness, and denying our only Master and Lord, Jesus Christ." When Jude was giving all diligence, that is, making careful preparation, to write a treatise on the subject of our common salvation, there was borne in upon his spirit the necessity for writing this letter, because there were certain men within the circle of the Church, who had crept in privily, and were being received and listened to, and whose influence was affecting the life of Christian people. They were "turning the grace of our Lord into lasciviousness, and denying our only Master and Lord, Jesus Christ."

Jude gave with equal clearness the purpose for which he wrote the letter in the words, "I was constrained to write unto you exhorting you to contend earnestly for the faith which was once for all delivered unto the saints."

The method of the letter is that of giving illustrations of apostasy, showing its nature and results; and also instructions for fidelity.

Here again, in another way, and from another view-point, and with other emphasis, the great theme is that of the Hebrew letter, the two great

THE MESSAGE OF JUDE 197

values of which were the revelation of the perils of apostasy, of how death comes through apostasy; and of the powers of faith, how the righteous man lives by his faith. The same two underlying thoughts are in this brief letter.

The central teaching of the letter is that of the peril of apostasy.

Apostasy is first defined as to its character and its characteristics. Secondly, illustrations of its nature and issue are given; Israel, Angels, Sodom and Gomorrah, Cain, Balaam, Korah.

The abiding appeal consists of an inclusive command; an exposition thereof; and finally an inspirational Doxology.

The central teaching has to do with apostasy; which is first defined.

When I speak of apostasy being defined, I am referring of course to apostasy within the Christian faith and fact. The illustrations are taken from the Scriptures and history of the Hebrew people; consequently they touch the underlying principle, rather than the immediate fact of the apostasy of which Jude was afraid as he wrote this letter to Christian people.

Apostasy is not finally intellectual; it is volitional; but it is closely united with the intellectual. It may be very difficult for us to say whether apostasy from Christ, the denial of faith, the turning of the back upon the Lord Himself, begins with intellectual doubt, or moral declension. If I were asked personally for an opinion—which I shall only give as a personal opinion—I should be inclined to say that the very order in which Jude has stated it is a revelation of the order in which it happens. First some moral declension, some disobedience to the Lord Himself, some turning of the grace of God into lasciviousness, the outcome of which is some denial of the Lord and Master Himself. My own conviction is that heresy within the Church is almost invariably the outcome of disloyalty to the teaching of the Lord at some point in the life. When a man turns the grace of God into lasciviousness, when he consents to act upon the idea that because he stands in grace, therefore his conduct is of very little moment, he is apostatizing. That is the most terrible of all apostasies. There have been periods when that apostasy has been formulated into a definite doctrine; the antinomian heresy declared that because a man is in Christ he cannot be lost, and therefore it

THE MESSAGE OF JUDE 199

matters little what his conduct may be, because nothing he can do can sever as between Christ and himself. That is apostasy in its worst form. No man can hold that doctrine without denying the Lord and Master. That is to deny everything for which He stood; to deny the real meaning and purpose of His dying, to deny the whole purpose of His heart, as He came to destroy the works of the Devil, in order to make possible to man a life of purity, to save man not merely from the punishment of sin, but from sin itself. To continue in sin that grace may abound is to deny the perfection of His Person; the passion of His heart that bore Him through the Cross; and His purpose for the establishment of the Kingdom of God in righteousness and holiness through the whole world.

Doubt is not apostasy. I believe there are a great many who, passing through a period of honest doubt and difficulty and inquiry in the presence of the great mystery of our Lord's Person, do not apostatize because they remain true to the measure of light they have, and they do not turn the grace of God into lasciviousness. In other words, apostasy, according to this first definition and whole argument, is not intellectual mistake, but moral failure on the part of those who name the name of Christ.

In verses twelve, sixteen, and nineteen, we have the characteristics of apostasy; they each begin with the same words. Perhaps there is no more forceful passage in the whole of the New Testament than that of verses twelve and thirteen. It is figurative but graphic. Reading it, one is conscious of the awfulness of apostasy. In verses sixteen and nineteen we have a description of those who apostatize, what they are in themselves, and what they do in the assemblies.

Between the declaration of the character of apostasy and the description of its characteristics, we have a series of very startling illustrations. In Israel the form of apostasy was that of unbelief; and the issue of it was that they were destroyed. The nature of the apostasy of Angels was rebellion; they kept not their proper habitation, they moved out of their God-appointed orbit; choosing for themselves, they wandered out of bounds; and the issue was that they are kept in bonds. They wandered out of the bounds of His law, and therefore they are kept in bonds, reserved in darkness until the final day. Sodom and Gomorrah afford a startling illustra-

THE MESSAGE OF JUDE 201

tion, in its recognition of the solemn fact that there light is given in some measure to every nation and man, and that men are judged by God according to the light they have. The apostasy of Sodom and Gomorrah consisted in their giving themselves over to all manner of lust and fornication. The issue was that of the age-abiding fire.

Then three persons are given as illustrations; Cain who was self-righteous; Balaam whose sin was greed; and Korah whose sin was presumption. All these are contrary to faith.

Go over the ground again. In the first illustration it is plainly stated, the sin of unbelief. The angels when they left their first estate, their proper habitation, did so as the result of unbelief. In the case of Sodom and Gomorrah it was failure of faith. The sensual life is the opposite of the life of faith. Sodom and Gomorrah, when they gave themselves to fornication, were answering the clamouring call of the carnal and sensual which is always a contradiction to faith. Cain's attitude was devoid of faith; his was the self-righteous attitude of life. Balaam's attitude was in contradiction to faith. In a sense Balaam had faith; he had belief intellectually. He failed in faith in that he did not obey. So also with Korah's presumption.

Where faith fails, morality fails. I pray you interpret that word morality in its widest sense, not as it is interpreted by the man in the street or by the magazine writer. The immorality of the angels was the denial of the government of God, and rebellion against it. Wherever you find it, immorality is denial of faith. Not the ending of intellectual conviction, that is not immorality. Immorality is refusal to obey the truth of which I am convinced, and that is also apostasy.

Where there is such apostasy, inevitably the judgment must fall. It is contained in germ within the apostasy. "My righteous one shall live by faith." If faith fail, God is not unfaithful; which does not mean that He will maintain the promise when the conditions are broken; but that He *cannot* maintain the promise when the conditions are broken.

Turning to the abiding appeal; we have first the inclusive statement. Jude wrote exhorting us to "contend earnestly for the faith." The one word translated "contend earnestly" occurs nowhere else. The root of the word is found in the

New Testament in other applications; where it is said for instance that Epaphras strove in prayer, we have the same word, which might be rendered agonizes. Here the word is intensified by its context, consequently our translation is, "contend earnestly." There is not the slightest suggestion of argument. We are not asked to defend the faith by arguing for it. What then is the thought of the word? It is that of passionate and determined effort. The word really has in it the thought of the abandon and cautiousness of the athlete. "Contend earnestly for the faith." The apostle did not mean, Lecture on Christian evidences. That may be a perfectly proper thing to do in its place. He did not mean, Form a league for the defense of the Bible. He did not mean, Argue with every man you meet that these things are so. The final argument for faith in the world is not the argument of words, but the argument of life. What he meant was this: Put into the business of your defense of this great faith passionate and determined effort; let there be the abandon and cautiousness of the athlete.

In the closing verses we have the exposition of the way in which we are to obey the command to contend earnestly for the faith, "building up yourselves on your most holy faith, praying in the Holy Spirit, keep yourselves in the love of God, looking for the mercy of our Lord Jesus Christ unto eternal life." We are to keep ourselves in the love of God; not to put ourselves there; we are in the love of God; being there, we are to keep ourselves in that love; which again does not mean that we are to remain there, but seeing that we are there, we are to behave as we ought to behave. We are in that love; therefore we are to respond to it, obey it. How are we to do that? By building, praying, looking. "Building up yourselves on your most holy faith," that is by answering the claim of the faith we possess, carrying it into all the activities of our every-day life so that we become stronger and grow perpetually. "Praying in the Holy Spirit." If our personal effort is that of building; our perpetual consciousnes is that of dependence, praying. All this with the goal in view, "looking," the eye ever fixed upon the ultimate consummation, the glorious issue.

If we desire to contend for the faith that is how we are to do it. The profoundest argument, indeed the only argument in favour of faith, is life homed in the love of God, building itself up on faith, forever praying in the Holy Spirit, and forevermore looking for the mercy of our Lord unto age-abiding life. Find the man or woman, youth or maiden, boy or girl, professing faith in the Lord Jesus Christ, holding in that sense the faith of Christianity, who stays in the love of God, builds up the life upon faith, never undertaking any enterprise save as it is conditioned by the underlying facts of Christianity, living forevermore under the Holy Spirit, in dependence upon that Spirit's coöperation, looking ever for the ultimate perfecting; such an one is doing more for the defense of the faith than all wordy argument. The faith is contended for by the whole business of life, by consecration characterized by caution and courage; the putting out of our lives of all the things that are contrary to the will of the Lord and Master, refusing to turn the grace of God into lasciviousness; never denying, but forevermore affirming in life, the Lord and Master of us all.

There is something else. We cannot contend for the faith and keep ourselves, save as we help others. How are we to help them? "On some have mercy, who are in doubt; and some save, snatching them out of the fire; and on some have mercy with fear; hating even the garment spotted by the flesh."

Finally, what is the inspiration of this life in which we contend for the faith? "Now unto Him that is able to guard you—as with a garrison—from stumbling, and to set you before the presence of His glory without blemish in exceeding joy, to the only God our Saviour, through Jesus Christ our Lord, be glory, majesty, dominion, and power, before all time, and now, and forevermore." The inspiration is the certainty that the Master is able to guard us from stumbling, and at last to set us before the presence of God with exceeding joy and without blemish. But He cannot guard us from stumbling if we deny Him. He cannot guard us from stumbling if we are apostate, if we deliberately continue in unbelief as in the case of Israel; in speculative attempts to act on our own behalf as in the case of the angels; in descent towards sensual things and fornication as in the case of Sodom and Gomorrah; in self-righteous satisfaction even in our worship as in the case of Cain; in greed as in the case of Balaam; in presumption as in the case of Korah. If in any of these things we are guilty of apostasy, He cannot guard us from apostasy. If we are abiding in the love of God, building on faith, praying in the Spirit, looking for mercy, then all hell cannot make us stumble, because He is able to guard us as with a garrison from stumbling.

A final word by way of application. First to the Church. What is the faith for which we are to contend? The faith once for all delivered to the saints; that is, the whole system of truth. What is the system of truth? That truth is centred in a Person. That Person is the Person of these New Testament revelations; the Person of the Gospels, the Acts, the Epistles. The Person is seen in the flesh in the first four pamphlets; but is interpreted by the Spirit in the apostolic writings. That is the faith. It is that truth embodied in a Person, operating in grace and holiness, for which we are to contend.

Then to the individual. What is the contending which defends the faith? Constant loyalty to Christ; ceaseless caution in the presence of things contrary to His will; courage and confidence. By these things we shall indeed defend the faith. It is possible for a man to attempt to defend the faith by argument, and successfully by argument to state the facts of the faith, while instead of defending it, he is actually destroying it by his own life, by his own character. Faith, and contending for the faith by obedience to the claims of the faith will forevermore make apostasy impossible.

THE MESSAGE OF REVELATION

A THE ESSENTIAL MESSAGE	B THE APPLICATION
I. The Central Teaching. Unveiling i. The unveiled Person. The Alpha and Omega. 　*a.* The Identification. 　　1. The Lord God. The Almighty. i. 8. 　　2. God dwelling with Men. xxi. 6. 　　3. The coming One. xxii. 13. 　*b.* The Vocation. 　　1. The Priest. Cf. ver. 5. 　　2. The King. The established City. 　　3. The Prophet. Cf. ver. 10. ii. The unveiled Power. 　　*a.* Personal. 1. Inherent. 　　　　　　　　2. Acquired. 　　*b.* Instrumental. 1. All material Forces. 　　　　　　　　2. All spiritual Forces. 　　*c.* Effectual. 1. Destructive. 　　　　　　　2. Constructive. iii. The unveiled Purpose. 　*a.* The Ultimate. 　　1. God dwelling with Men. 　　2. Men blessed in God. 　　3. God glorified in Men. 　*b.* The Progressive. 　　1. At War against Sin. 　　2. The Destruction of Sin. 　　3. The Patience of even Justice. **II. The Abiding Appeal** i. An opening Word of Courage. "Fear not." 　*a.* The Vision producing Fear. i. 17*a*. 　*b.* The Voice interpreting the Vision. i. 17*b*, 18. 　*c.* The Vision inspiring Courage. i. 19. ii. A closing Word of Caution. "I testify." 　*a.* No Additions. Speculative Deductions. 　*b.* No Subtractions. Unbelieving Denials.	**I. To the Church** i. This is preëminently a Book for the Friends of Jesus. ii. To know it is to be saved from Mistakes about 　　His Person. 　　His Power. 　　His Programme. **II. To the Individual** i. The new Creation as revealing the Meaning of Life in Christ. ii. The Processes as revealing the Principles of Life in Christ.

THE MESSAGE OF REVELATION

IN attempting to discover the message of the book of Revelation, it is well that we should remember that differing interpretations of detail need not detain or trouble us, because its essential message is not interfered with, whatever view may be held as to how the book should be interpreted in such matters of detail.

There are at least four schools of interpretation of this wonderful book. I simply mention them in passing. They have been described as the Preterist, the Historic, the Futurist, and the Spiritual. The first affirms that in this book we have Jewish history to the fall of Jerusalem, and to the fall of pagan Rome set forth in symbolic form. The second interprets the book as giving an outline of events through the whole of the Christian era. The third treats the book as giving the events associated with the second Advent of our Lord. The fourth deals with the book as being entirely spiritual, declaring that therein in signs and by symbols we have the revelation of the principles of the perpetual conflict between good and evil until the winning of the final victory. I am not going to enter into discussion as between these views. I believe there is an element of truth in every one of them. I do not think either of them exhausts the truth. However full of mystery this book is, it is the only book in the Bible which opens with a distinct blessing promised to the man who reads it, and keeps its words. That fact at least should arouse our attention, and give us to see that we ought not to treat the book carelessly, or lightly, or pass it over. I admit quite freely the difficulty of interpretation in the matter of detail; and there is no book in the Bible which I have read so often, no book to which I have tried to give more patient and persistent attention. As I have said, all the views to which I have referred may be partially true. The present study, however, is not concerned with them.

The first word of the Greek document is the keyword to the message as well as to the content. That is the word Revelation, the Greek word *Apokalupsis*. We have anglicized that word and now speak of the Apocalypse. In the Greek there is no definite article. The book opens with the word *Apokalupsis*, which means quite literally uncovering, disclosure. A literal translation is not always a correct one; for we must always understand the use of the word as well as its root meaning. Quite literally this word apocalypse means uncovering; far more beautiful and therefore nearer the truth for us is our word unveiling. That is the first word of the book. It is the key to the content, and it is positively, and inclusively the key to the message. An interesting fact is that this is the only occurrence of the word in the whole book; it is not found again. The word does not often occur in the New Testament. Paul uses it, and so does Peter. This is the one and only place in the writings of John where this word is to be found. It is as though it were reserved for this book. I do not mean that John reserved it, for it is quite possible that this book was written before his letters. It may be that if I could have talked to John the aged, after he had written the last of his words for his beloved children, I should have found that he did not know that he had never used the word but once, and only there. These are very human documents so far as the men who wrote them were concerned. It is in the recognition of the human that we come to the discovery of the Divine in the study of the Bible. While not now staying to enter into all that is involved, I believe that the Spirit presided over and led men in the arrangement of the Canon, as certainly as He presided over and led men in the writing of the books. I do not think the Spirit was withdrawn when the last inspired literature was given to the Church. I think the Spirit still presided over human choices until the Library was completely arranged. I repeat, therefore, that it is as though this word *Unveiling* were reserved for this book. We read the first word Unveiling; and it is as though the great doors swing open, and visions of glory appear, introduced by this word. We have been following from Genesis, through message after message, and at last we come to the final book in the library, and it opens with this word Unveiling. It is the ultimate book in the Bible; the final book in the Canon; and the attention is immediately centred upon a Person. It is "the unveiling of Jesus Christ, which God gave Him to show unto His servants, even the things which must shortly come to pass: and He sent and signified it by His angel unto His servant John." The Unveiling of Christ, the final truth about Christ is in this last book of the Bible. That is the key to its message.

Let us first consider the essential message. The central teaching is all suggested by the word Unveiling. This book is for the friends of Jesus. The proportion of our understanding of secret things is the proportion of our love for the Lord. There are too many things assumed here for the book to be apprehended by any save those who know the secret of the Lord.

First we have the unveiled Person; described as "The Alpha and the Omega"; a phrase which occurs three times, and only at the most remarkable situations. The message concerning Him is concerned with identification and vocation. The threefold use of that title identifies the Person; and shows the vocation of that Person in human history. Let us observe the three occasions.

It first occurs in the eighth verse of the first chapter. The "Even so, Amen" of verse seven is not the language of the one speaking before; it is the introduction to the affirmation of verse eight, and should be read in close connection with it, and is more forcible, I think, in the older form, "Yea, amen. I am the Alpha and the Omega, saith the Lord God, which is and which was and which is to come, the Almighty."

The next occurrence is in chapter twenty-one, verse six, "They are come to pass. I am the Alpha and the Omega, the beginning and the end."

The third is in chapter twenty-two, verses twelve and thirteen, "Behold, I come quickly; and My reward is with Me, to render to each man according as his work is. I am the Alpha and the Omega, the first and the last, the beginning and the end." That is the unveiling of the Person. The whole book is about that Person. Everything circles about that Person.

The first affirmation is characterized by simplicity; there is no ambiguity, there can be no mistake as to the meaning; "I am the Alpha and the Omega, saith the Lord God, which is and which was and which is to come, the Almighty." There is no verse in the Bible more explicit than that as a description of absolute and positive Deity. Thus in the first occurrence of the strange yet wonderfully symbolic and beautiful description, "the Alpha and the

Omega," the first and the last, the beginning and the end, it is used of God Himself. He is described by the conceptions of the Old Testament, condensed into brief statements, "The Lord God, which is and which was and which is to come, the Almighty." All the titles of God in the Old Testament are represented in that description. The qualities of every Old Testament title for God are in that wonderful passage.

The next occurrence is in the chapter of the final triumph. The millennium is described in six verses in the twentieth chapter. Beyond it there is conflict, and a great assize, and then the Kingdom of the Son is established, which must not be confused with the thousand years. It is in that unmeasured period that the city of God, descending out of heaven, God dwells with men; and concerning that ultimate triumph the words are employed; "I am the Alpha and the Omega, the beginning and the end." The process began when the Word Who was with God, and was God, "became flesh and tabernacled among us (and we beheld His glory, glory as of the only begotten from the Father), full of grace and truth." It will end with the ultimate victory. "Behold, the tabernacle of God is with men, and He shall dwell with them. . . . I am the Alpha and the Omega." That again is evidently the language of God.

The final occurrence is in the promise, "Behold, I come quickly; and My reward is with Me, to render to each man according as his work is." Who now is the speaker? The answer is immediately given; "I Jesus have sent Mine angel to testify unto you these things."

The first reference is patently to the God of the Old Testament, the Sovereign Lord, the Almighty God, the Becoming One, Who is and was and is to come, the Almighty. The last is linked to that simple declaration, "I Jesus have sent Mine angel to testify unto you these things." Thus the identification is complete. Jesus is Jehovah.

In these connections the Person is unveiled as to vocation. The first declaration was made in answer to an ascription of praise; "Unto Him that loveth us, and loosed us from our sins by His blood." The answer was "I am the Alpha and the Omega, saith the Lord God, which is and which was and which is to come,

THE MESSAGE OF REVELATION 219

the Almighty." That reveals the Person as Priest.

The next was made in connection with the fall of Babylon. The ultimate victory is won; the Kingdom has come; then the word is again spoken, "I am the Alpha and the Omega, the beginning and the end." That reveals the Person as King as well as Priest.

At the close of the book when the solemn warning is given that the words of the prophecy are not to be sealed, that the great teaching is to be the open secret of all those who read it; then again the voice is heard, "I am the Alpha and the Omega, the first and the last, the beginning and the end." That reveals the Person as Prophet.

Thus the Person is Jehovah—Jesus, at once Priest, King, and Prophet. The whole of the Old Testament is answered. The Pentateuch sighs for a Priest, but never finds Him. The historic books cry for a King, but He does not appear. The prophetic books attempt in broken words to speak the Word, the abiding Truth; but they were never harmonized, and final. The Old Testament says, Humanity needs a Priest, a King, and a Prophet. Here we have the Priest, the King, and the Prophet unveiled; and He is the Alpha and the Omega, the One from Whom all came, to Whom all proceeds, and through Whom the end is assured from the beginning. This One is the mystic, mighty, very God of Gods; and this One is Jesus. That is what this book teaches. No man can read it, and escape from the conviction that this is what the writer thought.

In the second place we have in this book the unveiled power of the Person; and it is revealed as personal, instrumental, and effectual.

The personal power is first inherent, and secondly acquired. He is, as we have seen, the essential Being; and we cannot read this book without feeling the awfulness of the power of God. We are made conscious of how terrible are the powers which are against God, in the figurative language which describes them as beasts, dragons. That is only the first impression. The final impression is that all these beasts and dragons are in the grip of God and cannot escape Him. That is a revelation of the inherent power of the unveiled Person. Then there is the acquired power; we see not the throne only; but also the Lamb in the midst of it, as it had been slain. That is power won out of some mystery of passion and pain and suffering. The book opens with the anthem of this acquired power, "Unto Him that loveth us, and loosed us from our sins by His blood."

The instrumental power of the unveiled Person is also unveiled. All elemental forces, earthquakes, lightnings, thunders; forces of the air; plagues; He makes use of. Spiritual forces also; angels, good and evil; all of them are under His command.

The effectual power of this One Person is seen to be both destructive and constructive. When we get rid of the idea that God can destroy, we get rid of the idea that God can construct. There must be destruction in order to construction in a world like this. The two activities are seen operating through all this book, and always through the same Person.

Thirdly we find the unveiled purpose, both ultimately and progressively.

The ultimate purpose of God is to dwell with men; man is to be blessed in God; God is to be glorified in man. We do not find in this revelation any reference to the highest glory of all. We must go to the Ephesian letter for that, and see the Church telling the wisdom of God to the ages to come. Here the glory is that of the Kingdom established in this world. This is the programme of God's final methods in the world. The ultimate note is that of the tabernacling of God with men; the city of God coming out of heaven; the realization of the Divine purpose on earth.

The progressive purpose of God is that He is at war against sin. He is destroying sin. I thank God for this book. Symbolic as it is, full of signs and wonders, the significance of which I have not yet been able to understand in detail; it nevertheless clearly presents this picture of God, the Alpha and the Omega, at war with sin; and it is as full of comfort as anything within the covers of the Divine Library. Persuade me for a single moment that God is going to make peace with sin, and I become the most hopeless man in the world. Let me see God with drawn sword fighting against sin; then I see a God of such infinite love, that I know that "though a wide compass first be fetched," the kingdom of the world shall become the Kingdom of this One.

The abiding appeal consists of an opening word of courage; and a closing word of caution.

When John was in Patmos he saw a vision of his Lord, a wonderful vision, symbolically revealing sublime things with which we are not going to deal in detail. When he saw that vision, he became as one dead; then there came to him the touch of the human hand, and the sound of the human voice, and the great "Fear not." "When I saw Him, I fell at His feet as one dead. And He laid His right hand upon me, saying, Fear not; I am the first and the last, and the Living One; and I was dead, and beheld I am alive forevermore, and I have the keys of death and of Hades. Write therefore the things which thou sawest, and the things which are." If you take the "therefore" out of the verse you have lost much. The "therefore" links the command to write with the great "Fear not." Write *therefore* the things you have seen, the things that are, and the things which shall be; write these visions and fear not.

Because I have said, "Fear not," therefore write. Write without fear. That is indeed a great word of courage to the man who writes the book, and to the man who reads the book. Be not afraid, because I am He that liveth, and I have the keys! Do you not feel that you could walk with Him through hell itself? Let us see the end of the whole matter. Let us watch the process of that righteous judgment that makes no peace with sin until it have established righteousness on the earth. Sin slew Him; but He slew sin. He was alive, and was dead; but is alive forevermore. The great "Fear not!" I hear it now, not only through the reading of the book, but above the clamour of the hour in which I live, amid the clash of arms, amid all the babel of earth's confused noises. "Fear not." This unveiled Person fills the vision. It is He that was dead but is alive forevermore. "Therefore will we not fear, though the earth do change, and though the mountains be moved in the heart of the seas."

Then there is a closing word of caution, "I testify." No additions must be made to this book, no subtractions from it. No additions; no speculative deductions. Take the things written and attempt to understand them; ponder them, but beware of speculative deductions. No subtractions; no unbelieving denials, no declaration that these things cannot be, because we cannot understand them. The Person as He is revealed; the power as it is unveiled; the purpose as it is

THE MESSAGE OF REVELATION

declared; without addition or subtraction. That is the final caution of the book.

In making application of the message of this book first to the Church, I would say again what I have already said. This is preëminently a book for the friends of Jesus. To know it is to be saved from mistakes about His Person, about His power, about His programme.

No man who denies the absolute and final Deity of Jesus can accept this book, he must get rid of it.

No man who has any panic in his heart as to the issue can believe this book. There is no book in the Bible to which I turn more eagerly in hours of depression than to this, with all its mystery, all the details which I do not understand. I go back to it, to the throne, and to the Lamb as it had been slain; and my puzzled mind and troubled heart feel the healing virtue; and I hear the song, and am ready for another day's fighting, for I know that Jesus shall reign.

No man who reads this book expects that the world is going to be converted by gospel preaching without judgment. There must be a period of judgment. God will have the double harvest.

There will be the harvest of evil; evil must work itself out to its final manifestation. It is not to be smothered. It is to be seen, not upon the house-top of the earthly city merely, but in the universe of God.

To the individual this book says, Behold the new creation; and by observing that understand the truth about thyself. If any man be in Christ, he is a new creation. Study well the beauty and the glory of life governed by this Person, and know the meaning of thy life in Christ. Study well the processes of life in the new creation, and understand the principles of thy life in Christ. Know that this new creation within thy experience can only come to its final perfecting, as God fights within thee against sin and slays it. The ultimate victory is not reached in a moment. Pardoned, justified, made nigh, we are, in a moment; but all the processes are necessary for the subjection of the territory, and the establishment of the Kingdom; thunder, earthquake, as well as the gentle and caressing touch of the dawning of the morning. Jesus Who is the Lamb in the midst of the throne is God; and in His presence is the place of worship; and in His power is the place of refuge.